Green Growth, Smart Growth

Green Growth, Smart Growth

A New Approach to Economics, Innovation and the Environment

Ralf Fücks

With a Foreword by Anthony Giddens

Translated by Rachel Harland

ANTHEM PRESS

Anthem Press India
An imprint of Wimbledon Publishing Company
India Private Limited (WPCIPL)
WPCIPL is a subsidiary of Wimbledon Publishing
Company Limited (UK)

This edition first published in India 2015
by ANTHEM PRESS INDIA
www.anthempress.co.in

First published in UK and USA 2015
by ANTHEM PRESS
www.anthempress.com

Originally published as *Intelligent wachsen: Die grüne Revolution*
in Germany by Carl Hanser Verlag München, 2013

ISBN-13: 978 93 80601 75 5 (Pbk)
ISBN-10: 93 80601 75 1 (Pbk)

FOR SALE IN SOUTH ASIA ONLY

Digitally Printed at Replika Press Pvt. Ltd

For Clara and Charlotte. You will live to see it, one way or another.

There are a thousand paths that have never yet been trodden—a thousand healths and hidden isles of life. Even now, man and man's earth are unexhausted and undiscovered.

—Friedrich Wilhelm Nietzsche, *Thus Spoke Zarathustra*

Simply carrying on is criminal; merely preaching self-denial is naive. The intelligent approaches lie somewhere in between.

—Peter Sloterdijk

Contents

Foreword

Our civilization—industrial civilization—is a very recent arrival on the historical scene. It has existed for no more than a couple of hundred years, a trivial slice of historical time compared to earlier forms of society, some of which survived in recognizable form for several millennia. In the short period of its existence, however, the industrial order has had a gigantic and all-pervasive impact upon the world and upon the physical environment. It has created the first truly global society, in which the level of social, economic and cultural interdependence of peoples across the world is massively greater than has ever been known before. Hundreds of millions live at, or beyond, levels of prosperity previously known only by a tiny number of ruling elites in previous ages. Quite rightly, billions of others aspire to similar standards of living.

And there are indeed billions of people today—world population has reached seven billion today and is heading towards nine or ten billion. In 1850 there were less than one billion people in the world, and at that time this was a peak. It is a staggering change. The story of the rise of the industrial order is one of opportunity and of risk—both of which operate at a far higher level than was ever true in previous history. How can there be enough food to provide for the needs of 10 billion people? Water is already scarce—won't the pressure upon this finite resource become unbearable? Deforestation is proceeding apace across the world, while the list of threatened species grows. If all this isn't enough, the expansion of modern industry is altering the world's climate, and possibly in an irrevocable way. Factor in the existence of nuclear weapons of fearsome destructive potential and the accumulation of risks is huge.

It isn't surprising that there are many who doubt our capacity to cope with this range of dangers—which are all the more serious because they overlap with one another in their consequences. Some give our civilization no more than a 50/50 chance of surviving the twenty-first century in recognizable form. The risks are all too real—there is no point in trying to minimize them. Moreover, because none of them existed in their current guise until even a few decades ago, we have little or no prior historical experience to draw on in trying to deal with them. It isn't just their novelty; their sheer scale is unprecedented. For example, it is awesome to think that, as collective humanity, we are in the process of altering the world's climate and on a permanent basis. Think of the power of nature, as witnessed in hurricanes, tsunamis or periods of extreme drought. Then imagine what things would be like if their intensity were to increase dramatically, as climate change models predict will happen if we don't mend our ways.

Yet the other side of risk is opportunity. The very human capacities that have created such awesome destructive power offer the chance of breakthroughs that can generate an altogether more beneficent future. Radical shifts in our current modes of life will be needed to realize such a scenario, but the very changes that have created such dangers for us can serve to revitalize world society and move it onto another trajectory. Such is the prime message of this book. Ralf Fücks rejects traditional forms of green philosophy, which place the emphasis upon frugality and upon limits to growth. On the contrary, ingenuity and innovation are the name of the game. A new model of sustainability is needed, driven by ingenuity and the capacity of our technologies to extract more from less. The most serious risks we face are common to humanity as a whole. They direct our attention to new levels of collective action, global in their implications and consequences, even if many of them start from the local or regional level.

The view endorsed by Fücks could be called utopian realism. Radical change is needed if growth is to be compatible with sustainability: there has to be utopian element in our thinking. Yet the necessary utopian moment has to be conjoined to realistic modes of realizing the needed changes. Without the utopian perspective we cannot see beyond the trends and mechanisms that dominate world society at the moment. Yet utopianism is vacuous unless the means are created to realize the values it embodies.

Let me take one particular example of how such an approach might work. We know that in order to minimize climate change there must be a worldwide switch from fossil fuels in energy production—away from coal, oil and gas, and towards renewables. Moreover, it must happen relatively quickly, since it is the consumption of fossil fuels that is the prime source of the greenhouse gases that are causing shifts in the world's climate. Isn't this just wishful thinking, since the fossil fuel industries are so firmly established and have huge inertia? The proportion of the world's energy generated from renewable sources, after all, is tiny by comparison. Yet the very process of intensifying globalization, making possible the very rapid introduction of new technologies more or less anywhere, might mean that the inertia is more apparent than real. Consider the mass introduction of smartphones into Africa and other less developed parts of the world. It is a process that has happened within just a few years. As a result, some African countries have been able to leapfrog the existence of fixed phone lines and move directly to direct mobile communication. An analogous process could happen with renewable technologies—rapidly and on the large scale, especially if further technological advances are made in the area of energy storage.

"All that is solid melts into thin air." It was an adage that Marx coined to describe the restlessly innovative character of modern capitalism. That process can happen far more rapidly today than was true a century ago. Consider as an example the advance of the internet, which had barely begun even twenty years ago but which is now truly universal in its impact. It has already changed the character of politics, the economy and civil society. Some of the emerging social and economic forms it is helping create could be crucial for the transformations Fücks envisages. New forms of grass-roots politics emerge, integrating the local and the global; the sharing economy is itself becoming a global force; new types of environmental movements and consumer initiatives are proliferating.

There are no guarantees here. The twenty-first century world looks, and is, disturbingly fractured and dangerous. Yet Fücks is surely right to call for the rehabilitation of the principle of progress and to anchor it in innovation.

Anthony Giddens

Preface and Acknowledgments

This book is not another warning about the end of the world. It is neither a penitential sermon on environmentalism, nor an appeal to frugality and self-restraint. Far from having exhausted the era of technological, social and democratic progress, we are on the brink of a new stage of industrial modernity: a shift from a fossil-based to a postfossil economy, from the ruthless exploitation of nature toward growth in tandem with it. The pages that follow tell the story of this great transformation—a process of economic and cultural change that is already beginning to take shape today—and they do so in the conviction that the danger industrial civilization poses to our future can be overcome using the means of modernity: science, technology and democracy. It is by no means certain that we will win the race against climate change and dwindling resources. That will require nothing less than a great leap forward—a green industrial revolution. But it is far more encouraging to look at the future as a world of possibilities than as one of doom and gloom.

Key Elements of the Approaching Green Revolution

- A revolution in energy production: By the middle of the century renewable energy sources must account for as much of the world's energy consumption as possible.
- A revolution in efficiency: Greater prosperity from fewer resources.
- Zero waste, zero emissions: Integrated value chains whose waste products are fed back into biological or industrial cycles.
- Bioeconomics: Natural materials and biological processes as the basis of a sustainable mode of production; the synthesis of biology and technology (bionics).
- Recultivation: Large-scale reforestation and the conversion of degraded soil into fertile arable land.
- Agricultural greening: A broad range of cultivation methods ranging from small-scale organic farming to high-tech urban agriculture; the integration of agriculture, food processing, biochemical production and energy generation.
- Sustainable mobility: Electric vehicles, attractive public transport systems, car sharing, the expansion of transnational railways, optimized transport chains, climate-neutral air travel.
- Environmentally friendly construction: Buildings that communicate with their environments and produce more energy than they consume, reusable materials, vertical greenhouses, roof gardens, green facades.

None of these changes are going to happen by themselves. It will take a combination of forward-looking policy, an active civil society, responsible consumers, innovative businesses and scientific research to bring them about.

While this book was only possible thanks to the wealth of food for thought provided by my work with the Heinrich Böll Foundation, a think tank and global policy network affiliated with the green movement, the views expressed in it are entirely my own. It addresses a range of questions that are the subject of controversial discussion far beyond the green community. If it breathes new life into the debate and inspires enthusiasm for change it has fulfilled its purpose. The original German edition was discussed in economic circles as well as among environmentalists. This is precisely the kind of alliance needed to advance the ecological transformation of industrial society.

There are a number of people I would like to thank for their part in the project, while absolving them of any responsibility for the final product. The first is Karin Graf, who kindly but firmly persuaded me to take on the challenge. Helmut Wiesenthal, Willfried Maier, Dorothee Landgrebe and Annette Maennel read and provided feedback on various drafts of the manuscript and I am extremely grateful for their encouragement and criticism. My discussions with Peter Siller were also a great help, while Margret Kowalke-Paz brought the footnotes and bibliography up to a professional standard. I owe a debt of gratitude to Martin Janik—my editor at the Hanser publishing house in Germany—for his advice, his suggestions on the text and for providing the impetus I needed to finish the manuscript, and I would equally like to thank Tej P. S. Sood and Brian Stone of Anthem Press for making the book available to an English-speaking public. Rachel Harland did a terrific job on a sensitive and competent translation. Last but not least I want to thank Marie, my wife, for her patience at an exhausting time: writing a book alongside a full-time job is a rather antisocial business, but I hope it was worth it.

Introduction

The Decline of Modernity or the Beginning of a New Chapter?

In 1972 a group of young researchers led by Dennis L. Meadows sent shock waves around the world with their study *The Limits to Growth*. Today the growth debate is experiencing a renaissance, albeit an acutely schizophrenic one: environmentalists, cultural critics and even economists are calling for an end to rampant growth, while at the same time all Europe is clamoring for a halt to the downward spiral of the economy. Saving alone is only leading us deeper into crisis; a new cycle of growth is key to breaking the vicious circle of debt and unemployment. So far, however, a sustainable economic revival remains wishful thinking. Rather than working toward an ambitious Green New Deal designed to modernize public infrastructure and catapult the European Union to the forefront of innovation, governments are barely muddling through. The only way for Europe to get back on its feet is to use the crisis as an opportunity for serious progress, both toward greater political integration and the renewal of our economy. Europe has the potential to become a pioneer of the green industrial revolution. How it lives up to that potential will determine both the prosperity of future generations and the continent's role in the world going forward.

In the face of a growing global population with all its needs, desires and ambitions, it is verging on escapism to dream of a postgrowth society. It might seem appealing to old Europe to withdraw from global competition into a state of self-sufficient introspection, but in the eyes of the rest of the world that would be a withdrawal into insignificance. Europeans themselves would soon discover that postgrowth society is no idyll, but a stage for social drama and distribution conflicts—as the Greek nightmare of recent years has shown. No less out of touch, of course, is the idea that we can return to the resource-guzzling, energy-intensive growth of the last century. That would mean closing our eyes to the environmental crises mounting before us. Climate change, the ongoing loss of fertile land and the water shortages looming in populous regions are clear signs that our current economic system is destroying the biophysical basis of its existence. We are close to exceeding the load limits of vital ecosystems and face severe upheaval if this trend is not stopped.

If continuing as we always have done is a crime against the prospects of future generations and crude appeals to self-denial are futile, what is the alternative? That is the central question of this book. It discusses the need to move toward an ecological modernity—a society in which the idea of progress, though still fundamental, takes on a new narrative: the story of man's coevolution with nature, whose potential we have barely begun to unlock. The current crisis does not spell the end of technological civilization; it is simply a period of transition from the fossil-powered industrial age to a more environmentally friendly mode of production fueled by the sun. This new system is already beginning to take shape. In the future, a pan-European network of renewable energy sources will provide us with climate-friendly electricity and heat. Buildings are becoming miniature power plants that produce more energy than they consume. Urban mobility nowadays involves a fluid network of public transport, bikes and electric cars that drivers can rent when necessary and leave at their destinations. Electric batteries serve as storage devices that collect excess energy and feed it back into the grid when demand is high. As technology grows more compact, material input is being reduced; computers, machinery and engines are becoming smaller, lighter and more efficient. Integrated value chains enable optimal use of natural resources. Waste flows back into biological and technological cycles. Energy efficiency and recyclability determine appliance design. Ultrafiltration plants convert wastewater into drinking water. Agroindustrial centers combining farming, horticulture, animal husbandry, food processing and energy production in closed-loop cycles are springing up around cities. Food production is returning to urban environments. Vegetables, fruit and mushrooms are grown in old factories, vertical greenhouses and rooftop farms all year round. Waste heat and carbon dioxide from industrial plants are used to operate greenhouses and cultivate algae. Soil recultivation, modern closed-loop recycling and improved plant breeding methods allow for sustainable increases in agricultural output. Biotechnology—the technological application of biological processes and resources—is becoming a leading area of scientific research. Artificial photosynthesis has made it possible to convert sunlight, water and carbon dioxide into synthetic fuels. Bioreactors use organic waste and cellulose to make chemicals. The metabolic rift between nature and the economy is beginning to heal. The earth is not a static mass, not some narrowly limited habitat, but a dynamic system full of undiscovered possibilities. Intelligent growth means growing with nature.

In large parts of the environmental community this kind of confidence is considered strange to the point of suspicion. Anyone who embraces inventiveness and innovation is soon accused of worshipping technology. We prefer to wallow in fatalism: The last 150 years of turbulent growth in the Western world were an exception that can neither be extended chronologically nor expanded geographically. The prosperity of industrial societies is based on the ruthless exploitation of nature. Continued growth and sustainability are mutually exclusive. Resources are running low. The party is over. Only the poor populations of developing countries have been living sustainably. If they emulate our prosperity we face an irreversible collapse. Our standard of living cannot be globalized, so we must economize radically. Unless we start paddling backwards of our own accord, a series of crises and catastrophes will cut civilization down to a size nature can endure.

I do not share this outlook. Yet no one can be sure that such bleak warnings will not come to pass. Despite all the climate conferences and declarations of intent, global greenhouse gas emissions reached a new high in 2014. If this trend continues, climate change will take on ominous proportions. We are in a race between innovation and disaster where victory will require nothing less than a green revolution. There is no master plan for this, no step-by-step guide setting out what is to be done. Like every revolution it will be an open-ended process. We must, however, be clear about the direction we mean to take: Are we heading for new shores or organizing our retreat? Are we embarking on a new age of entrepreneurship or a period of rationing in which our primary focus will be the just distribution of reduced resources? These are very different messages and tones. The one we opt for will generate its own specific dynamics and alliances.

The boom in cultural pessimism we have experienced since the financial bubble burst in 2008 should come as no surprise. It is a pattern we are familiar with from previous crises of capitalism.[1] Confidence is giving way to self-doubt as anxiety about the future spreads through the middle classes. The majority of Germans no longer believe that their children will be better off than them. The shift of global economic power toward the Asia–Pacific region is reinforcing the feeling that Europe has had its day. Critiques of capitalism on the left are merging with conservative unease toward consumer society. Yet, interpretations of the current rifts and tensions as symptomatic of a final crisis of growth society overlook the fact that crises act as catalysts for the modernization of capitalism: the welfare state was a reaction to mass poverty and the rise of the labor movement, Roosevelt's New Deal was a response to the Great Depression of the early 1930s and social democracy arose out of the destruction wreaked by National Socialism and war.

Today we are on the verge of another major transformation. It is manifesting itself in a number of areas simultaneously:

- Globalization has reached a new level. It now encompasses literally every corner of the globe. New technologies, ideas, movements and lifestyles become global phenomena. A conflict between tradition and modernity is pervading every culture and continent.[2]

- The balance of the global economy is shifting from the transatlantic to the Pacific axis. The old industrial nations are losing their monopoly on high-end products and technologies; the chasing pack is jumping straight into the high-tech age.
- As the former Third World makes rapid advances, billions of people are rising out of humble circumstances. What was once considered the Western way of life is being adopted by a global middle class. Pressure on natural resources is mounting as a result.
- The global mobility of capital and goods is being paralleled by increasing human mobility—despite all the attempts countries are making to assert control over their borders. A new transnational elite is emerging.
- Both in the business world and in civil society modern communications technologies are condensing time and space, facilitating worldwide action and cooperation on a scale and at a pace never seen before.
- The digital world—an infinite, globally accessible flow of information, pictures, ideas and communicative acts—is taking on its own reality with consequences for the analog world (the world of things). The virtual and real worlds are merging.
- Our knowledge of the world is growing exponentially. Never before have there been so many researchers around the globe working on new discoveries and solutions. The pace of innovation is increasing. To the extent that it has been digitalized, the corpus of human knowledge is potentially available to all. Education is becoming our most important resource.

- Neuroscience, information technology, genetic research, biotechnology and nanotechnology are converging under the banner of the life sciences. The boundaries between biology and technology are becoming blurred. Humans are creating nature.
- The conflict between the rapid growth of the global economy and the excessive strain being placed on vital ecosystems is forcing the synthesis of ecology and economics: we are witnessing a shift away from the exploitation of nature toward cooperation with it, from fossil fuels toward renewable energy sources, from linear production chains toward material cycles and from the maximization of output toward the optimization of processes.
- Agreements modeled on the Antarctic Treaty are placing transnational ecosystems of crucial importance to human civilization under the stewardship of the international community as global public property. The Montreal Protocol on Substances that Deplete the Ozone Layer is another example of how collective commitment can stem an ominous trend.

Millions of people around the world are already involved in this new stage of the Industrial Revolution: researchers and engineers, architects and urban planners, entrepreneurs and investors, environmental activists and critical consumers, journalists, artists and countless citizens doing their bit, big or small, for a better world. Protests and alternative movements are just as indispensable to this new evolution of capitalism as science and technology, not to mention the policy makers at all levels—from city hall to the UN—responsible for charting a clear course toward ecological modernity.

From the Natural World to the Human World

A return to nature is not a realistic option for a world of soon to be nine billion people. There are too many of us for that and our impact is too large. We have long since left behind the so-called natural way of life. On our long march through history we have arrived at the Anthropocene—an age in which the earth is predominantly shaped by humans. As early as 1873 the Italian geologist Antonio Stoppani spoke of the beginning of a new anthropozoic epoch in which humans had the power and universal reach to rival the great forces of nature. Around the turn of the millennium this notion was taken up again by Paul Crutzen, winner of the Nobel Prize in Chemistry for his research on the depletion of the ozone layer. In an article entitled "Geology of Mankind" published in the scientific journal *Nature* in 2002 Crutzen outlines humanity's growing influence on the biophysical world.[3] He suggests dating the beginning of the new age to the invention of the steam engine by James Watt in 1784. Humans have been enriching the carbon content of the atmosphere and thus altering the earth's climate ever since, bringing to an end 10,000 years of climatic stability during which temperatures only fluctuated on a scale of one degree Celsius. Crutzen believes that scientists and engineers have a responsibility to guide humanity through this new period of crisis toward a sustainable system of environmental management.

There is barely a corner of the planet left that does not bear the trace of human influence. Vast areas of the earth's surface have been shaped by people. Only a little under a quarter of its land area—notably the ice-covered polar regions and large desert areas—still counts as wilderness. Our activities affect the oceans, the animal and plant worlds, soil fertility and the water cycle. Not even the earth's climate or the ozone layer are purely natural phenomena anymore. The history of the human race can be read as a tale of human expansion into the natural world. Man has been modifying the topography of the planet since being banished from paradise. The creature has turned creator, becoming a powerful agent of evolution. This development began back with early attempts at arable farming and the domestication of wild animals. As the tools humans used to tackle nature grew more powerful, the tracks they left grew wider and deeper. Forests were cleared and rivers dammed; new farmland and settlements were wrenched from the seas; railways, canals and roads were built. Settlements became cities and wilderness was cultivated. New kinds of animals and plants came into being; many others disappeared, never to be seen again. Modern genetics is just another stage on this long road of ecological and human change. The boundaries between nature and culture are breaking down; civilization and the biosphere are merging into a single hypercomplex system. The journalist Christian Schwägerl reviews the scientific literature on this topic in his book *The Anthropocene*. He quotes the American geographers Jonathan Foley, Navin Ramankutty and Erle Ellis, who call for a change in our perspective on the planet. In their assessment, the "view of the world as 'natural ecosystems with humans disturbing them'" is outdated. It is more accurate to say that the earth has become a collection of "human systems with natural ecosystems embedded within them." In the Anthropocene our task is no longer simply to preserve nature, but to sustainably cultivate the biosphere.[4] Every new stage in the transformation of nature has been accompanied by fear. Warnings about human hubris, sorrow over the losses that progress brings, the sense of being caught beyond rescue in a raging maelstrom, the admonition that all wealth is illusory—none of this was invented by the environmental movement; it has accompanied every groundbreaking achievement throughout history, from the construction of the Tower of Babel to the invention of the railroad. In the version of the Faust legend written by German author Johann Wolfgang von Goethe, Mephisto's final remark on the restless entrepreneurship of the protagonist is: "The end will be annihilation."[5] Goethe depicts finance, industry and the domestication of nature as forms of progress towards doom. Elements temporarily tamed by force are ultimately more powerful than any engineering prowess. Around the same time as *Faust*, Mary Shelley's nightmare novel *Frankenstein: The Modern Prometheus* appeared. Shelley's title identifies her tragic hero as a descendant of the ancient fire bringer who defied the gods and paid dearly for his sacrilege. Frankenstein likewise flouts the divine order when he brings a humanoid creature to life. By the time he begins to fear the consequences of his genius it is too late. His calamitous creation is beyond his control. It becomes a monster that turns against humanity. Both Goethe and Shelley anticipated the ambivalent implications of the revolution in science and technology at a time when it was still in its infancy.[6] They cover all the themes that have become almost commonplace in critiques of progress today, from the disturbing acceleration of life to the illusion of limitless growth. Warnings against megalomania, against the fantasy that men (like the gods) can and may do anything, are a central topos. The motif of the sorcerer's apprentice who cannot get rid of the spirits he has conjured is another that survives in contemporary discourse.

Flexible Limits

To limit or not to limit? This question has been debated since antiquity. In fact it encompasses a dialectical unity. Without limits neither individual nor social life would be possible. Conversely, the history of civilization has been one transgression of cultural, technological and natural limits after another. It is not hard to detect the echoes of the age-old debate in current controversies over genetic engineering and synthetic biology. *The Limits to Growth* is the name of a seminal text of the modern environmental movement that shaped the thinking of an entire generation. Its title became a familiar phrase. The computer models developed by Dennis L. Meadows and his research group seemed to demonstrate beyond doubt that continuous economic growth would lead to ecological collapse in the foreseeable future. Unless we voluntarily stepped on the brakes, the book claimed, runaway environmental pollution and the depletion of natural resources would force us to reduce our production and consumption. The earth was losing its balance; devastating shortages were decimating the population. The message was forceful and clear: the age of human expansion was coming to an end. Self-restraint or ruin—*tertium non datur.* Considered in the cold light of day, this position is not new. The British theologian and economist Thomas Malthus, a contemporary of Goethe and Shelley, predicted severe famine as a consequence of population growth beyond the level global food production could sustain. When his *Essay on the Principle of Population* appeared the global population was approximately one billion. Today there are seven billion of us. Our life expectancy has more than doubled and the standard of living of today's middle class would have turned the aristocracy of Malthus's time green with envy. Admittedly there are around a billion people who do not have enough to eat, but they are not underfed because of insufficient agricultural output. The hunger problem is a problem of both poverty and waste: too much grain goes into the production of animal feed and too much is lost on the way from the field to the consumer.

Thanks to the Promethean powers of ingenuity, science and technology, the apparently rigid limits to growth have turned out to be flexible. No less important is democracy, which has countered impoverishment with suffrage for the poor, trade unions and freedom of the press. Today the global environmental movement, in cooperation with scientists and pioneering corporations, is acting as a catalyst for ecological reform. There is no guarantee that its efforts will ultimately succeed. Progress and destruction, improved and compromised human circumstances, new beginnings and losses are always inextricably intertwined. But that does not mean they cancel each other out. The history of modernity is not a zero-sum game. In spite of all the setbacks and catastrophes it is a story of progress spurred on by two forces: constant revolution in science and technology, and the expansion of democratic freedoms. It is only in conjunction with democratic and social rights that the history of technology becomes a tale of progress.

The participation of the broad masses in economic progress has always been hard fought, and that is still the case today. After a leveling phase in postwar capitalism, the gap between rich and poor has been widening again since the 1990s. While at the top of the social ladder wealth is growing, the number of working poor is also rising. In Europe as well as the US, the real income of the broad majority is stagnating or even decreasing. The fact that economic growth is no longer experienced as progress for all is feeding doubts about the point of the model as a whole: Why should people bother making an effort at school, in their apprenticeships or at work when it never gets them anywhere? What does a higher gross national product matter unless it results in greater prosperity for everyone? Equal opportunities and social leveling are not only matters of justice: they are central to the financial dynamics and political acceptance of market economies. Ecological innovation and social participation must go hand in hand, and not merely with respect to compensatory fiscal and social policy. Given the increasingly unequal distribution of wealth, the old idea of workers having a stake in productive property is becoming relevant again. We also have to consider the conflicting aims of a green economy. Not everything sold under the label of sustainability is genuinely sustainable. Replacing petroleum with biofuels might sound like a good idea at first, but when the conversion of corn, soy or palm oil into biogas and ethanol undermines food production, increases soil erosion and accelerates the destruction of rain forests the blessing becomes a curse.[7] In spite of all its drawbacks and deficiencies, for the vast majority of people the benefits of economic growth are beyond question. The life expectancy and living standards of billions of people around the globe have risen rapidly. They also have more opportunities for self-determination, more personal choice and a greater degree of freedom. All this is intrinsically linked to the economic upturn that began with the Industrial Revolution and has continued apace—various prophecies of doom notwithstanding—since globalization was boosted by the collapse the Communist world order. As industrialization spreads, the concept of human rights is also spreading around the globe. Education standards are improving on a broad scale. More and more young people are studying abroad, while the Internet facilitates a global exchange of information and ideas. There is of course no guarantee that this success story will continue. It would be negligent to ignore the warning signs that have been accumulating in recent years, from the turmoil in the financial system to the fever symptoms being exhibited by our ecosystem. The hunt for scarce resources has set a new spiral of rearmament in motion. A return to armed geopolitics seems particularly likely in the Asia–Pacific region and in the post-Soviet sphere. The interdependence of the global markets and the bloating of the financial sector make the system more susceptible to crisis. It is not my intention to understate these dangers. But while it is easy (and crowd pleasing) to paint the future as bleak and forbidding, it is more worthwhile to look for the elements of a new beginning—a new model of environmental and social progress—emerging in the midst of the crisis. That is what this book does.

Uneasiness with Growth

Until the Industrial Revolution exploded, human intervention in the environment was local or regional in nature. Its effects could be serious but its scope was limited. That changed with the advent of the fossil age. Coal and oil generated a huge boost for industry, transportation, agriculture, urban planning and consumption. Unfortunately this has had an unintended side effect: the constant enrichment of the carbon content of the atmosphere is intensifying the greenhouse effect. Temperatures are rising, the polar ice is melting and geothermal cycles are in chaos. The effects of environmental as well as financial crises are being felt around the world, while the erratic economic growth of the developing nations, led by China, is accelerating the stress on the environment. When there are billions of people driving cars, using computers, living in comfortable houses, traveling by plane and eating steaks it abruptly becomes clear that our present resource-intensive mode of production is unsustainable. We have already reached the point where the costs of growth based on plunder outweigh the benefits. Loss of fertile land, depletion of drinking water reserves and inevitable climate change may not appear in any country's national accounts, but we will still have to pay for them at some point, and that point is getting closer. The longer we wait to change course, the greater the eventual drop in prosperity will be.

Global CO_2 emissions must be halved by the middle of the century in order to stabilize the earth's climate. The overwhelming majority of the scientific community agrees on that. The contentious issue is what we do with this understanding: Must we, the privileged minority, drastically limit our demands while hoping that the societies of Asia, Latin America and Africa resist the temptations of modernity? Should we follow the example of Diogenes in his barrel, for whom freedom was contingent on frugality, and the quest for luxury, professional success, power and glory just another form of slavery? Does salvation lie in heroically resisting the charms of consumer society, just as Odysseus once ordered his men to stuff their ears with wax while he tied himself to the mast of his ship so as not to succumb to the song of the Sirens?

Antipathy to the notion of an expansive culture geared toward the acceleration and intensification of life has a long tradition. It currently seems to be enjoying a revival. Doubts about growth society are mounting against the background of the ongoing financial crisis, the excesses of the financial industry, the uncertainty of the middle classes and increasingly tough competition on the global markets. Measure and moderation rather than greed and stress, security rather than risk, and values rather money are the order of the day. This is the intellectual breeding ground for contemporary critiques of growth, which in many respects seem to revive the concerns of the 1970s. They incorporate a whole host of motifs. Many people think economic growth is only possible at the cost of nature. Others believe that European economies are in any case only capable of minimal further growth and that we should adjust to the prospect of a future without it sooner rather than later. From this perspective the political pursuit of growth is an expensive fiction and "prosperity without growth" the motto of a new realism.[8] As far as capitalism is concerned, there are no intrinsic limits to growth. It is predicated on the promise of constant gains, putting it at odds with the basic green idea that limitless growth is impossible in a limited world. What some people find fascinating about the capitalist economic system—its infinite cycle of new products and new needs—seems sinister to others. And then then there is the uneasiness with a culture that demands success at all costs. The short-lived heyday of neoliberalism, market deregulation and unfettered profits is over, while desire for greater balance between material prosperity and immaterial values is growing. Love, friendship, decency, joie de vivre: the best things in life are free! Many young people place greater importance on family and friends, control over their work and idealistic commitment than on consumption and professional success. They subscribe to the sentiment of Wolf Biermann's wonderful verse: "Better that we have prosperity than prosperity has us."[9] Their priorities are a secure livelihood, good health care and the ability to plan for the future. The more troubled the world seems, the more defensive, preservative values prevail over lofty hopes and ambitions. This does not seem to be a purely cyclical phenomenon, but evidence of a more deeply rooted change. Isn't it wonderful that the love of money is now passé and that values are once again considered more important than quick success? Of course! My daughters' generation no longer distinguishes between the political and private spheres. They seek to live out global justice in their daily lives. Many eat a vegetarian diet, care about fair trade and are immune to fashion and brands. They campaign for human rights and equal opportunities. They see work as more than just a way to make a living: it should be meaningful. And they are prepared to work hard but are not set on getting to the top at all costs. That should give us hope for the future.

And yet, there is a barely palpable but nonetheless perceptible fatigue hanging over the debate on escaping the growth trap—a feeling that Europe's best days are behind it. While Asia is now driving global growth, China is preparing to overtake the United States and Africa is beginning to awaken from decades of stagnation, Europe is living off past glories. "Let it be!" is the response from some quarters. We should bow out with dignity. Peter Gauweiler, the maverick of Germany's Christian Social Union party, thinks that Europe needs to reconnect with its local traditions, sings the praises of regionalism and suggests that we are better off out of international trade. The European Union as a collaborative effort to keep up with the big boys? No thank you! We know only too well where that leads. Another German, the unorthodox conservative thinker Meinhard Miegel, talks of the "exhaustion of the expansionist mode of thinking, feeling and acting that led to the introduction of the euro."[10] He strongly criticizes the corrupting influence of deregulation, bemoans our current lack of security and states with some satisfaction that not only Europe but half the world is showing signs of fatigue. In his view, any attempt to stimulate growth by injecting credit into the economy is futile. The simple fact is that Europe is fully grown. Its economic vitality has been exhausted. The task now is to ensure that society can still function in reduced economic circumstances. In short: we must organize our retreat without allowing the fabric of society to tear apart.

I agree with the diagnosis that it is pointless for Europe to chase after old growth, where "old" means financed by debt and resource intensive. Continuing as before will solve neither the economic nor the environmental crisis. But does it follow that we must now say goodbye to growth forever? By no means. "Zero growth doesn't solve a single problem; it only creates new ones," states Martin Jänicke, the long-serving director of the Environmental Policy Research Centre at the Free University of Berlin.[11] From an environmental perspective, zero growth just means that the consumption of natural resources remains constant, which achieves nothing. Calls for us to leave the gilded cage of consumerism fail to address the nature of production itself. Marx was absolutely right in this regard: cultural criticism cannot replace analysis of a mode of production. Demanding reduced consumption only *seems* radical. It demonstrates a failure to understand the central element of every ecological transformation: a fundamental change in the dominant mode of production with consequences for agriculture, energy, transportation and urban planning. We would see that if we stopped our European navel-gazing for a moment and turned our attention to the rest of the world.

When it comes to the dynamics of global growth over the next few decades, the debate on postgrowth society misses the point. The extent to which the global economy grows will not be decided in Europe. China, which is currently experiencing annual growth rates of 7 to 9 percent, will of course not remain the locomotive of world growth forever. Nonetheless, until the middle of the century the global growth rate is likely to be above, rather than below, 3 percent. The billions of people standing on the verge of industrial modernity will see to that. They have set their sights on an improved standard of living and will massively boost the demand for housing, food, consumer goods, transportation and services of all kinds. Economic growth generally results from two factors: firstly from an increased input of capital and labor and secondly from scientific and technological innovation, which leads to higher productivity. In the coming decades there will be no shortage of either of these things.

The aging societies of Europe and Japan are the ones slowing down. But they too would do well to invest more in education, science and innovation if they want to tackle demographic change without a drastic drop in prosperity. In the long term this is the best way to compensate for declining manpower resources. Whether Europe continues to attract skilled immigrants in future remains to be seen—the appeal of other, more dynamic areas of the world is growing. But even on the old continent there is still plenty of room for sustainable growth. The ecological modernization of physical capital and infrastructure requires significant investment. New, resource-efficient technologies replace old plants and machinery more quickly in a dynamic environment than in stagnating or shrinking markets. When revenue, income and tax receipts fall, investment in modernization drops too. It would be fatal to let that happen. We have only just embarked on an energy revolution that necessitates enormous investment in wind and solar power plants, transnational electricity grids and energy-saving technologies. The transportation sector is undergoing a similar revolution. Electric vehicles, car sharing and a flexible network of public and private transport are going to change the face of our cities. Investment in building renovation is long overdue. Indeed, our entire technological apparatus and public infrastructure is due for a fundamental overhaul similar to that which took place in Germany at the end of the nineteenth century and in the period following the Second World War. There is also a great need for investment in the education sector (particularly in vocational training and continuing education), while the demographic changes taking place will entail substantially increased funding for health care provision too. None of this will be possible unless economic productivity is maximized.

With respect to private consumption, most Europeans are far from living in the lap of luxury. Very few people have more money than they can spend. Even in affluent Germany half of households had less than €1,311 of disposable income after deductions for tax and social security in 2009—hardly an excess of riches.[12] On the contrary, these households are suffering from a lack of purchasing power. The further east you travel, the clearer it becomes just how fallacious the idea of postmaterial prosperity—let alone overabundance—is. Look beyond Europe and the situation is worse still. Even today the vast majority of the global population is living in precarious circumstances. Billions are on the breadline, without electricity, running water or adequate health care. And the global population is expected to grow by another two billion before the middle of the century. Ultimately the needs, desires and ambitions of these people are what is going to drive economic growth. The question is not *whether* the global economy will continue to grow, but *how* it will grow. Given the mass poverty in the world, zero growth is neither a realistic nor a desirable prospect. Nor can we continue as we have been doing. The third option, the one advocated by this book, is ecologically sustainable, socially inclusive growth.[13] Perhaps even an economy founded on the synthesis of nature and technology will eventually come up against absolute limits to growth. Only time will tell. And it may be true that for a growing number of people material needs are becoming less important than the desire for a work–life balance and self-fulfillment. But the vast majority of the earth's inhabitants are going in the opposite direction. There are more than enough energy supplies to fuel the industrialization of the developing nations. Coal and gas are still in plentiful supply. Even our current oil reserves are greater than those of 40 years ago. Most metals and minerals are still available in large amounts. When the supply of specific raw materials lags behind demand, prices rise. Higher prices in turn lead to new deposits being tapped and scarce materials being used more efficiently or replaced with alternatives.

The main obstacle to economic growth is not the exhaustion of raw materials. Much more dangerous for the planet is the recklessness with which the available resources are being exploited. Even if only 10 percent of the estimated reserves of coal, oil and gas were to be extracted and burnt, the resulting intensification of the greenhouse effect would take us well beyond the critical threshold of a two-degree (Celsius) rise in the global temperature.[14] And greenhouse gas emissions are not the only problem associated with industrial society's hunger for resources. The extraction and processing of raw materials generally goes hand in hand with high demand for energy, water and chemicals. It leaves behind desolate landscapes and contaminated groundwater. Especially in those developing nations where the public institutions are weak and the ruling elites corrupt, a wealth of raw materials can become a curse. We must thus make more efficient use of natural resources, implement closed-loop cycles for critical raw materials and replace them little by little with environmentally friendly alternatives. At present that means green technologies (like wind and solar power plants) that incorporate precious metals such as copper, silver, platinum and palladium. We must also establish a global resource management system to ensure both maximum transparency and high environmental and social standards. New alliances between industry and human rights or environmental organizations are playing a growing role in this area. They establish criteria for the sustainable use of raw materials and award quality seals to better inform consumers.[15]

The critical limit to economic growth lies in the resilience of vital ecosystems: the climate, soil and water. Climate change in particular has the potential to become truly catastrophic. Unless the CO_2 concentration of the atmosphere is kept under four hundred parts per million we risk losing everything. The climatic consequences of exceeding this threshold are incalculable. It follows that the atmosphere can absorb at most another 840 billion tons of carbon dioxide. That might sound like a huge amount, but it isn't. In 2011 global emissions climbed to a record 34 billion tons. Extrapolating from this number, we will have used up our CO_2 balance within 25 years. By the end of the century we can expect a temperature rise of four to six degrees—hence the dramatic need for action. We don't have much time left to turn things around and it can't be done without radically improving energy efficiency and switching from fossil fuels to renewable energy sources. In order to speed up this process we need global agreements that limit and set prices for CO_2 emissions. In the future we will also extract carbon from the atmosphere, whether by intensifying reforestation efforts, replenishing the humus layer or using carbon dioxide as a raw material in chemical production.

The findings of climate science show that we must act urgently, but they by no means dictate the volume of goods and services that can be provided to humanity in the future without destabilizing the climate. That quantity will be determined by two dynamic factors: the transition from fossil fuels to renewable energy sources and the efficiency with which we use scarce resources. An economy based on solar power and biological material cycles doesn't cause environmental problems. The limits to economic growth are determined by the resilience of the biosphere in combination with human ingenuity. While the former is limited, the latter is potentially limitless. In the long term, only the transition to a low-resource, climate-neutral mode of production will allow for further increases in economic prosperity: green growth or collapse, those are the alternatives. The key to sustainable growth lies in the separation of value creation from the consumption of natural resources.

Modernizing Modernity

An end to the growth of modern industrial society is neither desirable nor likely to solve our problems. It is undesirable because there is still too much poverty in the world that cannot be overcome by redistribution alone, but also because appeals to self-restraint all too easily end in virtuous tyranny. What would be worth striving for in a future where everyone were assigned a meager yet inviolable emissions and resource allowance? And what if old Adam (or rather Eve—after all, it was she who defied the ban on eating from the tree of knowledge) will not abandon his quest to go higher, further and faster? Must he be coerced into higher understanding? The logical consequence of the belief that environmental crisis can only be overcome by radically reducing human activity on earth—less production, less consumption, less travel, less data generation—is an environmental state of emergency. But once environmentalists start telling people what they can and cannot do they have already lost. The vast majority of people on this earth are dreaming a very different dream. While old Europe is wallowing in self-doubt, frightened by the bitter winds of globalization, they are pursing the comforts of modern life that most of us have long taken for granted. They won't let anyone or anything take that dream away from them.

It is true that things could end badly if the developing nations follow our example as they play economic catch-up. In societies like ours, with their falling population figures and growing number of elderly people, it is primarily the demand for social and cultural services that is growing. The countries of the South are still concerned with concrete material growth: housing, food and all sorts of consumer goods. The scale of this growth is illustrated by the Chinese automotive industry. In 1990 there were 509,000 vehicles produced in China (cars, buses and trucks). By the turn of the millennium that number had risen to more than two million. After that production advanced at a tearing pace. Since 2009 China has been the world's number one producer by some distance. In 2011 more than eighteen million vehicles came off its assembly lines—around three times as many as in Germany, which is renowned for its automobile production. The rise in the number of cars has been particularly rapid. Nearly fourteen million new cars were registered in 2010, while in Germany there are approximately three million per year on average. Relative to the size of its population, the number of cars in China is still well below the figures for highly industrialized nations. In Germany there are over five hundred vehicles per thousand inhabitants; in China there are 77. There is no risk that China will reach German levels. Over the coming decades the car is going to lose its dominant position in the major cities. But beyond the metropolitan areas the industry still has enormous potential for growth. The Chinese government expects the number of vehicles on its roads to more than double (to approximately two hundred million) by 2020. Rail and air travel will also increase considerably during the same period. And China is only the leader of a chasing pack that includes all of Asia, while Latin America and Africa are heading in the same direction.

The key question is not *whether* mobility is growing around the world—that is not even up for debate. The critical issue is the energy and resource efficiency of the transport systems and vehicles that will be used by billions of people for local and long-distance travel. A proportional increase in current traffic levels would be the last straw for the global climate, making it imperative that we move toward climate-neutral, resource-efficient transportation as quickly as possible: fast and comfortable public transport networks, electric cars, planes that run on biokerosene or hydrogen, and pedestrian- and cyclist-friendly cities. If we can quadruple the energy efficiency of our transport systems—and this isn't rocket science—we can double the amount of traffic worldwide while halving CO_2 emissions. As long as there are sufficient renewable resources to meet the remaining energy demands, climate neutrality will be within our reach.[16] What does this tell us? We must help societies undergoing modernization to skip as much of the fossil age as possible. In rural areas of Africa only 10 percent of households have electricity. Energy shortages are a major obstacle to economic and social development. One way or another, the continent's energy consumption is going to rise steeply in the coming decades. The pivotal question is whether coal and oil or sun and wind will form the basis of its economic ascent. The developing nations still have the chance to build their cities, industries, energy supplies and transport systems with maximum resource efficiency, but they need help in the form of money and technology. The prospects for sustainable growth will improve if prosperous industrial nations lead the way. Europe still has the scientific, technological and financial potential to break the vicious circle of economic growth and environmental destruction. And we have positive experience to draw on. Since the 1970s the old industrial nations have made substantial progress in improving the quality of the environment. Pollution caused by all kinds of toxic substances has been drastically reduced. Rivers and forests have recovered and the smog over cities has thinned out. We can continue these success stories. The next stage is to decouple economic growth from resource consumption and CO_2 emissions. There is every reason to believe this is possible. Since the fall of the Berlin Wall, Germany's economy has grown by around a third, while greenhouse gas emissions have fallen by 25 percent.[17] We have considerable improvements in industrial resource efficiency and the success of alternative energy sources to thank for these numbers. Denmark has seen a similar reduction in its CO_2 emissions, with Copenhagen on its way to becoming the world's first climate-neutral capital city by 2025.

The German experience has demonstrated that economic growth, environmental progress and falling emissions can go hand in hand. That is our most important message to the developing nations. Why shouldn't Europe participate in a growing global economy with intelligent services and sustainable products? Our strengths are knowledge and skill—things the world can never have enough of. The distribution of the fruits of growth is a separate issue and will be decided in the struggle for a just society. As we have seen over the last 20 years, growth in no way guarantees better conditions for the working classes. But a dynamic economic environment always provides greater opportunity for social mobility than times of economic stagnation. The fairy tale of jobless growth does not stand up to empirical scrutiny and the financial positions of social security systems mirror economic activity. Not even increased tax funding for social benefits can change that: tax revenue is dependent on economic growth too. Higher taxes for the rich can only paper over this fact for a limited time.

The Synthesis of Technology and Nature

Until now the metabolic relationship between humans and nature has been based on the *consumption* of natural resources: the richer and more powerful the human world grows, the poorer nature becomes. This has been the case since the rise of the early empires, if not before. Even the ancient Greeks and Romans ruthlessly plundered the forests of the Mediterranean region to obtain timber for their cities and fleets. When their empires fell, they left behind barren, sun-scorched expanses of land. Things are still done this way today: never before has the consumption of natural resources been so extreme, the level of greenhouse gas emissions so high or the danger to species diversity so advanced. While the productive property of the industrial nations has grown rapidly, the ecological systems on which human civilization depends are threatening to collapse. The rate at which natural capital is being lost is rising in proportion to material wealth.[18] This can and will not continue. The excessive strain being placed on ecosystems of vital importance to humanity makes it imperative that we change course. By overloading the atmosphere with greenhouse gases we are pushing the earth's climate to tipping point. Fertile land is being lost due to erosion and salinization, while at the same time the demand for food and agrarian raw materials is growing. Water shortages pose a threat to agricultural production.

We have reached a crossroads: either we succeed in establishing a sustainable mode of production or our planet is headed for serious crises. Technologies, processes and products are not the only things at issue. The relationship between humans and nature has to change. From now on we must take responsibility for both the natural and human worlds. In the Anthropocene, politicians, corporations and consumers are accountable for climatic stability, species diversity and the preservation of fertile land. We must look after the natural world, meaning that politics in the twenty-first century must become *geopolitics* in the literal sense of the word.[19] The atmosphere, the oceans and the Arctic ecosystems must be declared global public property and managed collectively. Humanity has gone well beyond the point of simply letting the earth be. Our task now is to shape it into a great landscape garden. A garden is a planned natural space, a symbiosis of beauty and utility. This approach has been practiced for centuries in the cultivated agrarian landscapes of the Alps, the vineyards on the River Rhine and the hills of Tuscany. These are landscapes shaped by farmers, paradigmatic for a sustainable economic system mindful of the natural basis of its production. With the rise of big industry a different perspective prevailed—one that regarded nature above all as a resource, an apparently inexhaustible store of raw materials and a dumping ground for the excrement of industrial society. The economy grew and grew, swallowing up the treasures that slumbered in the soil and the forests. In return it filled nature with trash, emissions and sewage. That amounts to plunder.

Now we are faced with another paradigm shift: the transition to a new economic system that works with the productive forces of nature rather than against them. Up to now our conception of nature has been shaped by the scarcity of natural resources that have to be used as efficiently as possible: Raw materials, freshwater supplies and fertile soil are finite—so the conventional wisdom goes. The natural world is a shrinking habitat for a growing number of people. This sounds obvious, but in fact it is shortsighted. Not the scarcity of limited resources but the amazing productivity of nature, the immense richness of evolution is the basis for a sustainable economy. We do not yet know what possibilities the combination of natural creativity and human intellect—the synergy of biosphere and noosphere—will yield.[20] A green economy in which evolution and technology form a productive synthesis is beginning to take shape. Leading thinkers in the field of environmental policy have come up with various terms capturing the essence of this vision: technology of alliance (Ernst Bloch), biocybernetics (Frederic Vester), efficiency revolution (Ernst Ulrich von Weizsäcker) and natural capitalism (Amory and Hunter Lovins, Paul Hawken). They conceive of a future society that is dynamic, rather than static, of growth with nature rather than meek submission to a predetermined natural order.

The primary productive force of postfossil society is solar power. Until now the phrase “solar power” has primarily been associated with solar electricity. It is easy to lose sight of the fact that the conversion of sunlight into carbon compounds is the basis of all life on earth—the energy source for the world of plants and microbes on which all other creatures depend. In the long term an environmentally friendly economy must also build on photosynthesis as a source of biological and chemical raw materials. Biotechnology will be one of the leading technological disciplines of the twenty-first century. New technologies, materials and products will imitate the inventions brought about by millions of years of evolution.

At the same time, resource efficiency must be continually improved. In this context the old green slogan “less is more” takes on a new meaning: the generation of greater prosperity from less energy and fewer raw materials. That sounds a bit like alchemy, but it isn’t magic. The chemical industry has already demonstrated how to increase production while lowering resource consumption. It has taken the principle of closed-loop material cycles and the cascade usage of raw materials and energy further than other sectors. Resource efficiency is one of the reasons why German industry is so competitive on the world market. Going green is a recipe for success in economic terms too. Over the last 20 years the country has shown how a highly industrialized society can lower CO_2 emissions without compromising its competitiveness. The German energy revolution has paved the way for an upsurge in wind and solar power production around the world. Many countries are watching very closely how Germany deals with the challenges arising from the rapid growth of renewable energy. If wind and solar power were to become its dominant energy sources the electricity system would have to be completely restructured. If the success of the transformation continues, others will follow. That in itself is a reason to persevere.

Combating Ecopessimism

Environmental discourse has traditionally been dominated by two big words: dangers and limits. There are good reasons for this. In order to break the business-as-usual routine and galvanize the public it is absolutely necessary to raise alarm. But alarmist discourse without alternatives turns people off. If we want to get members of the public, businesses and governments involved in environmental reform we have to talk about opportunities and potential. The debate over nuclear power is an instructive example in this regard. There has been a strong antinuclear movement in Germany since the 1970s and the catastrophic potential of nuclear power has been clear to everyone since the Chernobyl disaster in April 1986. But it took another 20 years before politicians finally agreed to abandon the curious idea of using nuclear chain reactions to produce steam. The German government had just decided to extend the operating life of its nuclear power plants when Fukushima happened. Always quick to sense which way the wind is blowing, Chancellor Merkel announced a U-turn, shutting down almost half of the country's nuclear reactors in one fell swoop. There was hardly any protest from the business world and no warnings that the lights would go out the next day. The reason for this was that, unlike in 1986, there was a widespread alternative to nuclear energy on hand: renewable energy. Wind power and solar electricity had already proven themselves. Since the Social Democrat–Green coalition government had passed the German Renewable Energy Act into law on April 1, 2000, a new branch of the economy had emerged, creating hundreds of thousands of jobs. Broad sections of the public were (and are) convinced that this is where the future of energy provision lies.

The decision to phase out nuclear power, then, was not merely a hazard control measure. It marked the start of a new, intriguing age of renewable energy—the beginning of a green revolution. There is no predetermined script for this revolution. Now that the process of environmental change has been set in motion it will generate its own dynamics. The number of new inventions is rising, new technologies are emerging, venture capital is flowing into young companies and new markets are developing. What yesterday was still science fiction is being surpassed by reality today. Who, 30 years ago, could have imagined the world we live in today? Since then the Soviet Union has collapsed, the Berlin Wall has come down and the division of Europe is history. China has become a world power. A Deutschmark is something you might find in a museum. Europe's forests haven't died out and there are salmon swimming in the Rhine again. The digital revolution has completely changed economics, politics and daily life. Germany has become a pioneer for wind and solar power. The Arab world, which for a long time was considered the epitome of stagnation, is at the center of a political hurricane. In other words: the present cannot tell us what the future will be. We cannot be sure that everything will be alright, nor do we have to give up on the idea of progress. Instead we have to redefine it. If environmentalists put all their passion into prophesying doom they will ultimately achieve nothing. The public will experience a frisson of fear, nod in agreement and continue in their old habits for as long as possible. Change will only come about if we help people to see beyond the dangers to the opportunities for a better future.

Proponents of the green industrial revolution are often accused of worshipping technology. Of course, even hard-bitten critics of civilization concede that there must be some technological innovation, but ultimately they see it as akin to attempting repairs on the Titanic. Our primary focus, they claim, should not be on changing our mode of production but on changing humanity and its habits, desires and behavioral patterns. We must convert from self-indulgence to self-restraint. No matter what you think of this kind of preaching, dispassionate analysis tells us that reduced consumption will not save the planet. The human race is too big for that and every year we are being joined by millions more people, all striving for access to the comforts of modernity. There is no going back from the level of individuality, mobility, comfort, communication and plurality that characterizes modern societies. A political program geared toward the minimization of production and consumption would result in a virtuous authoritarianism exercised in the name of the environment. It is imperative that we avoid this. The object of environmental politics is not to alter the human mindset, but to reorganize our mode of production and consumption.

Does that mean, then, that we can rely on technological innovation alone? Absolutely not. Changes to our everyday behavior and the revolution of industry and technology are closely connected. The days of guilt-free consumption are gone. We have to take responsibility for the consequences of our behavior. That means not only considering the retail prices of products but also their social and environmental impact, especially when it comes to our diet. What we eat influences more than just our personal well-being. It affects land use, cropping systems, animal breeding, water consumption, freight volumes and CO_2 emissions around the globe. Our hunger for meat and dairy products is the main force behind the industrialization of farming. The growing number of people reaching for poultry, beef, salami, yogurt and milkshakes in the supermarket are driving mass animal husbandry. As a result, a growing share of grain production is having to be diverted for use as animal feed. The prices of staple foods are rising and the pressure to further intensify agricultural output is growing. Anyone who laments the reduction of cows, pigs and chickens to agricultural machines and is appalled by monster stalls housing tens of thousands of animals ought to examine his or her diet. Less meat and more grains, legumes, fresh vegetables and fruit—try this and you will discover that it is no real deprivation. Given the merits of vegetarian cooking, restricting oneself to a good piece of meat once in a while does not have to mean renouncing all gastronomic pleasure. It's not a question of self-denial, just of a different kind of enjoyment.

Admittedly, not even a change in our conception of good food will transform the agricultural landscape into a preindustrial idyll. Global demand for food is going to rise, and agricultural raw materials are playing a growing role in industry and in the energy sector. The pressure on farming, soil and water supplies will continue to mount. To that extent, our individual behavior is only part of the solution. We cannot address these problems without political reform and scientific innovation. But no matter how insignificant the impact of our personal conduct, we should always do our best to avoid inflicting harm on other living things. Fair trade and organic products, ethical consumption and sustainable investments are more than short-term fashions. They are precursors of a new economy. The more people reflect on the ramifications of their lifestyles, the greater the effect will be.

Only a combination of technological innovation, political leadership and individual action can generate the depth, breadth and speed of ecological transformation necessary to avoid turbulent crises. It is far from certain that we will succeed in this. It is quite possible that over the next few decades the world will become a very inhospitable place—hot, dry and hostile to life. But even if it is too late to limit the greenhouse effect to two degrees Celsius, we should still be doing all we can to reduce CO_2 emissions as drastically as possible. The more successful we are, the more future generations will have to work with as they adjust to climate change and attempt to cool the earth down again.[21] We have already reached a point where a three-pronged strategy is required: we must maximize the reduction of new greenhouse gas emissions, reclaim carbon that has already accumulated in the atmosphere and adapt as best we can to unavoidable climate change. Regardless of how successful it is, no strategy for innovation or politicocultural reformation will bring about a harmonious, crisis-free future. A world of nine billion people will never be idyllic. Nonetheless, we must do everything in our power to steer progress in a new direction and avoid the social Darwinian precept of every man for himself.

Chapter 1

A Changing World

There are two schools of thought about economic growth. Strongly desired by some as a means of righting the debt-laden ship of state, others regard it as a deluded notion from which we must free ourselves as quickly as possible. Forty years after the Club of Rome's study *The Limits to Growth* became the manifesto of the environmental movement, antipathy to economic growth is making a comeback. The unsustainable burden it places on the environment, modern civilization's insatiable appetite for energy and the growing discrepancy between resource consumption and limited reserves of raw materials are fueling calls for a postgrowth society. Other commonly encountered motifs include weariness with a life devoted to consumption, laments over permanent pressure to perform and the ubiquitous acceleration of life, a feeling of helplessness toward financial markets gone wild and growing middle-class uncertainty in the face of a new period of economic hardship that demands more effort in return for less security. Recent surveys show that the majority of Germans do not connect the term "prosperity" with material improvements in their standard of living, but with a life free from worries about unemployment, old age and illness. The more uncertain the future appears, the more important qualities such as certainty and security become. Fewer and fewer people still believe that future generations will be better off. When the idea of progress through growth loses traction, questions of distribution take center stage.

Does the crisis raging in the financial markets prove right all those who predict that growth has had its day? *Growth financed by debt,* i.e. the constant debt-based expansion of government spending and credit-funded housing booms such as those that have had such an impact on the US and Spanish economies, has certainly hit the wall. The idea that we can maintain perpetual income and job growth by taking on more and more debt has proven to be insane. Throughout much of Europe a slowing economy and reductions in state benefits are having a negative impact on the standard of living of broad sections of the population. Demographic change is further strengthening this trend: a dwindling number of working-age citizens is having to bear increasing health care costs. So will growth soon be a thing of the past? Is the seemingly interminable effort to squeeze more and more from evanescent resources coming to an end? Is the oversaturation of the markets causing capitalism to flag? Is the global Monopoly game winding up as more and more people refuse to join in?

It seems unlikely. There is no end to growth in sight. On the contrary. We must not let the financial crises of recent years obscure the fact that the global economy is in the middle of a historic growth phase driven by four basic factors:

- Firstly, the *global population* is expected to grow from just over seven billion today to at least nine billion by the middle of this century. Even though rising prosperity, better education and greater self-determination for women are causing demographic growth to level out, this increase is inevitable thanks to the high birthrates of generations that have already come into the world. At present the global population is growing by an amount equivalent to the population of Germany—a little over eighty million people—every year, with the greatest demographic growth taking place in Africa: by 2050 there will be more than twice as many people living there as there are today. That alone will drive up demand for food, goods and services of all kinds.

- Secondly, the *global labor force*, which today amounts to around three billion people, is set to almost double by the middle of the century: every year umpteen million young, energetic people are crowding into the job market, looking for productive work. To put it another way, the growing demand for goods is being accompanied by increased manpower potential. In China alone the working population is going to increase by approximately two hundred and fifty million people over the next two decades—an increase greater than Europe's total current manpower potential.
- Thirdly, we are at present witnessing billions of people strive with all their might for a share in the spoils of modern civilization: homes with running water and electricity, a plentiful supply of food, household appliances, medical care, education, computers, cell phones and transportation. They aren't concerned with the question of how much is enough; they work hard and invest in their children's education in order to escape poverty and gain access to things we take for granted. The momentum of billions of people playing catch-up is a powerful force for growth capable of transcending any economic crisis. The *global middle class* is going to grow rapidly in the course of this trend. By the middle

of the century the number of people with purchasing power of between $10 and $100 per day is expected to rise from around one billion to four billion. Demand for high-end consumer goods and services will grow to many times the current level as a result.

- Last but not least, the pace of innovation is increasing at a breathtaking rate. While the most recent groundbreaking innovation—the digital revolution—is still in full swing, new waves of innovation are already breaking: renewable energy, electromobility, biotechnology, materials engineering, robotics, nanotechnology and medical engineering—a wide range of new technologies, products and services are making themselves felt. The capabilities of computers are growing rapidly, facilitating research projects on an entirely new scale. High-powered search engines and information networks allow worldwide access to all the data anyone could want. The boundaries between scientific disciplines are becoming blurred; new knowledge is being generated in interdisciplinary networks and the production of knowledge is being globalized. Never before have there been so many scientists working on new ideas and projects in so many countries. The Asian emerging nations in particular are constantly expanding their capacity for innovation. Within the last five years Chinese applications to the European Patent Office have increased fivefold. According to the president of the Patent Office, Benoît Battistelli, at this rate China will oust Germany from third place within a few years (the United States currently holds the top spot, followed at some distance by Japan and Germany): "We can no longer say that China is merely the world's factory: it is positioning itself to become the world's research laboratory too."[1]

China as a Forerunner

The new economic miracle is primarily a phenomenon of the emerging nations, which are undergoing the process of industrialization in fast forward and causing a dramatic shift in the balance of the global economy. Owing to their growth dynamic, the newly industrialized countries are together expected to account for around two-thirds of gross world product by 2030. In contrast, Europe's share is going to shrink drastically. Extrapolating from current economic and demographic trends, the American economic historian Robert W. Fogel has projected that come 2040 the 15 Western European EU countries, which by then will account for only 4 percent of the world's population, will be generating about 5 percent of GWP. The US, with 5 percent of the population, will be generating 14 percent, and with 17 percent of the global population China will have reached no less than 40 percent of GWP.[2] Linear projections such as these should of course be taken with a grain of salt, but they illustrate a process of economic continental drift that is going to fundamentally alter the world's political architecture. And there is in any case nothing very bold about the prognosis that China is likely to overtake the US as the world's largest national economy before the end of the current decade. The Berlin-based social scientist Helmut Wiesenthal points out that from the perspective of world history this development is not particularly sensational: In rising to economic dominance, both China and India are returning to positions they occupied right up to the beginning of the nineteenth century. Prior to the Industrial Revolution they were the two largest economies in the world. Now they are reconnecting with a proud history that never vanished from their collective memories.[3] In some respects this is also true of Turkey, as the successor to the Ottoman Empire. It is the only European borderland capable of keeping pace with the other emerging nations. Even during the financial crisis of 2011 the Turkish economy grew by an impressive 8.5 percent.

The societies of Asia, Latin America and Africa are just starting to catch up, having long been peripheral players in the global market. For the vast majority of people that was an unenviable position to be in—cut off from education and health care with no prospect of social mobility. The Asian tigers were the first to break the vicious circle of poverty: South Korea, Taiwan and Singapore led the way, followed by Malaysia, Thailand, the Philippines, Indonesia and Vietnam. Since the 1980s China has taken on the role of global growth locomotive. For 30 years the Chinese economy has been expanding at an annual rate of 8 to 10 percent. Not even the most recent global financial crises have managed to slow its self-perpetuating dynamism. The country's formidable rise is being driven by an extravagant *investment ratio* that has risen from around 30 percent at the beginning of the 1970s to over 40 percent today—approximately twice the level of Germany or the US.[4] A high investment ratio means expanded production capacity and modernized infrastructure, but also investment in educational institutions and the constant growth of a society's skilled labor force, accompanied by an increase in its potential for innovation. China is swiftly progressing from imitation mode to innovation mode. In 2012 there were three times as many people employed in research and development there as in Germany, and the gap will continue to grow. Judging by its technological standards, its diversity and its capacity for innovation, the Chinese economy is not only growing is size, but also in quality. This development has been accompanied by a massive increase in national income. Income per capita has risen at an annual rate of around 8 percent over the last 30 years. Despite glaring inequality in the distribution of wealth, this has led to unprecedented improvements in the circumstances of hundreds of millions of people who have risen from bitter poverty to modest prosperity.

For environmental as well as demographic reasons China must make the transition from extensive to intensive growth soon. The effects of its one-child policy will soon catch up with it. The Chinese birthrate is approximately 30 percent below the mark of 2.2 children per woman required for stable population development, and the country's demographic development will likely reach a turning point before 2030. After that the labor force will shrink over time, while the number of elderly people will rise rapidly. The US Census Bureau estimates that within the next 20 years the over-65 age group will swell from 115 million to approximately two hundred and forty million people.[5] China's demographic structure is becoming more like Europe's, albeit at a much lower level of prosperity. Western Europe got rich before it got old. China is threatening to get old before it can get rich, which is why its political leaders are doing all they can to alter the nature of its growth by increasing productivity and enhancing the country's capacity for innovation. This is good news from an environmental perspective because it will make the Chinese economy less resource intensive in the medium term.

Up to now China's CO_2 emissions have been rising roughly in parallel with the growth of its gross domestic product. They have doubled in the last 10 years and China has overtaken the US as the world's largest CO_2 producer. Although its emissions per capita are still well below the level of the old industrial nations, China is catching up quickly in this area too. According to the calculations of the International Energy Agency, its carbon emissions grew by 9.3 percent or 720 million tons in 2011. To put this in perspective, the *increase* in Chinese emissions was only slightly smaller than the *entirety* of Germany's CO_2 emissions that year. China's economic miracle is predominantly being powered by fossil fuels. The country burns approximately half the coal consumed worldwide. In 2011 its share of global energy consumption was 72 percent, while every week new coal-fired power plants with a capacity of around nine hundred megawatts are being added to the grid. Although for the most part the new power plants are substantially more efficient than old ones, this makes certain levels of future CO_2 emissions inevitable. At the same time, China is investing massive amounts in energy efficiency and renewable energy. In 2011 the People's Republic generated as much as 58 gigawatts of wind power—a quarter of the amount produced worldwide. Over one hundred gigawatts of electricity are scheduled to be generated by wind turbines in 2015 and Chinese companies now make up five of the world's ten largest wind turbine manufacturers. The electricity grid is being developed to direct wind power from the sparsely populated regions in the west to the population centers in the east.[6] Today China is also the world's largest producer of solar cells. To date the lion's share of its production has been exported, particularly to Germany, which has become the world's biggest market for solar electricity thanks to guaranteed feed-in tariffs. German electricity consumers have indirectly financed the development of the Chinese solar industry. But following a dramatic drop in the price of solar cells, China has increasingly been generating its own solar electricity. The government has set ambitious goals for improving energy efficiency. Sustainable growth has become an official mission statement. There are concrete economic reasons for this. A substantial share of the country's nominal growth is being gobbled up by devastating damage to the environment and public health associated with the existing development model. Wang Yuqing, former deputy director of the Ministry of Environmental Protection, estimates that in 2011 environmental damage amounted to 5 or 6 percent of GNP—more than half the economic growth for that year.[7] Air, water and soil pollution is jeopardizing drinking water supplies, eroding agricultural production and making people sick. Forty percent of the country's rivers are deemed to pose a health risk. Eight out of ten cities fall below already minimal air quality standards. Drought is spreading and the contamination of soil with heavy metals is increasing.

If China wants to avoid environmental and economic collapse it must alter its growth model, shifting from extensive to intensive use of natural resources, from the ruthless exploitation of people and nature toward a gentler economic system and from the dominance of energy-guzzling industries to stronger growth in the service and high technology sectors. It has a few decades to execute a development that took more than one hundred and fifty years in Europe. At the 18th Party Congress in November 2012 the Chinese leadership declared the preservation of environmental balance to be an urgent priority. Delegates unanimously approved the adoption of a corresponding article into the charter of the Communist Party. According to the declaration, developing an environmentally friendly civilization is a long-term plan of vital importance for the life of the people and the future of the nation that will also serve to make China more beautiful.[8] There is also growing pressure from below to take action against massive environmental pollution. Protests against environmental plunder are on the rise. In July 2012, for example, the inhabitants of the port city Qidong in eastern China resisted the construction of a pipeline intended to channel wastewater to the sea from a paper factory belonging to the Japanese company Oji Paper located around one hundred kilometers away. The people were afraid that poisonous wastewater would wipe out the fishing grounds they live off. Several thousands took part in the protests. In the course of the disturbance they stormed the headquarters of the city government, destroying computers and overturning tables. The mayor eventually announced on camera that the project had been abandoned.

The exploitative model of growth pursued by China up to now has reached its environmental and political limits. Its current crises are symptomatic of a turbulent transition to a new model of growth founded on innovation and quality. While the country's economic boom has thus far been based almost entirely on exports, in the future domestic demand will play a crucial role. As ever, China will not let outsiders tell it what to do. But it is adaptive and ambitious. The West should be doing everything possible to support it in its transformation from black to green superpower. It is in the interests of the whole world for China—an economic giant with an enormous ecological footprint—to make the leap into a postfossil future as quickly as possible, rather than repeating all the sins of the old industrial nations.

Globalization

China is at the forefront of a much wider-reaching development characterized by the economic rise of the southern continents more generally. *Globalization*, having received a shot in the arm from the collapse of the socialist world order at the beginning of the 1990s, is helping the former Third World catch up with the established industrial nations. It allows for the direct transfer of advanced know-how, modern technologies and management methods between nations. Multinational companies are not only distributing their production plants around the globe; they are also internationalizing their development divisions. Open capital markets are advancing the integration of old and new economies. Online communication and global logistics systems constitute the nervous system of a global division of labor. China is transforming itself from the world's workbench into a high-tech nation. Nowadays the country trains more engineers than the US. At the 2012 Hannover Messe, the world's largest industrial fair, five hundred of the five thousand exhibitors were from China, which wants to become the global leader in innovation by 2020—an ambitious but not unrealistic goal. South Korea has demonstrated that it is possible to make the leap from agrarian society to high-tech economy within four decades. India has become a center for the software industry and Internet services. Brazil is developing into a great energy power with the capacity to process its own abundant natural resources. In 2010 per capita income in Brazil was higher than in Russia; with an annual income of more than five thousand dollars, about half of the population now counts as middle class.

The flip side of this development is that the old industrial nations have lost their technological monopoly. The American management guru Vijay Govindarajan has spoken of "reverse innovation": new products and services are increasingly being invented in the up-and-coming countries of the South and spreading around the world from there. Even high-value goods are no longer exclusively the domain of the North. Cars, machinery, chemicals, computers, cell phones, consumer electronics, software, solar cells and wind turbines are being produced all around the world. The emerging nations are becoming increasingly competitive in export markets. In 2011 alone China exported 850,000 cars, primarily to other emerging nations—an increase of 50 percent over the previous year. And who knew that the production of pharmaceuticals had likewise migrated to Asia? Today China and India, rather than Germany, are the world's pharmacy.[9] The United States now obtains almost 80 percent of its pharmaceuticals from these two countries; in Europe their market share is between 45 and 70 percent. Affordability is still the main advantage of Chinese products, but manufacturers are dedicated to improving quality and design.

The revolution in the international division of labor is perhaps nowhere more starkly evident than in Britain, the birthplace of industrialization. Where once the manufacture of textiles, steel, locomotives, ships and cars boomed, now only remnants of industrial production survive. As recently as the early 1950s a quarter of the world's industrial exports came from Britain. Today its share has fallen to less than 3 percent. Manufacturing now accounts for just 10 percent of British economic activity (compared with 23 percent in Germany—German industry has managed to compete on the world market as a producer of high-value goods). Britain's working class, so rich in tradition, has been decimated along with its industry; the unions have lost their power. Whereas in 1952 there were still 8.7 million jobs in industry, 60 years later only 2.5 million remained. Alongside this development, the polarization of income and wealth has become more and more extreme. Until the financial bubble burst, bonuses in the City of London—one of the world's leading financial centers—were becoming increasingly prodigious, while the number of working poor was rising too. Throughout Europe there is a widening gap between globalized elites and those whom global economic competition has left behind. The new, cosmopolitan world of business is a profitable place for those with the requisite qualifications, the multilingual and mobile. In contrast, those with little more to offer than their physical capabilities are in a precarious position: unstable working conditions, wages that are barely enough to live on, unemployment and the prospect of poverty in old age are the downside of a globalized economy in which knowledge is everything and manpower in plentiful supply.

No wonder broad sections of the population are afraid of or even hostile to globalization. In the first round of the French presidential elections in early 2012 the antiglobalization parties of the extreme right and left achieved a combined 30 percent of the vote. Even the two frontrunners François Hollande and Nicolas Sarkozy scrambled to outdo one another with protectionist watchwords and promises to protect France from the bitter winds of global competition. France is a particularly telling example of the failure of statist industrial policy. State involvement in key sectors and attempts to prop them up with preferential contracts and subventions have hastened rather than hindered the decline of French industry on the global market. Its share in the value creation of the national economy is now as small as that of British industry—a circumstance that should give pause for thought to anyone who advocates building a fence around Europe in order to shield our industry from international competition. Regression to protectionist policy would likewise be politically fatal: the global integration of production and circulation not only creates economic interdependency; it connects the nations and peoples of the world in a continuous process of exchange. It provides the foundation for a genuinely global society. For the first time in history, diplomats and tiny groups of elites are not the only ones communicating with each other across continents. Cosmopolitanism is no longer merely a nice idea; it is being lived out by students and scientists, businesspeople and engineers, executives and artists. And it is impossible to separate the globalization of politics and culture from economic globalization, which is ultimately what really unites nations.

A further welcome effect of worldwide economic integration is the *globalization of norms and standards*, both with regard to matters of employment law—such as the prohibition of child labor, the right to unionize or workplace health and safety regulations—and the improvement of environmental standards. Reality may often fall below these standards and working conditions are brutal in many of the Asian sweatshops that manufacture consumer goods for the world market. But in addition to global standards for occupational safety and environmental protection, today there is also a global public ready to sound the alarm as soon as any breaches are revealed. If European and American businesses are not careful they can find themselves in hot water over appalling conditions among their suppliers. The resulting damage to their reputations has a direct impact on revenue and profit. Moreover, every break in global supply and production chains results in considerable losses. For this reason companies like Bayer and BASF have implemented uniform environmental and safety standards across all their production plants worldwide. They don't engage in ecodumping when they build new factories in developing countries. In fact, internationalization leads to incremental improvements in working conditions and environmental standards.

The New Economic Miracle and Its Cost

The integration of the global economy over the last 20 years has led to increased prosperity for hundreds of millions of people. Between 1960 and 2000 global income per capita grew by an average of 2.5 percent annually, with a slight upward trend. Since then it has been growing at a rate of 3 percent. GWP has grown at an annual rate of 4 percent over the last decade.[10] The economies of the southern continents (with the exception of Africa) are growing almost three times as quickly as those of Europe and the US. While social inequality *within* states has increased in the wake of globalization, the gap *between* the old and new industrial nations is getting smaller. The portion of the global population living in poverty is shrinking and the middle class is expanding.[11] One indicator of this is the sharp increase in the number of cars being registered in the former Third World. China is about to overtake the whole of Europe as an automobile market. In the first quarter of 2012 more new cars were put into circulation in India than in Germany, and Brazil is close behind.

Despite the extremely unequal distribution of wealth in the emerging nations, prosperity is not only rising at the top. According to the World Bank, in the period from 1992 to 2008 the number of people surviving on less than $1.25 per day fell from 41 to 22 percent of the global population (from 1.9 to 1.3 billion in absolute terms). The number of people without access to clean drinking water fell by half. This means that two Millennium Development Goals have been met five years ahead of schedule. Global food provision has also improved significantly over the last 40 years. In Africa around 25 percent more food is being produced per capita today than in 1992; in Latin America the increase has been slightly greater. However, efforts to contain hunger are at risk of stalling in the face of rising food prices caused not least by a growing demand for energy crops (biofuels). After having fallen to 820 million in 1997, the number of people starving in the world has risen to over a billion again as a result of the global economic slump caused by the financial crisis of 2008–9. The hunger scandal is a poverty scandal: there is no lack of food in the world, only a lack of income among the poor with which to buy it. The increase in extreme weather phenomena associated with climate change—droughts here, floods there—is also contributing to the crisis and the impact on the poor is all the more severe: hundreds of billions in development aid for the Third World notwithstanding, agriculture has been systematically neglected in many countries. There is still a lack of warehouses, cooling facilities and freight options.

Nevertheless, in both economic and social terms things are looking up for billions of people. A growing number are gaining access to the comforts of modern life—electricity, heated homes, a plentiful supply of food, higher education, transportation, professional medicine and consumer choice. Since 1992 energy consumption per capita has risen by an average of 5 percent annually. Education standards and access are improving and infant mortality is declining. The downside of this success story is the growing pressure on natural resources. According to UNEP, three million square kilometers of jungle—an area eight times the size of Germany—have been lost since 1992. Deforestation and fire clearing are decimating rain forests, especially in South America and Africa. While living standards are rising for most people, in the past 20 years one in eight animal species has disappeared. The expansion of residential and commercial developments is encroaching further and further on the habitats of flora and fauna. CO_2 emissions have also risen owing to the industrialization of the emerging nations. According to the International Energy Agency they increased from 22 to 31.6 billion tons between 1992 and 2011. The biggest increase took place in China, where up to now economic growth has primarily been fueled by coal-fired power plants. Approximately half the coal produced worldwide is burned in China.

Boon and bane, social progress and threats to its longevity go hand in hand. Putting a stop to social improvement is not the answer to this dilemma. Instead we must employ sustainable means to secure prosperity for all.

That is where our focus should be: on steering the huge increase in the production of goods and services that is going to take place over the coming years in a sustainable direction. The consequences of multiplying our current coal and oil consumption, land use, waste flows and carbon emissions would be dire. Our planet cannot bear more of the same forever. Ecological footprint analysis is a method used to plot current resource consumption against the earth's capacity for regeneration.[12] One of the key figures it takes into account is the land area required to compensate for current environmental consumption. The bottom line is that humanity is already exceeding the load limit of the environment by a factor of 1.5. We are eating into our capital. This number obscures stark differences between the various continents. If we were to globalize the current energy and resource consumption of the US, we would need seven reserve planets. Even in the case of Europe we would need four globes. Of course, purely quantitative analysis is misleading: the size of our ecological footprint depends not so much on the overall size of our economy as on our mode of production and consumption. Until now highly industrialized, relatively prosperous societies have been responsible for the bulk of the demands on our natural resources and the concentration of greenhouse gases in the atmosphere, so they must lead the way toward a low-resource, CO_2-neutral economic system. Yet the ecological footprint of the emerging nations, led by China, is rapidly growing in size. If they use the same methods as the old industrial nations to get rich, they will contribute significantly to the future destruction of the planet. It is thus in the interests of both groups to construct a new, sustainable foundation for economic activity.

Average growth of 3 to 4 percent would see GWP double in under 20 years. This is not an unrealistic prognosis. American *per capita income* has been growing at an annual rate of just under 2 percent for two hundred years. The newly industrialized nations are well above this level (China currently by 7–8 percent), and the global population is set to grow by another two billion people before the middle of the century. Although the enormous growth of the developing nations will eventually level off and is becoming increasingly susceptible to crisis, we can expect it to continue rising steeply for the next few decades.[13] Even the Club of Rome's relatively skeptical report on the world in 2052, which is informed by the expectation of massive crisis, assumes that

- gross world product will more than double (in real terms) by then,
- consumption expenditure per capita will rise from the current average of $7,500 per year to $12,000,
- annual capital expenditure will rise to more than three times the current level and
- global energy consumption will increase by more than 50 percent.

These prognoses are relatively conservative in comparison with similar scenarios developed, for example, by the World Bank and the OECD. In all probability we should count on substantially higher rates of growth. The majority of the developments mentioned are going to take place in the Southern Hemisphere, but the United States will remain a growing giant too. Its population is expected to rise to just under four hundred million by 2050. In entrepreneurial market economies a growing supply of labor leads to greater potential for growth. That being the case, we must assume that in the medium term Europe and the US will develop in very different ways. For the foreseeable future old Europe will be an exception to, rather than typical of, developments in the rest of the world, even in comparison with other countries whose population growth is approaching its peak. Even as their demographic growth gradually levels out they will be doing everything they can to maximize economic growth, improve living standards and cover the rising costs of aging populations.

No matter how chaotic the development of the global economy proves to be in the coming decades, there will ultimately be an enormous increase in the amount of goods and services provided. The number of new buildings that will be constructed between now and the middle of the century corresponds approximately to the number standing today, and this construction will be accompanied by rapid urban growth. The amount of traffic in the water, on land and in the air will increase exponentially, as will the demand for food. Given our present energy system and level of resource consumption we are not equipped to deal with all this. Continuing to pursue our current growth model would push the earth beyond its limits. Zero growth is not a solution. Unless we mean to surrender to a cynical fatalism and wait for severe crises to trim humanity down to an ecologically sustainable size, we have to tackle the problem head on by separating economic growth from the consumption of natural resources. That is the essence of the green industrial revolution discussed in this book.

Does the North Have to Shrink in Order for the South to Grow?

Most advocates of prosperity without growth concede that the economic growth of the developing nations must be allowed to continue for a certain period of time. In their view, however, the same does not apply to highly developed industrial societies. In fact, they argue, the wealthy countries of this world must rein in their consumption in order for the have-nots to outgrow their poverty. The German philosopher and political activist Rudolf Bahro, a radical evangelist for cultural revolution, once stated: "It is an unavoidable requirement of any altruistic solution to the North–South conflict that the machinery of production here shrinks, rather than grows, in order to prevent our combined needs from further exceeding the finite limits of the earth."[14] From this perspective, the sum total of what is materially possible on earth is a fixed magnitude defined by the fertility and resilience of the planet. As this limit has already been passed, global justice can only be achieved by redistributing what we have: economic development in the South requires the North to shrink.

This notion has all the charm of moral intransigence and political radicalism. But neither the premises nor the conclusion make sense. The earth is only finite in a spatial sense, not with regard to the productive potential inherent in the interplay of solar power, photosynthesis and human ingenuity. It is impossible to deduce absolute barriers to growth from the load limit of the atmosphere. The crucial factor with respect to climate change is not how much we produce but the carbon intensity of our mode of production. Conversely, simply reducing production and consumption will not prevent environmental ruin. How much do we expect to gain from the self-imposed moderation of affluent countries when it comes to lowering resource consumption and CO_2 emissions? Twenty percent? That would require Greek levels of austerity. Yet the OECD countries have been set the goal of reducing greenhouse gases by 90 percent. Even taking an optimistic view, self-denial can only bring about a fraction of the necessary environmental relief. The lion's share must come from product and process innovation.

Making do with less of the same (less travel, less consumption, less comfortable homes) will not save the planet. That will require changes to production processes, energy systems, agricultural methods, transportation networks and urban planning principles, especially now that the economies of the Southern Hemisphere are growing faster than those of the North. Germany currently accounts for just 2.5 percent of global greenhouse gas emissions, and this number is falling. In 2010 the EU as a whole accounted for 13 percent. According to the prognoses of the International Energy Agency, the European share will drop to 9 percent by 2030. China is now at almost 25 percent, an increase of over 200 percent since 1990. The belief that European sacrifices can compensate for increased CO_2 emissions in developing countries is completely out of touch with reality. Besides, no one seriously expects the US to adopt such a course of action. Everything rests on the successful implementation of radical efficiency reforms capable of drastically lowering the resource consumption of the North while simultaneously steering southern growth in a sustainable direction.

No matter how you look at it, it makes no sense to expect the old industrial world to accept a reduction in quality of life for the benefit of the southern nations. Who is going to tell five hundred million Europeans that they must drastically scale back consumption in order to make room for billions of people in developing countries to improve their standard of living? Merely redistributing wealth between the haves and have-nots won't get us very far: it will take a 50 percent reduction in global greenhouse gas emissions to keep climate change within manageable limits. The kind of brutal austerity program required to achieve such a reduction would be anything but a positive example to the emerging societies of the South. To put it another way: the only way to convince up-and-coming nations to take an environmentally friendly path is to ensure that it entails no drop in prosperity. As long as we continue to equate the long overdue reduction in emissions and resource consumption with declining value creation we are blocking the way to a global climate alliance.

That is not to say lifestyle changes are pointless. There is still a need for action in this regard, particularly when it comes to our dietary and travel habits: we should be eating less meat on health grounds as well as for environmental reasons, and at least in cities a combination of public transport, bikes, rental cars and our own two feet is both more efficient and less expensive than traveling by car. You don't have to be a self-righteous ascetic to see the benefits of a healthy and comprehensive diet and a more intelligent approach to transportation. Environmentalism and hedonism are no more opposites than technological innovation and behavioral change. But we should neither kid ourselves nor others: the bulk of the necessary environmental relief has to come from permanent improvements in resource efficiency and a transition to renewable energy.

This is precisely the lesson of international climate change negotiations. The eagerly awaited 2009 UN Climate Change Conference in Copenhagen failed primarily because neither the newly industrialized countries nor the US were prepared to accept binding caps on their CO_2 emissions, which they saw as restrictive to their prospects for growth. They couldn't get past the idea that increased prosperity goes hand in hand with rising CO_2 emissions. Unless we can get away from this equation, climate protection efforts don't stand a chance. There will be no global convention on climate stability until the central players are convinced that rising prosperity can be accompanied by declining resource consumption. Ottmar Edenhofer, chief economist at the Potsdam Institute for Climate Impact Research and a prominent member of the Intergovernmental Panel on Climate Change (IPCC), insists that even green growth is no substitute for a global climate treaty imposing binding caps on the emission of greenhouse gases. Conversely, however, without convincing examples demonstrating the feasibility of environmentally friendly growth there will be no such agreement. Both in the global economy and in matters of climate policy the balance of power is shifting from the old to the new industrialized nations. In 2008 China's CO_2 emissions surpassed those of the US for the first time; three years later they were already one and a half times as high. And China is only the harbinger of a wave of fossil-powered industrialization that is sweeping across broad regions of the former Third World. The rapid increase in the greenhouse gas emissions of the newly industrialized countries has already invalidated previous calculations on the prospect of limiting climate change to two degrees Celsius.[15] Unless we are intent on chaos, the pace of environmental innovation must be drastically accelerated in order to replace fossil fuels with renewable energy sources and substantially reduce CO_2 emissions. To the extent that old Europe can be considered any kind of global model anymore, this is where we have to lead by example. Instead of disengaging from global growth, our ambition should be to become a pioneer of *green growth*. We are ideally placed to take on this role thanks to high public environmental awareness, a broad spectrum of business and research know-how, a highly skilled workforce and a diverse infrastructure for the advancement of environmentally friendly technologies and products.

Growth and Social Progress

No matter what criteria you apply, whether life expectancy, infant mortality, education standards, health care, women's rights or democratic freedoms, the economic growth of the last two hundred years has gone hand in hand with social progress. Average life expectancy is probably the best yardstick for this. Even since the middle of the last century the global average has risen from 45 to 67 for men and from 48 to 72 for women. In 1950 just 1 percent of the global population had a life expectancy of more than 70; today 57 percent do. Admittedly there is extreme inequality in the distribution of social wealth, but even the situation of the working classes has improved beyond all expectation. From the perspective of a day laborer in the early days of industrialization, most workers in the Western world today lead a fairytale existence, both with respect to their private lifestyles and their social and political rights: a five-day week, guaranteed annual leave, continued remuneration in case of illness, comprehensive medical care, the chance to go to school, the prospect of social mobility, the right to vote and the freedom to plead their interests without being bludgeoned or thrown in prison. Go into any history museum and you will see for yourself the virtually unimaginable improvement in the position of the working classes that has taken place over the last 150 years. In spite of all its hardships, the history of industrialization in Europe has been a story of cultural progress. It is now being repeated in other parts of the world. All this progress would be inconceivable without the enormous increase in labor productivity and the constant process of technological innovation that have driven social wealth to previously unknown levels and provided the basis for the institutionalized class compromise of the welfare state. Long-term economic growth has facilitated social leveling in the form of rising wages and public redistribution policies. It has likewise paved the way to shorter working hours and access to education and culture for growing sections of the population.

This story is not over. For billions of people it has just begun. Their aspirations, their pursuit of a better life for themselves and their children are driving global economic growth. In turn, economic growth is the basis for rising investment in education, health care and better water provision, and as a result for increased life expectancy and a better standard of living. All over the world there is an evident correlation between improved education standards for women, the material prosperity of families and birthrates. The poorer developing countries are the ones with particularly high birthrates, generally in conjunction with high infant mortality.

Ultimately governments do not decide whether an economy grows or shrinks. That is determined by the farmers who increase their crop yields, the women who open small businesses, the immigrants striving to build new lives for themselves, the shopkeepers who expand their product ranges and the companies that invest in new products and services. Policy can boost or hinder the economy. Corruption, a lack of legal certainty, high national debt and extreme inequality with respect to land ownership and wealth hurt economic growth. Investment in education and health, a stable energy system and a good transport network drive it. But the people pursuing their dreams are the really important ones, at least in societies with market economies, where producers and consumers are the key players. Should we be trying to stop people from improving their personal circumstances, curbing enthusiasm for the new and reining in entrepreneurial spirit in order to wipe out economic growth? That would not only demonstrate great arrogance on the part of the replete North toward the hungry South. It would also be an own goal from an environmental perspective: the environmental crisis will only be overcome with accelerated structural change and fast-paced innovation, not by neutralizing the economy. We need more, rather than less, inventiveness and entrepreneurial spirit.

It has not yet been determined whether the future will be better than the past for most people on earth. But fatalism is just as misguided as the faith that somehow everything will be alright. If things *are* to be alright there will have to be fundamental changes at all levels of politics, the economy and our everyday culture. Take global food provision, for example: even the soon to be nine billion people in the world will have enough to eat *if* investment in the agricultural infrastructure of developing countries is increased, cropping systems are improved, soil erosion is halted and the production of biofuels is not conducted at the expense of the world's food supply. Due to competing claims for land use, the recultivation of barren soil will also be necessary. None of this will be easy, let alone in the relatively short amount of time we have to secure to the livelihood of a growing global population. But it is feasible. Instead of furrowing our brows and warning against megalomania, we must harness an *enlightened culture of action* in order to develop solutions for the self-inflicted problems of mankind.

Demographic Change

If we only had to worry about Western Europe, the valiant crusaders of the antigrowth movement could relax. The real action is elsewhere. There is a certain irony in the fact that antipathy to growth resonates most strongly in places with economies that are struggling to grow. In Germany growth rates dropped from an average of 8.2 percent in the 1950s to 1.1 percent in the period from 2000 to 2010. There is nothing to say that the situation will never improve again. As discussed above, that will largely depend on our capacity for innovation and investment activity. Continued, long-term global economic growth bodes well for German industry. Nonetheless, demographic change in Europe is dampening the continent's potential for growth. The main issue is the drastic decline in the working-age population that has already set in and will intensify in the coming years. For the time being Europe is a demographic anomaly. Only Japan is in a similar situation: there too society is aging rapidly while the population shrinks. The percentage of elderly people in the US is also rising, but in the context of a total population that is still growing.

There have of course always been times when the populations of whole areas were drastically depleted by natural disasters, epidemics, overuse of environmental resources, slavery and devastating wars. But for the first time in human history the majority of European countries are experiencing long-term population decline during a period of considerable prosperity and lasting peace—a complete reversal of the evolutionary paradigm we have known up to now. Population growth has previously always gone hand in hand with the development of the forces of production, from the development of arable farming to modern industrialization. Improved nutrition, hygiene and modern medicine have all played their part in reducing infant mortality and increasing life expectancy.

It is estimated that in around 8000 BCE the total number of people on earth was approximately twenty million. At the beginning of the Common Era there were around two hundred million. The billion threshold was reached circa 1830. About a million years had passed since the emergence of Homo sapiens in prehistoric times. From then on, as industrialization set in, demographic development accelerated rapidly. By 1930 there were already two billion people on earth. It only took another 30 years to reach the next billion, then 15, then 13, then 12, then approximately 11 years to arrive at the current count of over seven billion people. The faster the pace of economic, technological and cultural development, the faster the global population has grown.[16]

According to the prognoses of demographers, population growth is now going to slow down again. Birthrates are dropping as prosperity, education standards and the number of women in employment rise; in several countries they have even fallen below the reproduction rate necessary to maintain population size (an average of 2.2 children per woman). This not only includes most European nations but also Russia and, since the beginning of the century, China as well. However, the global population will continue to grow until at least the middle of the century. The relevant predictions anticipate that by then it will have reached a minimum of nine billion. Even in China, despite rigid reproductive policy, we can expect the population to rise to as many as 1.4 or 1.5 billion. The crucial point for our discussion here is that China's manpower potential, i.e. the number of people for whom jobs and incomes must be found, will conceivably increase by another 250 million people. Against this background the Chinese government (*every* Chinese government) will obviously stick to its growth policy for the foreseeable future.[17] More than half the global population growth is expected to occur in Africa. Without sustainable economic growth most people in the developing countries will have no prospect of escaping an impoverished and uncertain existence.

The projections of Germany's Federal Statistics Office indicate that by the middle of the century the country's population will drop from its current level of around eighty-two million to just under sixty-nine million. That assumes an annual gain of one hundred thousand people due to immigration. If net immigration were to double, the population would fall to around seventy-four million.[18] If the birthrate remains at the current level of 1.4 children per woman, the age structure of German society will change drastically: whereas in 2000 there were 23 people over sixty-five for every 100 people of working age, by 2050 there would be 57.[19] Depending on the level of immigration, the potential labor force (defined as the number of people aged between twenty and sixty-five) will drop from 50 million today to somewhere in the range of 35 to 39 million. In contrast, the number of people aged over eighty, of whom there were just under 4 million in 2005, is expected to rise to 10 million.

These numbers anticipate serious intergenerational distribution conflicts that would become unavoidable if real economic performance were to decline during the same period. Even an aging society needs growth in order to update its infrastructure, modernize its economy and guarantee high social standards. A society in which manpower potential is significantly declining while the number of people in need of care is rising is more reliant than ever on high productivity. In order to absorb the effects of demographic change we also need

- Europe to become more open to the immigration of young, hardworking people;
- a higher percentage of women in the workforce;
- a more flexible retirement age and a higher percentage of older workers;
- a culture of lifelong learning and
- a commitment to saving that allows us to finance productive investments and establish supplementary private retirement schemes.

In addition to (not as an alternative to!) establishing an accelerated innovation policy, we must begin to reduce our society's dependence on growth. First and foremost this means cutting national debt. High public debt demands maximum economic growth. The alternatives are draconian tax rises and harsh cuts to public services. Clearing our debts must thus take priority over new benefits legislation. An economy that exhibits only modest growth must also limit its claims on the public purse. Extending people's working lives and capping pension increases are not popular measures, but they are necessary. Given the decline of the labor force, taxes and deductions on earned income can no longer serve as the predominant source of funding for public spending. In the future we will see a shift towards consumption and resource taxes. Investment income must also be taxed at a higher rate. Demographic change is stretching the welfare state to its limits, making it all the more important for society to help itself. Civic commitment, voluntary work, neighborhood initiatives and cooperative projects are becoming more important than ever.

It should be noted, however, that reducing our dependence on growth does not mean renouncing any chance of growth. In a world shaped by steeply rising demand for goods and services, Europe must remain in the game as a provider of sustainable products and solutions. Failing this, we face a downward economic spiral accompanied by intensified conflicts over the distribution of a shrinking national product. The key variable in all this is not absolute GDP size but economic output per capita. As long as this remains high (preferably continuing to grow), even a shrinking society can preserve its prosperity.

Chapter 2

The Limits to Growth — The Growth of Limits

In 1972 a team of scientists led by Dennis L. Meadows created a huge sensation when they published a study commissioned by the Club of Rome entitled *The Limits to Growth*.[1] The book is one of the rare publications that we can say changed our outlook on the world. It sold 12 million copies and was translated into more than thirty languages. All the big newspapers and magazines devoted cover stories to it. While it was not until 35 years later that former US vice president Al Gore used the slogan "An Inconvenient Truth" for his campaign to raise awareness about climate change, this tagline would have been even more appropriate for the earlier publication. It became the bible of the global environmental movement. The metaphor of the limits to growth entered general usage and Meadows himself became a respected scientific and moral authority.

Even though none of the predictions of 1972 have come true, today it is regarded as common sense far beyond the green movement that unlimited growth is not possible on a limited planet. To challenge the notion that the limits to economic growth are physically predetermined, fixed magnitudes and to suggest that human ingenuity is capable of expanding them is to risk being excommunicated for heresy, though the authors of the report themselves indicated that the scenarios it addressed were not inevitable: "Is the future of the world system bound to be growth and then collapse into a dismal, depleted existence? Only if we make the initial assumption that our present way of doing things will not change. We have ample evidence of mankind's ingenuity and social flexibility. [...] Let us use the world model as a tool to test the possible consequences of the new technologies that promise to raise the limits to growth."[2]

In this respect the warning of 1972 has been thoroughly effective, but Meadows has come to see himself as a voice crying in the wilderness whose appeals fall on deaf ears. And perhaps his bleak assessment is not entirely unfounded. The world has not renounced the golden calf of growth. With few exceptions its nations have failed to establish binding conventions for the protection of the natural world. It cannot be denied that the major ecological trends are still negative: greenhouse gas emissions are rising, species continue to die out, the rain forests are shrinking, pollution of the oceans is increasing, the degradation of agricultural land is advancing and drought is spreading. We are heading for large-scale environmental and social upheaval driven by a growing global population and a consumerist civilization incapable of reining in its appetite for more.

What Meadows underestimates, now as then, are the counterforces already at work in many areas: the hundreds of thousands of scientists developing environmentally friendly technologies and products, the inestimable number of environmental organizations and citizens' action groups effecting political and economic advances, the companies competing over environmental innovation, the expansion of modern environmental legislation and the establishment of professional environmental authorities, the growing public awareness of environmental matters and the coming-of-age of a new generation for whom environmentalism is no longer a foreign concept. Admittedly the environmental impact of the last 40 years has been rather mixed. On the plus side, substances harmful to the ozone layer have largely been eradicated from industrial production. There has also been a large-scale improvement in the quality of the air over Europe and North America. The biological condition of our rivers and lakes is noticeably better than in the 1970s. The environmental balance of the chemical industry, once one of the dirtiest and most hazardous branches of industry, has steadily improved. Heavy metal pollution, a massive problem in the 1960s and 1970s, has been successfully contained. Pesticides used in agricultural production are now handled more carefully than they once were. The use of substances associated with adverse health effects such as asbestos or DDT has been eliminated in many countries. The waste industry has been reorganized and unregulated dumping stamped out. Reusable materials are collected separately from other trash and recycled. Even Germany's forests—which seemed doomed 30 years ago—have recovered and Europe's woodland is growing again. In spite of various prophecies of doom, food security has increased. The energy consumption of many companies is falling in spite of increased production. The construction of nuclear power plants has stalled, while the availability of renewable energy sources is rising steeply. Alongside environmental progress, the average life expectancy on earth has increased by 10 years since the first edition of

The Limits to Growth and infant mortality has fallen by almost two-thirds.

The theories of the Club of Rome have played no small part in these successes. To the extent that they have helped set the ecological modernization of industrial society in motion they have been highly influential. The question is whether this transformation is advancing quickly enough to gain the upper hand before the full impact of the environmental crisis unfolds. In the first phase of environmental politics, which began in the 1970s, the main priority was to stop air pollution, save forests and rivers from biological death and get industrial society's classic contaminants—heavy metals, sulfur dioxide, nitric oxide and poisonous chemicals—under control. Now the priority is a massive increase in resource efficiency and an accelerated transition to renewable energy sources.

Excursus: First the Forests Die, Then the People

How many people still remember the commotion over forest dieback (*Waldsterben*) that was so prevalent in Germany during the first half of the 1980s and hastened the rise to prominence of its Green Party? "There Is Poison over Every Treetop," wrote the magazine *Stern* in 1981. Another German news magazine, *Der Spiegel*, followed this with a cover story drawing on a study published back in 1979 by the Göttingen-based soil scientist Bernhard Ulrich, who predicted that large sections of Germany's woodland would die out within five years. Indeed, forest dieback in substantial areas of central and northern Europe had already reached severe proportions by the 1970s, primarily as a consequence of the sulfur dioxide emissions released into the air over large areas of the continent from power stations and industrial plants. The term acid rain was familiar to almost every child at the time. Nitric oxide, ozone and heavy metals were also having an impact on the forests. Partial overaging and mismanagement (monocultures) intensified the problems. The first nationwide investigation into the issue in 1984 found that a third of all woodland trees had been affected, though a range of different phenomena were grouped under the heading of new forest dieback. The dramatic pictures of bald spruce trees, dead branches and canopies full of holes that galvanized the public at that time mostly depicted areas of the Harz region or the Ore Mountains, which had been hit particularly hard by flue gas from lignite-fired power plants in what were then Czechoslovakia, the GDR and West Germany. So the furor over apparently unstoppable forest dieback was not baseless. Yet, while tempers were running high on the subject in Germany (in France "*le Waldsterben*" always remained a loanword), the situation had already begun to change for the better.

Sulfur dioxide poisoning had already reached its worldwide peak in 1973. It had been discussed at the 1972 UN Conference on the Human Environment in Stockholm, which was the starting point for a series of international conventions on emission control. In 1979 the Geneva Convention on Long-Range Transboundary Air Pollution was passed. When it came into effect in 1983 it was the first international, legally binding measure for the reduction of air-pollutant emissions. It was followed by the Helsinki Protocol on the Reduction of Sulphur Emissions, passed in 1985, and a further convention on the control of nitrogen oxide emissions (the Sofia Protocol), which was passed in 1988. Protests against forest dieback thus became the catalyst for a first round of multilateral environmental protection agreements. Along with a whole range of national measures, these led to the successful reduction of air pollution and an improvement in the health of forests. Filtration systems for power plants and factories, catalytic converters for cars and large-scale forest liming had the desired effect. By 2003 sulfur dioxide emissions had decreased by an unbelievable 88 percent, while nitrogen oxide emissions had been cut in half.[3] The industrial collapse of the Eastern Bloc countries and the shutdown of coal-fired power plants in the former GDR also helped to reduce air pollution.

Echoing the findings of European neighbors, in 2003 Renate Künast, then the German minister for agriculture, declared forest dieback to be at an end. She stated that the negative trend had been stopped and the condition of forests had stabilized, though parts of the tree population still exhibited clear signs of damage.[4] Although Germany's forests suffered from the extremely hot and dry summer of 2003, the tree population recovered quite quickly. Today climate change is the greatest threat to their health. Rising temperatures, dry spells and severe storms will take their toll. But the forests are not going to die—in fact the tree population is growing again. Over the last two decades 17 million hectares have been added across Europe (not taking Russia into account), including one million hectares—10 percent of the total woodland—in Germany. Today European forests are denser and taller than they were 20 years ago. A total of 56 million hectares—30 percent of which are in Russia—are protected. This number is rising by approximately half a million hectares per year.[5]

What can we learn from this story? The threats to the environment are as real today as they were when *The Limits to Growth* was first published in 1972. Unless we do something to counteract them we face massive upheaval. Criticism of environmental fatalism does not give us carte blanche to continue unscrupulously as before. We cannot be sure that everything will be alright. Without fundamental changes to production processes and products, to our energy and transport systems, we risk chaos. The operative point is that while things could turn out that way, they don't have to. Cassandra-like prophecies have an important role to play in galvanizing us. But it is in our hands to determine whether or not they come true.

Meadows and his school clearly have little to contribute to a strategy of ecological modernization. If our ecological survival depends on the world exchanging growth for self-restraint in the near future there is in fact little hope that the collapse of civilization can be avoided. All our systems are programmed for continued growth over the next few decades, which is why it is essential that we separate the growth of the real economy from the consumption of natural resources (in other words, that we reduce the ecological footprint of the human race while the prosperity of the broad masses grows). But not everyone accepts this. Meadows believes that all efforts to reduce the consumption of natural resources to a sustainable level are futile as long as we are unwilling to make sacrifices: In his view, the environmental crisis can only be overcome by an absolute reduction in consumption among the more affluent members of the human race. Given that we have already exceeded the load limit of our ecosystem by 50 percent, nothing but a drastic reduction in production and consumption will help. Period. He is certain that no efficiency revolution or renewable energy source can absorb the consumer pressure associated with a growing global population. Unbridled consumption will gobble up any efficiency gains. Technological innovation can at best delay the collapse but not avert it. He has remained true to this position since 1972. Even back then he wrote that "technological optimism is the most common and the most dangerous reaction to our findings," and that it is only a distraction from the "most fundamental problem—the problem of growth in a finite system."[6] From Meadows's perspective even governmental measures for the protection of the environment treat only the symptoms of the growth disease afflicting modern civilization. An economic system and lifestyle founded on growth is damned to exceed the fundamental limits of the ecosystem sooner or later. When it does, severe crises will result: famines, economic depression and reduced life expectancy. Human civilization will be thrown back into survival mode.

The Authoritarian Tendency of Environmentalism

When the first edition of *The Limits to Growth* appeared in 1972 the authors predicted that per capita food and industrial production would slump from 2020 onward if economic and demographic growth continued unfettered and that a comprehensive resource crisis would leave the world reeling: The depletion of drinking water reserves, a decline in oil production, scarcity of industrial raw materials, overuse of arable land and endemic air pollution would culminate in a crisis of civilization. Eventually life expectancy would drop, decimating the global population. The recommendations that Meadows's team derived from their seemingly irrefutable computer models all involved strict limitations on economic activity and population development. This put them in latent conflict with a liberal political and economic order. Remarkably, the authoritarian aspects of the study were barely discussed (at least within the environmental community). Its authoritarian tendency is in fact perfectly logical if our only hope lies in "accepting the nature-imposed limits to growth."[7] If we do not freely subordinate ourselves to this reality we must either be coerced by a strong government or forced to by the breakdown of industrial civilization. If, as Meadows believes, growth is the root of all evil, it follows that environmental collapse can only be avoided by transitioning to a "state of equilibrium" in both demographic and economic terms—that a) birthrates must not exceed mortality rates and b) investments must not exceed capital consumption allowances.[8] The former condition requires a restrictive demographic policy, the latter broad state control over the economy. It is not difficult to see that such a society would be openly hostile to individual freedom and market economies.

Today Meadows merely believes that the onset of chaos has been delayed. The greenhouse effect and its role in exacerbating the global water and food crises has been added to the issues addressed back in 1972. Water shortages have a knock-on effect on agricultural yields. The clock is ticking. If we accept Meadows's position, a decline in industrial production and crop yields owing to our overuse of the planet's resources is inevitable. The global population will in turn be reduced to a size the earth can bear. Since the human race is evidently not prepared to moderate its demands voluntarily, environmental crises will force it to limit its numbers and its consumption. As the end of modern industrial civilization nears, democracy and freedom are likewise at risk: "If the physical parameters of the planet are declining, there is virtually no chance that freedom, democracy and a lot of the immaterial things we value will be going up." The idea that we can maintain our standard of living while the populations of poor countries gradually improve theirs is illusory, as is the hope that the great collapse can be avoided "through the magic of technology."[9] In Meadows's view, to speak of sustainable development is an act of great self-deception. It is too late for preventative adjustments. All that remains is the chance to prepare our societies as best we can for the coming environmental, economic and social shock. Democracies are predisposed to overuse the ecosystem: political parties and governments are constantly promising new benefits in an attempt to buy approval, while putting off the costs until later. In this regard mounting environmental debt is simply the flip side of growing financial debt: here too it is a case of buy now, pay later. Meadows is skeptical as to whether democracy and sustainability are compatible at all: "People are shortsighted. If they want to solve the world's problems—climate change, for instance—they must look to the next 30, 40 or 50 years, whereas politicians only think as far as the next election. That is why no binding climate convention has been established."[10] Here he mixes anthropological arguments with doubts about the capacity of democracies to translate long-term public interests into political action. The anthropological argument is that humans have a tendency to throw further than they can see. In other words, all our actions have long-term consequences that we are unaware of, and even if we recognize them we are not in a position to respond accordingly, because all our feelings, thoughts and deeds are determined by current impulses—the gratification of our needs in the here and now, fear of acute danger or the pursuit of instant pleasure. The Austrian philosopher Günter Anders refers to this condition as "the obsolescence of mankind."[11]

The profound cultural pessimism—the almost eco-Darwinian tenor—of these theories is impossible to miss. Humanity, having already overshot the limits to growth by some distance, is also incapable of a politics of retreat. Innovation is not a solution. Only major crises can reduce the human race to a sustainable size. Meadows remains both empirically and mentally trapped in a methodology that attempts to model the future based on present circumstances. He does account for increased resource efficiency and progress in the field of renewable energy, but only gradual progress capable of delaying—not preventing—collapse as long as the global economy continues to grow. From this point of view sustainable grow is an impossibility. In fact, the future success of an environmentally friendly economic system cannot be forecast based on the status quo—there are too many unknowns for that. We can only reinforce the potential for green revolution that is revealing itself today. It is uncertain whether the revolution will unfold rapidly enough to stave off looming turmoil. But it is far more productive to approach the future as a "universe of possibilities" (Ernst Ulrich von Weizsäcker) than to write it off. Meadows fails to grasp the openness of the future, the capacity of human inventiveness to overcome critical shortages. Yet this capacity for technological and social innovation is precisely what differentiates humanity from nature. It is also the reason why extrapolations from the present cannot predict the future.

The debate on the existence of rigid limits to growth to which humanity must subordinate itself on punishment of doom is not only of economic significance. Our attitude to the future—whether as an open, malleable space or an age of grim scarcity—is also of major importance to democratic politics. In an article written for the 20th anniversary of the Rio de Janeiro Earth Summit, the Norwegian environmental economist Jørgen Randers, a long-time associate and collaborator of Dennis L. Meadows, openly expressed sympathy for authoritarian models of political leadership.[12] The article develops Meadows's argument that parliamentary democracies are incapable of transcending short-term utility in the long-term interests of the species. Randers's solution to this dilemma is a benevolent dictator. For starters he invokes ancient Rome, where autocrats were installed in times of war to make quick decisions without long discussions. According to Randers, elected parliaments could learn from this and appoint benevolent dictators of their own for limited terms in order to establish climate policy that would truly benefit mankind.

It's hard to believe your eyes when you read this: Leninist vanguardism in environmentalist clothing. But it's only consistent, then, that Randers should next single out the Chinese Communist Party as a role model. In his eyes, China's single-party government is a "'benevolent dictator' that does what is right," which is why he has no problem with the party assuming the power it does. Randers is fascinated by the idea of a centralist, authoritarian system of leadership that can push through major projects without big public debates or consideration for the people affected. His remarks call to mind the famous Three Gorges Dam, which was erected with literally no regard for the losses involved: 13 large and 140 smaller cities as well as 1,350 villages were flooded; 1.2 million people were displaced from their homes to make way for the 600-kilometer-long reservoir and a further 300,000 were relocated five years after its completion in 2006. Public criticism of the Pharaonic project was forbidden; anyone disregarding the ban risked prison or attacks on life and limb. After making critical comments on a German public television program, the activist Fu Xiancai was brutally beaten. He has been paralyzed from the neck down ever since.[13]

But Randers does not discuss this. He cites the construction of tracks for high-speed trains as a praiseworthy example of the Chinese dictatorship in action: "Given the central decision-making structures, the land rights of a few residents are no obstacle to the progress of construction. Tracks and roads are built at an unbelievable pace, albeit at the expense of those whose interests are ignored." Well, you can't make an omelet without breaking eggs, can you?

Randers not only considers the political monopoly of China's Communist Party to be a plus; the country's lack of due process also seems to him like an advantage. When there is little chance of a successful challenge to the organs of power, environmental decisions—whether sensible or not—can be executed without delay. Only a benevolent dictator can shut down 10 antiquated paper mills with the stroke of a pen and replace them with a giant factory built to the highest environmental standards without having to consider the workers who will lose their jobs at the old facilities. Randers comments that "these decisions are of lasting benefit to the environment and would be hard to implement in a democratic society. There are major ecological advantages to this in the long term, though some people are disadvantaged in the short term." That being the case, it's a good thing there are no independent unions either.

Randers paints a rose-tinted picture of China's highly contradictory domestic situation when he claims: "The Chinese have solved the problem of climate change." They are still a long way from that. China's CO_2 emissions are growing at roughly the same pace as its economy; according to official data they rose at an annual rate of 7.5 percent in the period from 1997 to 2010, while unofficial calculations assume a rate of 8.5 percent.[14] At 7.2 tons per capita, the country's emissions are now significantly higher than the global average. The portion of energy coming from renewable sources has admittedly quadrupled since 1992, but coal is still the backbone of the Chinese energy supply. The Chinese leadership has ambitious plans for the development of solar and wind power, improved energy efficiency and reforestation, but the country is still far from achieving sustainable development. Randers's conception of the Communist Party as a benevolent dictator is likewise more wish than reality. It ignores the notorious corruption and financial self-interest of the *nomenklatura*—inevitable results of inadequate checks and balances, due process and public control. Ultimately he fails to recognize that the supposed advantages of autocratic rule prevent critical objections from being heard and alternatives seriously examined, resulting in simplistic decision making. That's why, when all is said and done, deliberative processes are more effective than authoritarian methods. They may take longer, but a thorough evaluation of the interests and arguments involved in an issue generally leads to better results. And ultimately the inclusion of critical voices provides an opportunity to create sustainable consensus, rather than just producing winners and losers.

We cannot simply dismiss the argument that parliamentary democracy has an inherently expansive tendency: It promises more kindergarten places here, day care subsidies there, guaranteed basic pensions, improved health care, free higher education and new concert halls—on credit if necessary. Any party defying the expectation that every new government will further expand the welfare state risks being voted out. Nevertheless, pessimists like Meadows underestimate democracy's capacity for self-correction, while overestimating the sustainability of authoritarian regimes. It is a caricature of citizens' powers of judgment to represent them as mere bargain hunters interested only in their own short-term advantage. People absolutely want to be informed, involved and taken seriously. They also insist on justice and a reasonable degree of fairness in the distribution of burdens.

The fact that Germany has become a pioneer for environmental protection and green technology is the result of decades of criticism and opposition. Anyone who admires authoritarian regimes fails to understand the significance of democratic feedback mechanisms for environmental learning processes. Citizens' action groups, critical media, political pluralism and free elections are indispensable catalysts of change. Aside from this functional rationale, we must also consider the fundamental motivating force of environmental politics. Its raison d'être is not merely the survival of humanity. Hannah Arendt's maxim that "the goal of all politics is freedom" applies to green politics too. The aim is to secure the freedom of future generations to determine the course of their own lives, and this goal must determine the means of our politics. Ogling authoritarian regimes corrupts the environmental cause.

Is Industrial Society Running Out of Fuel?

One of the central theses of *The Limits to Growth* was that the scarcity of industrial raw materials would force an end to growth. Industrial society was compared to an engine running at full speed that would run out of fuel in the foreseeable future. The team of authors investigated 19 raw materials essential to modern industry. They came to the conclusion that, assuming exponential growth, 12 of them would be running low within 40 years. Even a discovery of reserves five times as great as those known about at the time would only extend this period by a few decades.[15] One way or another, they argued, reserves of aluminum, copper, gold, silver, lead, zinc, natural gas, crude oil, mercury, molybdenum, tin and tungsten would be exhausted before very long, leading to a steep rise in the price of raw materials. The way the situation actually developed says more about the limitations of these kinds of prognoses than the inevitability of an end to growth.

Mercury is a classic example of how shortages and environmental problems can be overcome by substitution. Due to its association with adverse health effects mercury has largely disappeared from batteries, dental fillings and thermometers. As a consequence, consumption of it has fallen by 98 percent since the beginning of the 1970s and its price by 90 percent. In contrast, since *The Limits to Growth* was published gold consumption has risen by an amount eight times greater than the reserves known about back then. At the beginning of the 1970s there were 10,980 tons of gold available. Based on this the authors predicted that supplies would be exhausted by the end of the twentieth century at the latest. In fact, believe it or not, over the last 40 years 81,410 tons have been extracted, while the gold reserves available today are estimated to amount to 51,000 tons. Here, as with other metals, we observe a paradoxical phenomenon whereby known reserves increase along with consumption. That is not to suggest that reserves of these metals are infinite, but even if no more new gold reserves were ever discovered, more efficient extraction methods, recycling and substitution will allow us to extend the life of existing supplies far into the future. With respect to copper, in 1970 the known reserves totaled 280 million tons. Since then approximately four hundred million tons have been consumed, while the remaining copper reserves are currently estimated to amount to almost seven hundred million tons. The Danish statistician Bjørn Lomborg, a veritable enfant terrible of the environmental scene, gathered this data for an essay published in the journal *Foreign Affairs*.[16] Admittedly Lomborg goes rather too far in making an unconditional appeal for economic growth—without asking what form this growth should take—on the grounds that the doomsday scenarios put forward by the Club of Rome have not materialized.

There are shortages of only a few strategic resources on the horizon. In the medium term the supply of phosphorus, a vital component in the production of fertilizer, could become critical. Phosphates stimulate plant growth. Worldwide production could peak as soon as 2035, while depending on how demand develops, complete exhaustion of the natural reserves is expected in 80 to 120 years.[17] Phosphate fertilizer is indispensable to industrial farming, a fact that has led the science fiction writer Isaac Asimov to describe phosphorus as "life's bottleneck." The material waste that occurs in the long chain from mine to consumer is enormous, with estimates putting it at around 80 percent. Farmers overfertilize their fields many times over. The phosphorus that is flushed out advances the eutrophication of bodies of water. Up to now there has been little effort to reclaim the raw material from wastewater, sludge, slurry, plant remains and bone meal, but that will change as supplies shrink and prices rise. Environmentally friendly cultivation methods will take on new importance if phosphorus runs low. Another option is the use of sulfur-reducing bacteria to activate antisoluble phosphates present in soil. The acid they release makes the phosphate present in compounds in the soil available to plant roots. This method could significantly reduce the need for chemical fertilizers.

All told, the decisive raw materials crisis that was prophesied has not come to pass and nor is it imminent. That doesn't mean we are free to waste resources without restraint. From an environmental perspective there are good reasons not to extract every last trace of the raw materials stored in the earth's crust. The extraction of raw materials involves massive interventions in the landscape. Forests are cleared, groundwater is contaminated and poisonous chemicals are implemented in the pursuit of precious metals, ores, minerals and oil. Processing them requires large amounts of energy. Heavy industry is one of the main sources for the emission of CO_2 and other air pollutants, while hunger for resources drives political and military conflicts. Many of the countries that produce raw materials are ruled by more or less authoritarian regimes. The working conditions in the mines are miserable and the profits flow into the pockets of corrupt elites. In the midst of global competition for strategic raw materials, which is being intensified by China's resource hunger, little consideration is given to human rights or environmental protection. There is a temptation to conduct raw materials policy as mere procurement policy, with development and democratic goals falling by the wayside.[18] These are all good reasons to minimize resource consumption—by using limited raw materials sparingly, increasing resource efficiency five or tenfold and implementing waste-free material cycles. We must also establish binding social and environmental standards for the extraction and processing of raw materials. International conventions and new nongovernmental alliances reinforce each other in this respect. Without years of persistent lobbying by the Extractive Industries Transparency Initiative, America's Congress would probably not have enacted the Dodd–Frank Wall Street Reform and Consumer Protection Act, which requires raw materials companies listed on the

New York Stock Exchange to disclose their transactions country by country and project by project.[19]

With regard to energy provision, the lifeblood of industrial society, an exhaustion of reserves is even less of a concern. This is due first and foremost to the potential of renewable energy sources, which we have only fractionally exploited up to now, but also to the known reserves of coal, oil and gas. Contrary to popular opinion, there will be no shortage of fossil fuels in the coming decades. Ottmar Edenhofer puts the fossil fuel reserves still slumbering in the earth's crust at an unbelievable 12,000 gigatons (a gigaton is equal to one billion tons). The problem is not the *exhaustion* of fossil fuels but excessive *use* of them, and in particular the carbon dioxide emissions released when they are burned. According to the IPCC, of which Edenhofer is a member, the atmosphere can absorb a maximum of 230 gigatons more carbon without climate change rising above two degrees. Beyond that any rise in the CO_2 concentration of the atmosphere would have self-perpetuating, cumulative consequences such as the thawing of permafrost soil. In fact, given the pace at which oil and coal production is growing, we are heading for a temperature rise of closer to four degrees. Taking into account current plans to expand global oil production, the present production capacity of 93 million barrels per day will rise to around one hundred and ten million barrels per day by 2020. The United States and Canada are at the forefront of this development.[20] The other forms of environmental pollution connected with the combustion of oil, coal and gas are also telling: so-called side effects such as respiratory illnesses, damage to buildings, high water consumption and the contamination of bodies of soil and water are becoming problems in their own right, while the prices of fossil fuels are still too low to compensate for their incidental macroeconomic costs.

A New Petroboom?

While coal and gas are still in plentiful supply, experts are arguing about whether we have already passed the peak of global oil production. Country-specific investigations into production volumes indicate that 64 countries—including Russia, Mexico and Norway—have already reached or passed the point of maximum production.[21] According to a Citigroup study, Saudi Arabia, the world's largest oil producer, could become a net importer by 2030 if its domestic energy consumption continues to rise as it has been doing. The country already uses a quarter of its huge production output for its own purposes and its oil consumption is growing by 8 percent annually. If such excessive energy consumption were to continue, its export potential would shrink to nothing.[22] This calculation will probably remain academic, because like other countries Saudi Arabia will increase its investments in energy efficiency and solar power. But the rising domestic consumption of production countries will result in declining supplies on the oil markets. It remains to be seen to what extent the expansion of supply in other areas will compensate for this.

When the gap between supply and demand widens, prices rise. This is not a simple linear process, however, because rising prices promote the tapping of new oil fields and more intensive exploitation of existing ones, thus leading to an increase in supply. They also curb demand, whether by inducing more efficient use of existing supplies or a switch to different energy sources. Predictions of oil prices shooting through the roof in the coming years should consequently be treated with caution, especially as they are heavily cyclical. In fact, between June and October of 2014 the barrel price of Brent oil fell by no less than

20 percent—in spite of conflicts in the export countries of Iraq, Syria and Libya. Two fundamental trends underlie this development: stagnating global demand and the unexpected rise of the US to become the world's largest oil producer. Fracking, the extraction of unconventional energy sources from rock layers deep within the earth, has been key to this development. It has confounded every prediction made about the global oil and gas markets.

When the research group led by Donella and Dennis L. Meadows made their projections about the limits to growth at the beginning of the 1970s, global oil reserves amounted to six hundred billion barrels. Just under forty years later they totaled 1.2 trillion barrels; 760 billion barrels had been produced in the intervening period alone.[23]

As oil consumption grows, so too do the available reserves. How does this paradox come about? As a consequence of new production technologies, considerably more efficient exploitation of oil fields, the discovery of new deposits, the tapping of previously inaccessible areas (the deep sea, the Arctic) and the use of unconventional carbon hydride reserves (shale oil, tar and oil sand). When prices rise it also becomes profitable to extract oil in remote places and using elaborate techniques. From an environmental perspective this is bad news: switching to unconventional sources involves an increase in energy expenditure and emissions and has a destructive effect on sensitive ecosystems. At the same time—and this is the good news—rising prices lead to improvements in efficiency, thus making our economy less dependent on oil. We have seen evidence of this in the highly developed industrial nations since 2005: economic growth is no longer wholly dependent on oil consumption.

The discovery of new reserves and the emergence of new techniques for the production of gas and oil are causing geopolitical shifts whose full import is not yet clear. The

US, which for years was as dependent on oil imports as a junkie on a dealer, is now becoming a major power in the petroleum market once again. In spite of the devastating oil spill that occurred in 2010 in the Gulf of Mexico, more and more new oil production licenses are being granted. At the same time, the United States is experiencing a genuine natural gas boom. Its supply of shale gas in particular is enormous and since the end of the 1990s fracking has provided the technological means to make extracting it profitable. Fracking involves drilling down, often several kilometers, to the shale layer before continuing horizontally. A mixture of water, sand and chemicals is then injected into the drilling site at high pressure in order to break open the rock and release the natural gas within it. The same method is used to produce oil. The US has over twenty extensive oil shale formations. Oil can be produced there at a cost of $50 to $65 per barrel—while the current market price is around ninety dollars. In August 2014 America actually overtook Saudi Arabia as the world's top oil producer. US dependence on imports is decreasing as a result. As recently as 2005, 60 percent of the country's oil needs were imported; by 2012 that figure had fallen to 42 percent, with a strong downward trend.

Conservationists have strong reservations about fracking, and for good reason. Critics fear that it could cause chemical substances including carcinogens like benzene to penetrate groundwater aquifers. It also involves huge water expenditure. These objections could put a severe damper on the euphoria over the new gas boom. As seen most recently in the great summer drought of 2012, water shortages are becoming an acute problem, especially in the Midwest and the southern regions of the United States. Water consumption for gas and oil production is coming into competition with agricultural water use. Then there is the problem of unregulated methane emissions—an issue that has largely been ignored up to now: "Satellite observations of huge oil and gas basins in East Texas and North Dakota confirm staggering 9 and 10 percent leakage rates of heat-trapping methane. [...] 'At the current methane loss rates,' researchers write, 'a net climate benefit on all time frames owing to tapping unconventional resources in the analyzed tight formations is unlikely.' In short, fracking speeds up human-caused climate change, thanks to methane leaks alone. Remember, natural gas is mostly methane, (CH_4), a super-potent greenhouse gas, which traps 86 times as much heat as CO_2 over a 20-year period. So even small leaks in the natural gas production and delivery system can have a large climate impact—enough to gut the entire benefit of switching from coal-fired power to gas."[24]

On the basis of a comprehensive risk assessment, in September 2012 Germany's Federal Environment Agency recommended that the extraction of gas from deep rock beds should only be permitted under strict safety conditions and that fracking should generally not be permitted in protected drinking water areas. *At present* the agency advises against the large-scale implementation of fracking.[25] Its message can be read as "preferably not now, maybe later"—depending on how the technology stands the test of time. Given the need for gas power plants as a reserve for renewable energy sources and the significant role gas plays in the heating market, we are faced with an exemplary conflict: is it better to import natural gas from Siberia, where it is produced without any particular environmental qualms, than to produce it under controlled conditions at home? It will be some time before sustainably produced biogas or synthetic gas from renewable energy sources are capable of replacing natural gas to a significant degree. As in other European countries, public acceptance is critical to determining whether shale gas has a future in Germany, and that is unlikely to be particularly high. It is doubtful whether comprehensive information and early public involvement will change this.

In Austria even a clean fracking pilot project that was to be conducted without any toxic chemicals fell through in the face of public opposition. The frac fluid—the liquid cocktail to be injected into the rock—only contained water, bauxite sand and cornstarch. The plan was to run this mixture through a closed-loop water cycle and reuse it. A citizens' action group mobilized against the project using the slogan "wine country, not gas country" and it was unceremoniously cancelled, even before the first test drill to a depth of six kilometers could be carried out. A notice on the website of the oil and gas concern OMV, which developed the project in cooperation with the University of Leoben, stated succinctly: "At present the project is not economically viable." Whether that is the last word on the matter remains to be seen—the shale gas supplies in Lower Austria are apparently sufficient to meet the country's gas needs for 30 years. However, the situation in Poland demonstrates how untrustworthy such provisional estimates can be: predictions made about imposing shale gas reserves there have had to be adjusted down by a factor of 10 (from 5.3 trillion to somewhere in the range of 346 to 768 billion cubic meters) and ExxonMobil has pulled out of the exploration of Polish shale gas deposits. Complex geological conditions, lower reserves than expected and excessive bureaucracy have seriously dampened the dreams of a Polish gas boom.[26]

In America too there have been numerous local protests against fracking. Up to now the protesters have mostly been fighting a losing battle. Politicians and economists regard the new production methods as an opportunity to move toward energy independence and stimulate domestic value creation. The United States now produces more natural gas than Russia and the price of gas has halved since 2004. Major industrial consumers in the US currently pay two-thirds less than in Germany, with electricity savings of 40 percent.[27] These conditions are making America an attractive industrial location again, particularly for energy-intensive sectors such as chemical or aluminum production, and within a few years the US is actually going to become a net exporter of natural gas. In preparation for export, gas is cooled to the point where it condenses and can be transported by tanker. In this way six hundred cubic meters of gas can be fit into one, meaning that the volume to be transported is only a fraction of the original value. China, whose gas consumption is growing rapidly, is already buying into US production. Once the expansion of the Panama Canal is complete there will be a clear transport route to Asia. Including Canada, which is evidently determined to proceed in extracting oil from its tar sands regardless of any ecopolitical objections, North America will also be able to meet all its own oil needs. This constitutes a geopolitical revolution. Some commentators are even talking of a new era of excess oil in which OPEC will lose its power.[28] The downside of the new petroboom, however, is that the costs and risks associated with the exploration of new oil sources deep below sea level or in remote regions such as the Arctic are increasing. And while tapping new sources is becoming more and more costly, we are experiencing a decline in cheaply available reserves. As soon as more than half of an oil field's stores have been extracted the production curve drops off sharply, while production costs rise exponentially. If we have not yet reached peak oil, we have at least reached peak cheap oil.

In addition to climate change, then, there are strong economic arguments for gradually moving away from oil as the basic raw material of industrial society. Prices will rise going forward, while the security of the supply will decrease. Half of the oil consumed in Germany comes from the North Sea, where production is in constant decline. It peaked in 1999 at around six million barrels per day and this number is expected to fall to two million by 2020, increasing Germany's dependence on crisis-ridden production countries. Nobody today can predict how stable the Gulf states will be in ten years. Iraq and Libya are still fragile, Iran and Venezuela unknown factors. We cannot even be sure of Nigeria. The dependence of the global economy on unstable regimes is not exactly reassuring. Whichever angle you take, there are more than enough environmental, economic and political reasons to expedite the transition from fossil fuels to renewable energy sources. It is thus crucial that alternative energy sources become competitive. Among other approaches, that means imposing fees for CO_2 emissions anywhere in the world and putting a stop to complimentary usage of the earth's atmosphere as a dump for greenhouse gases. The fact that resource depletion is not going to end the fossil age makes it all the more urgent that we take these steps.

When crude oil becomes more expensive, the competitiveness of alternative fuels—first and foremost natural gas—increases. Although natural gas consumption has risen by 31 percent in the last decade, the known reserves are currently 60 percent larger than in 1991, with new sources constantly being discovered. The advantage of natural gas is that it only gives off half as much carbon dioxide as coal when burned to generate electricity. Gas power plants can be effectively combined with renewable energy sources because they can be flexibly managed, and natural gas can also be implemented as a basic material in the chemical industry or as fuel for vehicles. Using it to replace coal or oil lessens our impact on the environment. However, the new gas boom also has a dangerous side. The US in particular is in danger of stumbling into a natural gas trap. Prices are currently so low in America that energy efficiency and renewable energy are at risk of being forgotten. The number of contracts being issued for the construction of new wind turbines has nosedived; in California alone there are apparently 14,000 windmills standing unused. Erratic public policies for the promotion of renewable energy are contributing to this debacle. It is very tempting simply to ramp up gas and oil production rather than embracing efficiency and renewable energy: "Drill, baby, drill!" as the saying goes.[29] Yet America's wasteful energy consumption has long since ceased to guarantee better economic performance or quality of life. If the Obama administration does not succeed in its final attempt at implementing ambitious energy and climate policies, the prospects for a global climate convention will remain bleak and America will have again squandered the opportunity to take a leading role in the green energy revolution, despite meeting all the criteria to do so: cutting-edge technology, venture capital, entrepreneurial spirit and plenty of sun and wind.

While crude oil is not going to disappear from industrial production, in the medium term it is conceivable that it will lose its dominant role in the global energy supply as renewable energy sources and gas take on greater significance. It will gradually be displaced from the transportation sector by electric vehicles, gas and second-generation agricultural fuels, and it will no longer be used to heat buildings or generate electricity. Its usage should be limited to sectors in which value creation is extremely high and feedstock transitions take longer than elsewhere. This applies in particular to the chemical and pharmaceutical industries.

High oil prices are, however, making the extraction of fuel from coal (coal hydrogenation) more cost effective. This process was practiced on a large scale in the Third Reich in order to reduce German dependence on oil and produce fuel for industry and the armed forces. Today South Africa is among the pioneers of indirect coal hydrogenation using the Fischer–Tropsch process, during which coal is converted into synthesis gas at temperatures of more than one thousand degrees, with the gas being used as a basic material in the production of gasoline, diesel, heating oil and aromatics for the chemical industry. Three large plants provide approximately one third of South Africa's fuel. According to Wikipedia there are currently plans to build 25 more facilities for indirect coal hydrogenation around the world, 13 of which will be in the US and seven in China.[30] Coal hydrogenation is extremely energy intensive and releases massive amounts of CO_2. Its end products are even more harmful to our climate than oil-based fuels. Whether this technology becomes established on a global scale will primarily depend on its economic feasibility and the alternatives available. The introduction of CO_2 taxes or binding limitations on and an increase in the cost of carbon emissions in the context of a cap-and-trade system would be effective countermeasures. Ultimately, however, dirty methods of energy production will only be eradicated if cost-effective alternatives are available. It is thus crucial that the cost of renewable energy sources continues to fall. It will also take an improvement in vehicle fuel economy and a more intelligent transport system to check the growing demand for raw materials. Here, too, a combination of efficiency improvements and alternative drive technologies are required. No matter how you look at it, the conjecture that the industrial system is running out of fuel is both illusory and dangerous. In fact we are in the middle of a race between renewable energy and fossil fuels—with all the risks that entails for the climate.

The situation is similar with regard to other industrial lubricants, including the so-called rare earth elements, which are in fact not very rare at all: global reserves are estimated to total as much as ninety-nine million tons—a plentiful supply, given that annual consumption is currently around one hundred and forty thousand tons, although demand will continue to rise.[31] While restrictive Chinese export policy has led to shortages of some of these raw materials, that does not enable us to draw conclusions about long-term reserves. Though at present Beijing controls 95 percent of the global market for rare earth elements, it only possesses around a quarter of the known deposits. Growing demand and rising prices will lead to old mines being reopened and new ones being set up. At the same time—as with other metals—an increased recycling quota will extend the lifetime of natural supplies. Instead of shipping large quantities of electronic scrap from Europe to Africa, where it is cannibalized with no consideration for humans or nature, we should be recycling the resources it contains—including gold, copper, nickel, cobalt and a range of rare earth elements such as cerium, lanthanum and praseodymium—locally. Biotechnological processes will play a growing role in this area, e.g. the use of bacteria to reclaim palladium, which is present in trace amounts in industrial waste. British researchers are working on implementing palladium-covered microbes as biocatalysts in fuel cells.

Reserves and Prices

The American economist Julian L. Simon, who passed away in 1998, was a vehement opponent of the modern Malthusian assumption that exhaustion of natural resources is inevitable. At no point in time, he argued, can we know for certain how large the available reserves of a raw material really are, since new technologies enable us to tap new deposits. Furthermore, he insisted on the almost limitless extent of the human capacity to overcome critical shortages through innovation.[32] Simon's optimism that even in future there will be no sustained shortage of raw materials may be questionable, but his core thesis—namely that human ingenuity in combination with effective shortage pricing always finds new solutions for resource shortages—is historically sound. Of course, he didn't dispute that certain raw materials are in limited supply, even if new deposits are always being found. But even if iron ore, gold, copper, platinum etc. do run low at some point, we don't know the potential of the natural resources that will be available to us in future. The value of the forces of nature (wind, solar and hydropower) and of natural materials (iron ore, copper, cotton etc.) is only realized through the application of technological inventions. They only become resources once we have the capacity to use them. Before this they are merely part of the natural world. The oil under the Arabian Peninsula was useless to the ancient Egyptians. Coal only became a valuable raw material thanks to the steam engine and modern iron smelting, and the sun only became a source of electricity with the invention of photovoltaics. The possible uses of nature's potential as a source of prosperity expand in tandem with rapid developments in science and technology.

Simon famously made a bet with the entomologist Paul R. Ehrlich, who had come to prominence thanks to particularly drastic predictions about the famines and catastrophic shortages that would occur as a result of the population explosion. His book *The Population Bomb*, which appeared in 1968, had a major influence on the discussion about the inevitability of a resource crisis that culminated in the Club of Rome's study *The Limits to Growth* four years later. Simon challenged Ehrlich to name five metals with a total value of one thousand dollars that he believed would run short in the foreseeable future and thus substantially increase in price. Ehrlich chose chromium, copper, nickel, tin and tungsten. The wager period was 10 years. When that time was up in September 1990, the inflation-adjusted prices of all these metals had fallen and Ehrlich paid Simon the difference of $570.07. In fact, the prices of tin and tungsten had fallen by more than half. Ehrlich would also have lost if he had invested in petroleum, sugar, coffee, cotton, wool or phosphates: taking inflation into account, all these commodities had become less expensive, whereas during the same period the global population had grown by a record eight hundred million people. None of Ehrlich's other apocalyptic predictions came true either. Simon did however lose a similar bet over the price of wood with the forestry professor David South.[33]

It is of course not possible to make long-term predictions on the basis of 10 years, but Simon managed to show that—taking inflation into account—over long periods of time the prices of raw materials remained roughly steady or even dropped. Prices that rose significantly in the short term were offset by newly tapped reserves, improved procedural efficiency and the implementation of alternative raw materials. It seems counterintuitive, but accounting for inflation the prices of raw materials have actually fallen substantially since industrialization began. Taking the 2001 weighted price index for industrial materials as a yardstick, prices during the first great wave of industrialization around 1850 were six times as high. Raw materials prices reached their absolute peak at the end of the First World War, before falling sharply by the beginning of the second. The war industry's enormous consumption of resources and the rebuilding effort after 1945 then caused prices to rise again, before zigzagging to an all-time low between 1960 and 2001.[34] According to the calculations of the UN Food and Agriculture Organization (FAO), food prices are also substantially lower today than in the 1960s and 1970s, despite a wave of price increases between 2008 and 2012. If we assign the 2002 level a value of 100, food prices had a value of 250 in 1960, rose to a record 350 by the middle of the 1970s and declined continuously after that. They only began rising again at the beginning of the new millennium.[35]

There is good reason to surmise that the relationship between supply and demand on the raw materials markets is fundamentally changing now that the populous developing countries have embarked on industrialization and mass consumption. One indication of this is that in the decade between 2001 and 2011 the inflation-adjusted prices of raw materials rose by almost 150 percent. The implication is that the growth of the global economy has entered a new phase, in which the need for all kinds of resources is growing faster than the available supplies. That being the case, we can expect the prices of raw materials to continue rising. But it is also true that any future upward trend in the price of scarce resources will trigger its own countermovements. Rising prices increase the incentive to look for alternative processes and materials. New, more efficient technologies emerge, leading to the use of different raw materials—the switch from copper wiring to fiber-optic cables is a familiar example of this. Furthermore, raw materials prices are highly cyclical, a state of affairs that is being compounded by a growing volume of speculative raw materials certificates and options. After the high of 2011, industrial raw materials have become substantially less expensive against the background of the ongoing crisis in Europe, the weak performance of the US economy and the slowing Chinese boom: Within one year the price of iron ore dropped by 40 percent, the price of palladium by 30 and the price of copper by 25 percent. Gold dropped 15 percent from the high of September 2011, although it is an increasingly sought-after investment in times of crisis.[36]

All this notwithstanding, the issue here is not whether the available natural resources will suffice, in combination with solar power, to facilitate economic growth ad infinitum. Resource efficiency cannot be increased indefinitely, and even the conversion of sunlight into energy and biomass is tied to physical resources: soil, water and industrial raw materials. We can expect the need for all sorts of natural resources to increase for the next few decades and the pressure on soil, forests and oceans to grow. That is not to say, however, that the limits to growth have already been reached. In fact, shortages on the raw materials markets help promote the transition to a sustainable mode of production because rising prices lead to more efficient resource usage and accelerate the search for alternative materials. In this regard, times of crisis are invariably also opportunities to speed up innovation. It is always a mistake to think of the future as a mere extension of the present. The future of industrial society, its resource base and its production methods are no exception.

The upshot of the above is that the critical limits to growth do not (for the foreseeable future) lie in the exhaustion of energy sources and industrial raw materials but in the excessive strain being placed on vital ecosystems: the earth's climate, soil, oceans and reservoirs. As climate change has repercussions for all other essential ecosystems, the enrichment of greenhouse gases in the atmosphere is the most pressing problem we face. The core of a sustainable growth strategy thus lies in the decarbonization of the economy—in making the great leap toward postfossil, solar society. But there are other pressing challenges to tackle too: the reclamation and enhancement of agrarian land, the supply of freshwater to a growing global population, the protection of maritime ecosystems and the preservation of species diversity. The key lies in increasing resource efficiency—in generating greater prosperity from less energy and fewer raw materials. That involves more than just the optimization of production processes, buildings, appliances, vehicles etc. Production and consumption must be integrated in such a way as to minimize the loss of raw materials, water and organic matter. The greater the synergy, the less need there will be for fresh resources.

Thomas Malthus and the Relentlessness of Nature

The limits to growth have appeared to be within reach once before, in the early days of industrial society: At the end of the eighteenth century the British priest, economist and social philosopher Thomas Malthus prophesied that agricultural production would not be able to keep up with a rapidly growing population. He claimed that rising food prices and famines were inevitable and that the earth could not sustain more than a billion people—the approximate population at that time. In his *Essay on the Principle of Population* Malthus writes of a surplus of people for whom no place has been set at the "great banquet of nature. Nature orders [them] to withdraw, and she delays not to put this order into execution."[37]

Though he has been soundly refuted by the subsequent course of history, Malthus's thinking persists today, particularly with respect to the concept of fixed limits imposed on human civilization by nature. The transgression of these limits is seen as a second fall of mankind that must be atoned for with misery and death. Nature dictates what humans are capable of; it stipulates the limits of the habitat to which humanity is consigned. Malthus had only a limited conception of the capacity of human ingenuity to expand this space. He believed only slight increases in agricultural yields to be possible. Like the ideas of many of his spiritual children, his theory suffered from a fundamental error: it projected the status quo of his time into the future. How could he have foreseen the groundbreaking discoveries of Justus Liebig and his contemporary Gregor Mendel? The combination of agricultural chemistry and systematic plant breeding revolutionized farming and multiplied crop yields.

Since Malthus made his bleak predictions, the global population has grown sevenfold, increasing hand in hand with per capita calorie consumption—a classic example of the growth of limits. Although more than a billion people on earth today are underfed, it is not due to a lack of food. They are hungry because they are too poor to buy food, and because decades of mismanagement in many countries have hampered agricultural development. Energy consumption has increased by a factor of 40 and the global economy by a factor of 50 during the same period. In the twentieth century alone the global population almost quadrupled (from 1.6 billion to 6.1 billion). Such turbulent population growth had never been seen before. It made sense to fear chronic famine and a dramatic lack of resources, but instead life expectancy has risen continuously and standards of living, particularly in highly industrialized countries, have skyrocketed to previously unimaginable levels—because, rather than in spite of the growing population. In combination with modern technology and rising education standards, a larger population means greater economic potential—ultimately *people* are the most important productive force.

As the global population increases to nine billion and beyond, pressure on the environment will continue to mount. The danger of destabilizing essential ecosystems is obvious, and it would be negligent not to prepare for this eventuality. We need a plan B for coping with a whole series of crises: a global economic slump, water shortages, food crises and distribution conflicts over scarce resources. So much for crisis management. But our plan A must be to avert looming crises by minimizing modernity's consumption of natural resources without sacrificing modernity itself. The limits to growth that Malthus had in mind were eradicated by the first scientific and technological revolution. Now industrial society is coming up against new limits: declining species diversity and the loss of fertile land, the destabilization of the earth's climate, overfishing of the oceans and growing water shortages in many regions of the earth. The critical challenge is to find yet more intelligent solutions to these new crises. There are limits to what the earth, as the home of human civilization, can bear. Human inventiveness and our ability to respond to crises with technological, cultural and political innovation is unlimited. And the power of the sun as the source of a postfossil lifestyle and mode of production is almost infinite.

The Dead-End Street of Zero Growth

Taking the attitude that less is more might lead to happiness for individuals. Quality of life is no less defined by control over one's time, social relationships and satisfying work than by material goods. But zero growth in Europe is not the answer to the turbulent economic growth taking place throughout most of the rest of the world. The up-and-coming nations will negotiate on anything but their right to growth. It is on this very point that post-Kyoto climate diplomacy has failed. If the environmental movement becomes synonymous with antigrowth politics, the battle has already been lost. When billions of people rise out of poverty, the environment benefits too: environmental awareness increases along with prosperity. Rather than tilting at growth per se—like Don Quixote at windmills—we must change the *nature of growth*. The fixation of the debate on GDP gains and losses is misleading. GDP is a sum of money; it tells us nothing about the ecological footprint of an economy. The question we should be asking is not whether the monetary value of goods and services sold is growing, but how resource intensive their production was, what emissions they involve and how severely they pollute the biosphere. Rather than focusing on how much GDP grows or shrinks, ecologists should thus be focusing on the material side of the economy. Our goal must be to achieve zero emissions, not to freeze economic activity at its current level. Environmentally speaking, zero growth is no help at all; from an economic and sociopolitical perspective it gives rise to all kinds of problems: investors withdraw capital, ambitious citizens emigrate, the pace of innovation drops, infrastructure is eroded and pensions and healthcare come under even more pressure than before. Given the demographic change we are facing, we should absolutely be aiming to reduce both our personal and social dependence on growth, but it by no means follows that we should make a stagnating or even shrinking economy our goal.

The current European debt crisis has revealed the thoroughly schizophrenic nature of the growth debate. While the call for an end to rampant growth circulates in feature sections and conference halls, politicians and the bulk of the public are concerned with how best to revive it in crisis countries. Green politicians are no exception to this. The debate on postgrowth society is taking place in a nirvana, while in the real world the German government is being criticized for its one-sided austerity policy. The Greens and Social Democrats are broadly in agreement that the European response to the crisis lacks a growth component. Enforced saving alone is plunging the affected countries into a downward economic spiral, demand is slumping, unemployment and poverty are spreading and hope of a better future is disappearing.

The crisis is hitting the younger generation hardest. Millions are jobless, not earning enough to survive or without the material means to start a family. In many European countries there is already talk of a lost generation. In Britain 22.5 percent of young adults aged between 16 and 24 were unemployed in the spring of 2012. The corresponding figure for France was 23.3 percent, while in Spain and Greece half of young people were jobless. In Italy a quarter of those under 30 were neither in paid work nor had they completed an apprenticeship. With numbers this disastrous there is a desperate need for increased investment in educational opportunities for children and young people as well as reforms in vocational training. At the same time, it is clear that the job prospects of this generation depend on the European economies getting their act together with regard to sustainable growth. Job sharing, self-employment, voluntary work and publicly financed projects are important responses to the crisis, but in the long run they are no substitute for a renaissance of the productive sector.

The question is not *whether* Europe needs economic growth but *how* the forces of growth can be strengthened and *which direction* we ought to take: do we try to revive the old growth model, or do we use the crisis to expedite the ecological modernization of our cities, speed up energy reform on a European scale, overhaul our transport infrastructure and institute a major research and development program for environmentally friendly technologies?

Prolonged zero growth would be no more beneficial for Germany than it would elsewhere. The challenge of simultaneously coping with demographic change, reducing national debt to a manageable level, providing education and work for millions of young immigrants and, on top of all this, maintaining an efficient welfare state is daunting as it is. It would be almost insurmountable if the economy were to stagnate or shrink. Both government tax revenue and the financial positions of social security systems are linked to economic growth. The oft-cited theory of jobless growth doesn't stand up to empirical examination. Economic growth and employment levels have always been connected. Following the period of decline caused by the financial crisis of 2008–9, the number of people gainfully employed in Germany reached an all-time high. Contrary to popular belief there was a bigger increase in employment subject to social security contributions than in so-called tax-free minijobs. Since 2005 the number of jobs with social security benefits has grown from 26 million to more than twenty-nine million, although this rise is almost entirely due to an increase in part-time work.[38] Even if growth is far from being an unambiguously positive phenomenon, zero growth entails enormous economic and political stress and bitter distribution conflicts. In the short term it might seem possible to uphold a certain standard of living for the majority by massively redistributing the wealth of the rich, but no society can meet the demands of the future by redistributing present wealth. Sooner rather than later there comes a point when such societies start living off their capital. We have seen where that leads before, as in the former German Democratic Republic up to 1989.

If nothing else, economic growth drives the modernization of physical capital. Technological innovation occurs first and foremost during periods of economic growth, when investments are made in new factories, plants and machinery. Generally speaking, every new production plant is more environmentally friendly and resource efficient than its predecessor. If the economy stagnates, investment declines too, and with it the pace of economic modernization. This applies to private households and public authorities as well as to commercial enterprises. In times of zero growth or recession private households put less money into home improvements, new domestic appliances, vehicles etc. and the replacement of old appliances and vehicles with new, more environmentally friendly models stalls. Ultimately government investment is also tied to the rate of economic growth. If the economy slows, tax revenue declines, while welfare spending increases. Public investment drops as a result—particularly now that recourse to increased public borrowing is no longer really an option. This slows down the renewal of public infrastructure, which is dependent on government investment (or at least on state subsidies), with a knock-on effect on public transport as well as urban ecological modernization programs, research funding etc. Huge investment is required in all these areas in order to hasten environmental reform. In order to speed up the transfer of freight transport to the railways we must invest in the expansion of rail networks and the modernization of train technology. A combination of public funding programs and private investment is required to reduce the energy consumption of buildings. As a rule of thumb, the more dynamic the economy, the faster the modernization of buildings, transport systems, energy production, industrial machinery and the fixtures of private households takes place. The operative point is that in the process of modernization resource efficiency must grow faster than consumption. Without the stimulus of investment and innovation we are left with old machinery, production processes and structures, and thus with a negative environmental balance. Doing less of the same can at best delay environmental catastrophe, but not prevent it. Prevention will require a continuous process of environmental innovation, a process that is most likely to flourish in a dynamic economic environment.

Another popular theory, the claim that beyond a moderate standard of living increased income and consumer choice do not make people happier, smacks of autosuggestion. It is reminiscent of the fable of the fox who claims the grapes are too sour for him—when in reality they are hanging out of his reach. It is unsurprising that in times of crisis and fear for the future a desire for security and stable social relations takes the upper hand. Fear of failure overshadows hope for improvement. It would be an exaggeration to interpret this as an overture to postgrowth society. Even in prosperous societies the link between economic growth and quality of life still holds, as long as the fruits of growth are not monopolized by a happy few. When interviewed, the rich and successful are always asked: what does money mean to you? The smart ones answer: freedom. In fact, the same applies to the vast majority of the population. Increased income gives us more options with regard to how and where we live. In many respects it make us more independent. It allows us to live more comfortably, enjoy life more and give our children a better education. It improves our chances for a long and healthy life. It means bigger tax contributions to the public purse and thus helps to finance culture, education and social security—all things that even postmaterial society values highly.

The assertion that money can't buy happiness is at best half true. Such wisdom is poor consolation to those who have to watch every euro in order to make ends meet. It is closer to the truth to say that money *alone* cannot buy happiness, but that is hardly a new discovery. Let those who already have everything extol the virtues of frugality—the vast majority of people on this planet still want to improve their material standard of living. Not even the well-off middle classes in our own country are renouncing the comforts of consumer society; they are merely becoming more refined in their tastes. They no longer simply want more; the new trend is toward better, finer and more unique consumption. Fair trade and organic products are features of an environmentally enlightened hedonism, as are fancy road bikes, hybrid cars, car sharing, environmentally friendly homes, yoga and gyms. Frequent flying and extensive living spaces fully equipped with electronic appliances make the ecological footprint of this lifestyle far larger than that of people living on unemployment benefits who do not worry about the environment because they have other, more pressing concerns. Far be it for me to denounce the LOHAS lifestyle.[39] It is more or less my own. But we should not kid ourselves that green hedonism is an adequate response to the environmental crisis. Without a revolution in industrial production, energy provision, agriculture etc. the lifestyle of ecological modernity will not be sustainable.

Chapter 3

The Malaise of Modernity[1]

You see, where'er you look, on earth but vainness' hour.
Tomorrow will destroy that which was built today;
The meadow where the boy a-shepherding will play
Together with his flock, there now the cities tower.
That will be trampled soon which now is in full flower,
Tomorrow ash and bone who now defiance inveigh;
No bronze, no marble stands that will not pass away.
Now fortune laughs, but we are soon in hardship's power.

—Andreas Gryphius (1616–1664)[2]

The history of human civilization has always been accompanied by a basic sense of transience, vanity and futility in counterpoint to the impulse to reach for the stars. Since the very beginning, the aspiration to go faster, higher and further has been attended by an ominous feeling that everything is going to end badly. In the Old Testament story of the Tower of Babel, God punishes humankind for having the hubris to want to erect a city with a tower "whose top reaches to the heavens" by confusing their language "so they [cannot] understand each another." The people are forced to abandon the project and scatter all over the world. An unfinished section is left behind as a warning about man's presumptuousness. The story belongs to a series of lapsarian narratives telling of heavy punishments for the wrongdoing of mankind. God annihilates sinful, fallen humanity with the Flood and destroys the wicked cities of Sodom and Gomorrah in fire and brimstone. Interpretations of the end of whole civilizations in flood and fire as punishment for arrogance and intemperance are not exclusive to Christianity. Diluvian narratives are found in numerous traditions from all regions of the world. Apocalyptic visions of the consequences of climate change are themselves part of this convention. The simulation models used by the IPCC rely on empirical data and scientifically verified hypotheses about the interplay of greenhouse gases, climate change, sea levels, turbulent weather etc. It would be negligent to dismiss them as mythology. But the interpretation of climate change as a consequence of the excesses of modern civilization is not science; it is the modern version of age-old tales of destruction by fire and water as punishment for a sinful life.

Icarus was another mortal who tried to go too high. It is worth briefly reminding ourselves of this parable from Greek mythology, in which Daedalus—a renowned inventor, engineer, builder and artist—is commissioned by the Cretan king Minos to construct a labyrinth to house the Minotaur, the monstrous offspring—half man, half bull—of his queen's *mésalliance* with a bull. Daedalus's ingenuity has a hand in the earlier episode too: he constructs a fake wooden cow for Pasiphaë to hide in in order to copulate with the bull. Not only that, it occurs to him that anyone who unwinds a thread on the way into the labyrinth will be able to find the way out again. Thanks to his cunning, Theseus, son of the king of Athens, is able to kill the Minotaur and escape. In punishment for this, Minos imprisons the disloyal inventor and his son Icarus on Crete. As escaping by sea is of the question, the resourceful Daedalus decides to copy the birds. He makes artificial wings by attaching feathers to a light frame with wax. Before setting out, Daedalus impresses upon his son that he must not fly too high or too low: he must neither get too close to the heat of the sun nor to the moisture rising up from the sea. But the inevitable happens: Filled with the intoxication of flight, Icarus becomes cocky and ascends toward the sun. The wax in his wings melts, the feathers fall off and the careless boy falls into the sea. The moral of the story is clear: Icarus falls victim to his hubris. Earthly beings are not permitted to reach for the sun, which in the ancient world belongs to the sphere of the gods. Yet the story does not completely extinguish the dream of flight. Had the reckless Icarus remained on course, the adventure would likely have succeeded. And there is something else we can take from this saga: Man can expand his capabilities with the aid of technology modeled on nature. He can transcend his natural limits by learning from nature, as long as he doesn't become overconfident.

The Prometheus saga likewise describes the ambivalence of aspiration and fear, progress and risk we experience with each new advance into the realm of the gods. Prometheus, whose name means "farsighted," furnishes humans with divine qualities and capabilities: He grants them the wisdom of Athena and the skill of

Hephaestus as well as teaching them how to control the ills of nature. And he restores their ability to make fire, which has been taken away by Zeus in punishment for betraying the gods. The revenge of Zeus is fearsome. He sends Pandora, the all gifted, with a jar containing all manner of afflictions. Despite the warnings of his brother Prometheus, Epimetheus accepts the gift of the gods, and from that time on humanity is beset by fever, sorrow and early death. Only hope, the last gift, cannot escape, because Pandora quickly closes the jar again. This story is evidently a warning that every new technological development, every new attempt to reach for the sphere of the gods brings renewed misfortune on the world. With every invention, every technology for controlling natural phenomena such as fire, humanity moves another step further from its natural state, acquiring powers previously reserved for the gods: the ability to fly at the speed of sound, to communicate over long distances, to create light ("Let there be light"), to reroute rivers, to move mountains and to bring down thunder and lightning on enemies.[3] There is a downside to all these achievements: they can also bring down fear and suffering on humanity itself. Prometheus, whom the young Marx lauded as "the most eminent saint and martyr in the philosophical calendar," embodies defiance of the gods.[4] He doesn't submit to the natural–divine order of things, instead providing humans with new abilities that put them in control of their own destinies. He pays a terrible price for this hubris. Zeus has Prometheus tied to a cliff, where he is left without sleep, food or drink. And as if that were not enough, each day an eagle feeds on his liver, which perpetually grows back so that his suffering never ends. Eternal life, so ancient wisdom tells us, is eternal suffering. But do we let that frighten us?

Goethe's *Faust* as a Tragedy of Progress

> Grief and woe!
> A beautiful world
> [...] by your violence,
> has been destroyed.[5]

Every age interprets Goethe's universal drama in its own way. From our current perspective, given the horrors of the past and those still to come, it is logical to read *Faust* as an "exemplary tragedy about the progress of modern man."[6] Goethe certainly anticipated the drawbacks of capitalist modernity with spooky prescience: speculation and financial crises, war and environmental destruction, greed and violence. Love drugs, artificial human breeding and the curse of breathless acceleration are also among the subjects he deals with as he explores the inner workings of a mind that fluctuates between depression and delusions of grandeur. Faust restlessly climbs to ever higher heights, reckless in the pursuit of his goals. Always pressing onward, he consequently misses out on the joys of the earth. If in part I, the Gretchen tragedy, he still longs for love as the highest form of earthly happiness, in part II he is driven by quite different desires: "I wish to rule and have possessions!"[7] He transforms into a prototypical entrepreneur whose talent lies in directing the efforts of his workers toward a goal: "Prompt effort and strict discipline / will guarantee superb rewards: / to complete a task that's so tremendous, / working as one is worth a thousand hands."[8] It is not merely greed for wealth that motivates him, however, but "the dream and the will to found a private kingdom, [...] the will to conquer, [...] the joy of creating." These are the attributes of the modern entrepreneur as described by Joseph A. Schumpeter at the beginning of the twentieth century.[9] The project that Faust regards as the crowning glory of his life can be read as a parable about the early days of industrialization. Goethe illustrates changing attitudes to nature: The wild beauty of the sea is no longer something to be admired; it becomes an opponent that must be tamed. Contemplation gives way to the mastery of nature. In the eternal rolling of the waves Faust primarily sees squandered energy: "Imbued with strength, wave after wave holds power / but then withdraws, and nothing's been accomplished— / a sight to drive me to despair, / this aimless strength of elemental forces! / This has inspired me to venture to new heights, / to wage war here against these forces and subdue them."[10] He launches legions of workers to build dikes and canals and prepare the reclaimed land for settlement. What has been wrested from the sea must become part of the human world. The afterlife does not interest Faust since he believes his land project will make him immortal: "The traces of my days on earth / will survive into eternity!"[11] In anticipation of this highest happiness he can finally say "Tarry a while, you are so fair!"[12] But in doing so he loses a bet with Mephisto and pronounces his own death sentence. The spades that Faust—now afflicted by blindness—hears are not digging canals but shoveling his grave. And the land will not be taken over by people but by ghostly lemures, "patched together, half-live creatures / of sinew, ligament and bone."[13]

In a major feat of scholarship, the Swiss economist Hans Christoph Binswanger has interpreted Goethe's masterpiece as the primordial drama of capitalism. In his reading Faust is not so much concerned with glory as with the "continuation of the creation process by man."[14] The idea of walking in God's footsteps both fascinates and frightens us—all the more so now that we are no longer using spades and steam engines to tackle nature, but nuclear fission, genetic engineering and biotechnology. The power of technology was only really unleashed when paper money, reproducible at will, replaced gold as a method of payment. This allowed for the first large-scale investments made against the promise of future growth. In *Faust* the distribution of banknotes is described as a kind of black magic: as long as people believe in the process, something worthless (paper) is transformed into something valuable (money). Credit-financed exploitation of natural resources is similarly depicted as a continuation of medieval alchemy, albeit using different means: dirt is to be turned into gold. In Binswanger's words: "The aim is to maximize the monetary value of the world. In this sense the whole world is a goldmine." Anything we find in nature can be gilded, i.e. transformed into gold, just as the old alchemists dreamed. And money is itself a magic medium: it gives us power over people and things.

In Binswanger's view, the idea of limitless growth is analogous to the ambition of "overcoming time and transitoriness," qualities that are only granted to the immortal gods.[15] There is nothing very new about this interpretation. The assertion that all modern man's aspirations for more—his constant compulsion to go further—are attempts to escape his own mortality is a standard argument in psychological literature. Achieving immortality through one's works and deeds is perhaps the strongest motivation, the greatest dream of modern man, whether as an artist, politician or entrepreneur. The accumulation of possessions is just the base form of this need to be remembered after death. It is outshone by the fame of the discoverer, the scholar, the statesman, the inventor, the poet and the Olympic champion. Ought we to suppress this instinct in favor of a more contemplative, self-content mode of existence? Are we even capable of doing so? It seems unlikely.

The metaphor of a pact with the Devil that provides the starting point for *Faust* has likewise become deeply ingrained in our understanding of industrial modernity, and not only with respect to risky technologies and unscrupulous profiteering. There is even something inherently diabolic in our boundless thirst for ever-deeper knowledge of the secrets of nature. It was the satanic serpent who encouraged Eve to eat from the tree of knowledge, causing her to lose her innocence—the original sin for which we were banished from paradise. Since that time there has been no way back to primordial unity with God and nature, only the way forward to a world of our own. The myths of antiquity tell us "that the wresting and exploitation of knowledge are perilous acts, but that man must and will know, and once knowing, will not forget."[16] With the beginning of the Neolithic Revolution approximately twenty thousand years ago mankind stopped merely blending in with nature and began reshaping it in accordance with its own needs.[17] In modifying the world given to it, humanity is building a new one. The operative question is whether its destructive or creative side will take the upper hand. The more we learn about the earth and the more precisely we understand the interplay of its systems, the more likely sustainable management of the planet becomes.

Binswanger's interpretation of Goethe addresses all the ingredients that give modernity its ambivalent character—the creation of money, capitalist entrepreneurship, science, technological control of nature and the release of the individual from all traditional bonds. Modernity allows for real progress, creativity, brilliant inventions and dramatic improvements in the living standards of the broad masses, but this process of advancement has its price. Based on his reading of *Faust*, Biswanger identifies three areas in which modernity has suffered great losses:

The first is the "loss of beauty."[18] The world was beautiful before humanity began putting its stamp on it. The destruction and disfigurement of nature is strikingly illustrated in the fifth act of a *Faust* production put on by the Thalia Theater in Hamburg. Cardboard silhouettes of megacities are carried onto the stage to replace sets depicting a bucolic idyll. Naturally beautiful landscapes disappear; ranges of skyscrapers spring up. We are presumably all pained by the brutal urbanization of natural landscapes and the rash-like spread of concrete eyesores along coastlines. And yet, on balance this issue is not as straightforward as it seems in Goethe's work and Binswanger's reading of it. For one thing, most of the European landscapes we consider beautiful today are not unspoilt; they are the result of centuries of cultivation, examples of nature shaped by man and for the most part symbiotic products of peasant agriculture adapted to the natural landscape. This could be considered confirmation that ugliness first came into the world with industrialization, but what about the beauty of modern urban landscapes? That was my immediate response to the *Faust* scene described above: Surely these man-made mountains are impressive too? Why are we fascinated by Manhattan? As I write this, I am on the 29th floor of a hotel in Chicago, looking out onto an urban panorama of high-rise buildings that extends to the horizon and up at slender towers stretching skyward. It is a view might depress some people, but I find it uplifting.

Aside from aesthetic and psychological considerations, there is something deeply aristocratic about mourning the expansion of industry and urban development—mourning the loss of a world in which only a tiny minority were granted an uplifting existence. A world in which only the aristocracy and the senior clergy led lives of sublime leisure, while the peasant population and ordinary urban dwellers lived short, deprived, frequently wretched lives in miserable circumstances. They probably didn't regard nature as romantic and beautiful, but as an alien power from which they had to wrest their livelihood and whose wrath they suffered again and again. Drought, heat waves, plagues of insects, torrential rains, catastrophic floods, biting cold and violent storms were around before climate change, and in preindustrial times people were much more vulnerable to them than today. For most of the earth's inhabitants the world is currently a much better place than it used to be. Beauty is a world that provides the greatest possible happiness for the greatest number of people.

The second cause for lament identified by Binswanger is the "loss of security caused by the dangers technology conjures up."[19] This is another narrative that has accompanied the history of technology (as a means of dominating nature) like a perpetual echo. Up to now the high point of the struggle against the destructive forces of technological progress has been opposition to nuclear power and its military sister, the atomic bomb. Binswanger's analysis calls to mind the recent nuclear catastrophe in Fukushima, Japan as an example of how man-made technology can turn on man. Nuclear power is an extremely risky undertaking. It is produced by controlled nuclear chain reactions. The heat generated by these reactions is converted into steam, which is in turn used to drive turbines. The technology has been mockingly described by critics as a method of heating water using nuclear fission—in other words, in the most complicated and dangerous way conceivable. The process and its radioactive by-products must be reliably isolated from the environment. This applies both to the radiation given off by reactors and to nuclear waste, which has to be buried for tens of thousands of years. That alone is an insane undertaking, given that nobody can take responsibility for such a colossal period of time. Then there is the potential for catastrophe inherent in every reactor accident. Since we know from experience that there is always a danger of something going wrong when humans interact with machines and that in spite of all precautions absolute safety cannot be guaranteed, the operation of nuclear power plants always involves a residual risk. No matter how minimal this risk may be, accepting it means playing with the lives of tens of thousands, if not millions of people. We need only remember that during the meltdown at Fukushima the authorities were on the verge of evacuating Tokyo. When large amounts of radioactivity are released, broad swathes of land are exposed to radiation for decades and beyond, and bodies of water become contaminated. Both the people affected and their children suffer from radiation sickness and genetic defects. These temporal and spatial dimensions of nuclear accidents are what rightly frighten people. Even though many more lives have been lost in car accidents than in the major nuclear accidents of recent decades, nuclear technology engenders a stronger sense of vulnerability. The potential dangers outweigh the benefits, especially as there are plenty of alternatives to nuclear power.

On closer consideration, however, *Faust* is not about weighing up the advantages and risks of specific technologies. It evokes a more general fear: the fear that our efforts to dominate nature will end in catastrophe. While Faust assumes that inventiveness and labor will win out over the forces of nature, Mephistopheles plays the role of Cassandra. He can foresee the great flood sweeping in behind the dikes and dams Faust builds to contain the ocean and reclaim land for settlement: “And yet with all your dams and levees / your striving serves no one but us; / in fact, you’re now preparing a grand feast / for the water-daemon, Neptune. / All of your kind are doomed already; / the elements have sworn to help us; / the end will be annihilation.”[20] All man’s efforts are in vain; anyone who refuses to submit to nature will be destroyed by it. In modern environmental parlance we might refer to this as nature fighting back. Climate change, drought and storm surges are punishment for the hubris and excesses of mankind. Binswanger appears to adopt this apocalyptic view when he attests that Mephisto knows better than the blind Faust in his megalomania.

But is it actually true that technological efforts to control nature have made human existence less secure? There is good reason to be skeptical about this claim. In reality modern civilization, including modern farming, is much less vulnerable to the moods and evils of nature than earlier ages. We are much more resilient to cold spells and heat waves than our predecessors, and while as recently as the nineteenth century whole areas of cities were razed by fire, we barely perceive fire as a risk at all anymore. Plagues, which decimated populations time and again in the Middle Ages, have largely been eradicated, at least in industrial nations. Where they do reappear, as in the case of the Ebola epidemic, they result from a lack of education and the absence (or incompetence) of public health systems. Workplace accidents were much more common in the early stages of industrialization than they are today. Antibiotics and advances in modern medicine have drastically lowered mortality rates. In the industrialized world average life expectancy has more than doubled. Our control over our own lives has also grown immeasurably thanks to rising levels of education, the freedom of movement provided by modern modes of transport, equal rights for the working classes, gender equality and the basic level of social security provided by the democratic welfare state. None of this can be divorced from the enormous increase in social wealth that has accompanied the technological and industrial revolution of the last two hundred years.

But perhaps Mephistopheles is right nonetheless. There is a real danger that all this progress will ultimately end in annihilation. Prior to now our development has been based on the ruthless exploitation of nature and its productive forces. If we continue on this path, we face the collapse of ecosystems that are vital to human civilization: soil, water and the earth's climate. The demise of whole coastal regions due to rising sea levels, extended periods of drought and devastating storms are realistic scenarios if climate change speeds up. But scaling back our technological efforts to control nature will not save us. So what will? The supposedly idyllic existence of preindustrial times is no longer open to us. The path back to nature is closed. Our only option is to move forward, toward intelligent, sustainable use of nature's productive forces. Today, when thanks to its size and its technological know-how humanity has become more powerful than ever before, the need for a reflective culture of innovation, one that considers its consequences and understands the enduring ambivalence of progress, is all the more urgent. Every step beyond the current limits of science and technology, every advance into new terrain is a risk. We must never lose sight of the consequences nor discount the possibility of our blessings becoming curses. But while we must not meddle recklessly with creation, that does not mean we have to persevere timidly with the status quo. All we can do is try to structure the interminable process of scientific and technological innovation as a learning process in which adjustments can be made early if things get out of hand.

The third loss Binswanger addresses lies in "man's growing inability to truly enjoy the wealth he creates."[21] In this context Binswanger writes of a loss of the present. Life in the here and now is being consumed by worry, which increases rather than decreases as wealth grows. The rich look anxiously to the future, plagued by fear of failure and losing the wealth they have so laboriously scraped together. As markets become more global they are also becoming more volatile. Rather than being able to sit back and relax, shareholders incessantly monitor all possible predictors of future performance. "The investor is plagued [...] by concern about the future development of the economy. Never satisfied with the present, he becomes addicted to forecasts."[22] This is a keen observation, and yet it only tells half the truth. There is plenty of evidence to support Binswanger's theory. It is barely possible to keep track of all the media coverage on stock markets and investment tips nowadays. Stock exchange experts read the future in tea leaves. Anyone with private assets anxiously tracks the ups and downs of the capital markets and laments missing the best time to buy or sell. Entrepreneurs plan for uncertainty with regard to future supply and demand. The more pensions and health insurance are reprivatized, the more individuals worry about the future. Financial crashes can ruin our plans for our old age or our children's education overnight. Our material security is largely dependent on unruly financial markets too complex for any ordinary mortal to grasp. Then there are the environmental crises and political conflicts of a rapidly changing world to worry about. Despite previously unheard of social wealth, we are increasingly anxious about what the future will bring. If anything, our anxiety is actually increasing *as a result of* our wealth, perhaps because as prosperity grows the fear of losing it does too.

That being said, concern for the future has not prevented the privileged sections of humanity from making the most of life on the sun decks of the Titanic. And by "privileged" I do not only mean rich and famous. You need only stroll through the downtown area of a European metropolis on a sunny day to see how much the global middle class is enjoying life. The claim that people are no longer capable of enjoying the present comes across as elitist misanthropy. Despite all the laments about the terrors of acceleration, we actually have more time and more opportunities to enjoy the finer things in life than our parents and grandparents. Weekly and annual working hours have fallen continuously over time, while life expectancy, education standards, holiday entitlements and purchasing power have risen rapidly. There is a contrasting strand of conservative cultural criticism that rationalizes this trend as the product of narcissistic hedonism, a cult of the present and a propensity to seek refuge in consumption that misses the point of so-called real life. Sometimes it is the loss of religion that is said to be driving people into compensatory consumption, sometime fear of death or the need to escape inner emptiness. Whatever the claim, it is always accompanied by a wagging finger exhorting the supposed victims of the rat race and the terrors of consumerism to find their way back to a good and true life. On the one hand we are said to be missing out on the present because we are consumed with worry about the future; on the other we are accused of blocking out impending crises by throwing ourselves more senselessly than ever into the here and now. Whatever we do is wrong.

Sinners, Repent! The New Penitential Movement

The appeal for prosperity without growth calls to mind the self-contentment of an aging bon vivant discovering the virtues of measure and moderation after years of excess. Until the middle of the twentieth century Europe led the Industrial Revolution. The tiny half-continent sucked up the resources of the whole world to fuel unprecedented levels of economic growth and prosperity. Now the demographic curve is turning downward, the economy is slowing and growth rates are falling. There is a growing sense that Europe's best days are behind it and that it is in any case incapable of competing with the hungry emerging nations. The cultural studies scholar Harald Welzer, one of those now proclaiming the need to renounce growth, sums up this attitude nicely: "The future of the West is already behind it. You have to know when to let go."[23] The dream of a postgrowth society is the yearning of an academic middle class that already has everything its heart desires (except for the next iPhone). For the most part, the rest of the world is dreaming a different dream: one of social mobility and a rising standard of living.

Democracy is responsible for having extended the lifestyle of the rich and powerful—previously only accessible to a small, privileged minority—to the masses. It would probably take an authoritarian dictatorship over needs to enforce asceticism for all with massive restrictions on long-distance travel, consumption, fashion, communications technology etc. Industrial modernity epitomizes the Promethean principles that have spurred on the development of human society: inventiveness and a desire for new discoveries and experiences, but also a restlessness that refuses to linger in the moment because it is always in pursuit of something new. There have always been cultural countermovements preaching the need for frugality, self-restraint and a contemplative existence in harmony with nature. Ultimately, however, these penitential movements have only brought about the refinement and differentiation of cultural practices.

The project of civilization is not yet complete. Rather than attempting to slow human evolution to a static equilibrium, we must adopt a new approach—one of mindful coevolution with nature that involves us becoming less materialistic in our needs, albeit at a high level of material comfort. The populations of rich industrial societies are no longer solely interested in accumulating more and more possessions. We are witnessing a move away from the expansion of consumption in purely quantitative terms. Their focus is shifting to needs involving self-fulfillment, refinement, a sense of beauty, communication, self-awareness and worldliness. Beyond a certain level of prosperity the demand is not simply for more, but for higher quality. It would be self-deluded, however, to equate this development with a renunciation of the growth paradigm. Even qualitative growth requires a high degree of productivity and value creation.

In a passionate presentation at the Climate Change Conference in Copenhagen, contemporary German philosopher Peter Sloterdijk described the conflict between two opposing schools of thought on the environmental crisis.[24] Astonishingly his remarks provoked very little response. Evidently they failed to resonate with the prevailing environmental discourse in Germany. And yet, to all intents and purposes Sloterdijk agrees with the alarmist diagnosis of the environmental movement. His point of departure is what he calls the crisis of kinetic expressionism—his name for the "modern mode of existence, which has primarily been made possible by easy access to fossil fuels." This high-energy way of life must be radically modified because the climate change it is generating is a threat to the foundations of civilized life on the planet. At stake in the struggle for climatic stability is nothing less than "the chance to keep the process of civilization open and ensure that it continues." The twenty-first century will be an age of severe crises and major upheaval, and the looming meteorological reformation is of no less significance than the Christian Reformation of the early modern period. It will give rise to similar movements seeking to save humanity from the hell of climate change through sublimation, repentance and rebirth.

Succinct as ever, Sloterdijk delineates a future clash of the titans between modernizers and penitential preachers: "The idealistic party in this struggle will be represented by the agents of a new modesty who confront their materialist opponents with the demand that all forms of kinetic expressionism be reduced to an environmentally acceptable minimum. [...] The goal of this future moral code, which is inimical to expression and to emissions, is to completely invert the direction civilization has taken up to now. It calls for reduction where previously augmentation has been on the agenda; [...] it urges self-restraint where previously self-liberation was celebrated." Were this regime of rationing to prevail, "every individual would hold a small amount of emissions credit, accorded to him or her as a shareholder in the atmosphere and the other elements." In the language of the Wars of Religion, Sloterdijk describes this stance as environmental Calvinism. It demands self-denial, frugality and extreme virtuousness in the name of the survival of the species and a just distribution of scarce resources.[25]

Whether or not you think such a world desirable, the call for moderation is unlikely to bear fruit. Such appeals for a culture of self-contentment "are not only opposed by the full force of expressionist civilization but also contradict what we know about the forces that drive higher cultures, which would be inconceivable without the quest for self-preservation and the will to self-enhancement." According to Sloterdijk this combination predisposes humanity toward "a culture of abundance, waste and luxury." Billions of people in the southern continents are rapidly embarking on an age of expanding needs. Choice, consumer freedom, mobility, fashion, global communication, speed, mass culture, increased self-awareness and greater experience of the world—all this is inextricably linked to modernity. These phenomena are modes of existence rather than external attributes of the modern individual. Any attempt to radically restrict them would end in an inevitably coercive program of reeducation.

Improving Humanity

There is only a small step from saving the world through strict self-limitation to human reeducation programs of varying degrees of harshness. To see the disposition of the individual as the root of the problem is to equate improving the world with "improving humans en masse."[26] Only a radical change in the inner nature, the basic psychic configuration of modern man can hold back the apocalypse. Asked how humanity can escape its "miserable situation," Dennis L. Meadows answered: "We need to change our nature. [...] My fear is that our genes make us unequipped to deal with long-term issues like climate change."[27] Meadows's response has resigned overtones—he no longer believes that a devastating crisis of civilization can be avoided. His colleague Jørgen Randers is attracted to authoritarian forms of rule. Rudolf Bahro advocated the withdrawal of small spiritual communities from the megamachine of industrial capitalism. The project of bettering human nature has a long history. It can be divided into two main strands. The first is an ascetic variant that calls for the renunciation of everything inessential, of all trumpery and luxury, as a means of self-improvement and is represented in its extreme form by the hermit, who lives in solitude and relinquishes all bodily pleasures in the pursuit of saintliness. It became a potent mass movement in monasteries of the early Middle Ages: the abolition of personal property, strict discipline, total subordination of the individual to the life of the community and the organization of daily life around prayer and meditation. Celibacy is another manifestation of this outlook. The second major approach to human improvement involves more or less compulsory reeducation conducted by public authorities, from ideological indoctrination to reeducation camps. It was taken to extremes in the ideology and practice of communism, which sought not only to purify revolutionaries—to overcome bourgeois behavioral patterns in the purgatory of class warfare—but to produce a new type of individual, as required by the new society. Communism had no use for old Adam. Leon Trotsky, the theoretician of permanent revolution and practitioner of red terror, described the project of human psychic reform in prophetic terms: "Once he has done with the anarchic forces of his own society, man will set to work on himself, in the pestle and retort of the chemist. For the first time mankind will regard himself as raw material, or at best as a physical and psychic semi-finished product."[28] The labor camps of the Gulag were the pestle in which the old version of man was ground down; the cauldron of modern human genetics is the retort.

Rudolf Bahro: Subsistence and Spirituality

The idea of a new man is also found in the intellectual tradition of the environmental movement—especially in those currents that see consumerism as the root of all evil. On this issue, as elsewhere, Rudolf Bahro is the most radical proponent of ideas expressed in gentler terms by others. According to Bahro, the expansive dynamic of capitalist relations of production is mirrored in the structure of individual needs. The accumulation of capital and a psychic orientation toward consumption as the purpose of life presuppose one another, which is why the struggle between capital and labor does not lead out of the growth trap, but deeper and deeper into it. Higher wages and social benefits keep the growth machine running: "The short-term interests dictated to human beings in their capacity as wage laborers by the prevailing social relations are in contradiction with their longer-term interests."[29] History, he writes, provides only two models for resolving such deep contradictions: "Something like Plato's guardian state, which today would be a highly bureaucratic dictatorship, or a revolutionary mass movement with some particular goal in mind." The choice, in other words, is between a dictatorship over needs and sociocultural revolution. The chosen approach must not only bring the apparatus of production under societal control but also reprogram the human psyche: "The environmental crisis cannot be solved unless countless individuals are elevated above their purely immediate and compensatory interests."[30]

Appealing to reason is not enough to overcome humanity's constant aspiration for more. This is where Bahro's quasi-religious turn begins. He invokes the American Romantic Henry Thoreau, a contemporary of Marx, prophet of a simple life in commune with nature and pioneer of civil disobedience. Thoreau understood industrial modernity, with its constant increases in production and consumption, as a path to slavery: "Every superfluous possession," he said, "is a limitation on my freedom." This notion stands squarely in the tradition of the medieval Franciscans and Dominicans, who repudiated all personal property in the pursuit of freedom. In doing so they sought to emulate Jesus, another of Bahro's key witnesses: "Do not store up for yourselves treasures on earth. [...] For where your treasure is, there your heart will be also" (Matt. 6: 19–21). Bahro is adamant that reforming consumption requires nothing less than a psychological revolution. Ascetic self-fulfillment means "transcending the self and reaching out to other people, to humanity and to the universal spirit—indeed to anything, as long as it remains within humanity."[31]

Once a member of the executive board of the German Green Party, Bahro quit politics to concentrate fully on his inner life after realizing to his disappointment that the party had no intention of abandoning the Titanic and merely (in his view) hoped to postpone the collapse of civilization. This meant practical involvement in diverse communitarian experiments—including a trip to Oregon to visit Bhagwan Shree Rajneesh (aka Osho), then the guru of gurus, who had set up a center for spiritual enlightenment and sexual libertinism there—and work on his last great book, *Logik der Rettung* (*Avoiding Social and Ecological Disaster*), in which his diagnosis of the human psyche and his recommendations for treating it became more radical than ever.[32] As though peeling an onion, he pulls back the layers of his subject one by one in search of the impetus behind the "logic of self-exterminism" he identifies in civilization. Starting with the "industrial megamachine," he progresses to the excessive exploitation of capital, from there to "European cosmology" and the "uninhibited white ego," and from there to patriarchy, the "male *Logos*" and the "lost balance between man and woman," before arriving at an anthropological aberration that long predates capitalist modernity—human anthropocentrism and egocentrism.

If the reason for the fall of man lies in the alienation of individuals from the communities and humans from nature, errant mankind must embark on a long journey back to the origins of civilization in order to start over. This is the essence of Bahro's message in *Logik der Rettung*, which advocates for a refounding of culture based on a deep transformation of consciousness that reaches into the very fundaments of our genotype.

He proclaims the following principles for the new culture:

- "Prioritization of the original cycles and rhythms of life over development and progress. Greater happiness can only be achieved if we make less history."
- The replacement of industrial civilization with a "lifestyle of voluntary simplicity and frugal beauty founded in subsistence economics": "We must not harm or exploit animals, must not engage in tourism or drive cars, must abstain from most medications and refrain from doing business with banks, must not conduct positivistic research etc."
- Individualization must be overcome by way of a new social synthesis lived out in symbiotic communities based on elective affinities. "The viability of new communities is dependent on a commonality of vision and on basing everyday life around a spiritual practice in which *Eros*, *Logos* and work are reconciled and reinforce one another."

Bahro takes the program of cultural revolution to its logical consequence: the radical renunciation of modernity. He appeals to us to leave behind not only capitalism and big industry but the whole contemporary way of life. Neither is possible without the other. In doing so he is far more consistent than those critics of capitalism who turn on globalization and large-scale industrial production but would never give up the comforts they provide. Bahro would have called that having your cake and eating it. His program calls for a return to preindustrial modes of production and ways of life, the reintegration of humanity into natural life cycles, acceptance of sickness and death as fate, the organization of work and life within local communities and a stationary existence instead of global mobility—in other words, a "contractionary way of life" that scales material use down to a minimum and turns all development inwards: manual labor plus spirituality. It is reminiscent of the old Benedictine precept *Ora et labora, Deus adest sine mora*—pray and work, and God will always be with you.

"To have or to be?" Bahro radicalizes a question that has shaped the sentiments of an entire generation since the publication of Erich Fromm's bestseller of that name in 1976. But what if this opposition is misleading in itself? It is not a question of having or being at all: "It is a matter of becoming, of the unfinished evolutionary process of mankind and the world." This bold reply comes from Jan Bloch and Willfried Maier, who as early as 1984 published an anthology entitled *Wachstum der Grenzen: Selbstorganisation in der Natur und die Zukunft der Gesellschaft* (The Growth of Limits: Self-Organization in Nature and the Future of Society). While remaining very much within the spirit of utopian Marxism, they criticize the concept of the limits to growth on the grounds that it is used to support calls for humanity to integrate into a preestablished natural order.[33] The alternative they propose is coevolution with nature.

More than twenty-five years have passed since the publication of *Logik der Rettung*, during which time the "megamachine" has continued to grow in pace and scope. Rather than rejecting consumer society, billions of people are striving to access a modern middle-class lifestyle. There has been no return to subsistence economics, while technological innovation, the global division of labor, communication and urbanization are speeding up. If the renunciation of industrial modernity is the only thing that can save the human species from self-annihilation we might as well abandon all hope. Our best chance of stemming the coming crises would be to declare an authoritarian state of emergency. Bahro did not advocate that. He pinned his hopes on a spiritual revolution from below, with small communities catalyzing major transformation. Yet, despite its rejection of power and violence, there is something totalitarian about the project of completely reprogramming the human mind. Bahro attacks the hubris of a civilization that seeks to dominate nature, but the call to rebuild the deep structures of the human psyche reveals an even greater arrogance. In comparison, the project of ecologically transforming industrial society seems like an almost pragmatic undertaking, although it too amounts to revolution: a revolution not only of the technological basis of industrial society but of its relationship to nature too.

The Potential of the Earth

Can the diabolically hurried culture of twenty-first century modernity continue without causing irreparable damage to the biosphere on which human civilization depends?

Sloterdijk's response to this question remains speculative. He calls into question the axiom that the earth is a narrowly limited habitat whose potential can be precisely measured and predicted by science. The biophysical world is supplemented by two artificial worlds: the world of technology ("technosphere") and an intellectual world, the world of networked knowledge ("noosphere"). These spheres act as an extension of the natural world and multiply its potential. Sloterdijk takes up the Spinozian observation that nobody has yet determined the full potential of the human body and applies it to the earth: we do not yet know "what the earth would be capable of if the geosphere and biosphere were enhanced by an intelligent technosphere and noosphere. It is not impossible that the resulting effects would be equivalent to a multiplication of the planet."[34] Only if we continue to think of the relationship between man and nature as an exploitative one "will the earth remain a limited monad forever." If we instead follow a path of cooperative productivity between nature and technology, we can transform it into a hybrid planet "on which more is possible than conservative geologists believe."

What Sloterdijk outlines here is a vision of the expansion of natural limits to growth thanks to a triad of nature, intellect and technology. He extrapolates from a development that began back in the early days of arable farming and artificial irrigation and has been systematically ramped up since the beginning of the Industrial Revolution. The qualitative difference between his vision and the first 150 years of industrial society lies in a new relationship between humans and nature: the earth is no longer just matter, just a source of raw materials and a dumping ground for humans to exploit, but a congenial productive force. This does not wipe out the limits to growth, and especially not the scarcity of fertile land or the level of CO_2 emissions our climate can withstand, but there is no set limit on the number of people and their standard of living. The earth's potential is not a fixed quantity that can be precisely determined by science; it is the resultant of natural resources and human intelligence.

We should not think of ecological transformation as the return to a bucolic idyll. A return to a more contemplative life might be desirable for the individual, but it is not an answer to the environmental and social crises of our time. They demand a high degree of technological and social innovation, entrepreneurial spirit and dynamism. Acceleration, rather than deceleration, of technological and social change is necessary if we are to make the leap to a carbon-neutral economic system within the next few decades.

Chapter 4

The Green Industrial Revolution

The purpose of thinking about the future is not to predict it but to raise people's hopes.

—Freeman J. Dyson

"The human race is poised at a time before great change." This is how Ernst Ulrich von Weizsäcker, Karlson Hargroves and Michael Smith begin the introduction to their book *Factor Five: Transforming the Global Economy through 80% Improvements in Resource Productivity*. The book is a follow-up to *Factor Four*, an environmental classic published over fifteen years ago in which Weizsäcker and his coauthors Amory and Hunter Lovins coined the phrase "doubling wealth, halving resource use." What differentiates this school of environmental thought from the mainstream—especially in Germany—is its fundamental confidence that we can master the threat industrial civilization poses to itself if we "use the sophisticated understanding in areas such as physics, chemistry, engineering, biology, commerce, business and governance that we have accumulated in the last 1,000 years to bring to bear on the challenge of dramatically reducing our pressure on the environment." According to Weizsäcker, Hargroves and Smith, our task is to establish how "technologies, infrastructures, legal rules, education and cultural habits [interact] to produce economic progress while conserving a healthy environment."[1] This kind of hope for a better future is no mere sop. Even Weizsäcker accepts that *fossil-powered capitalism* has already exceeded the load limit of vital ecosystems. But if a massive reduction in production and consumption is not the answer to this problem, a solution must be sought elsewhere: the generation of prosperity must be divorced from the consumption of natural resources. That is the core principle of the green industrial revolution whose beginnings we are experiencing today.

The ecological footprint left on the earth by humanity is the resultant of three variables: population size, consumption levels and technology. In theory there are thus three ways for us to balance our environmental books:

1. By reducing the global population: an inhumane endeavor that reduces people to vermin.
2. By reducing our consumption levels: at best an option for people who have more than they need. Even heroic levels of self-denial would not reduce CO_2 emissions by the necessary amount: 50 percent of global greenhouse gas emissions and 90 percent in the old industrial societies.
3. Through technological innovation: in essence a combination of revolutionized efficiency, renewable energy and ecological material cycles.

We tend to regard sustainability first and foremost as a *quantitative* problem: industrial nations produce and consume more than the planet's ecosystems have to give.

But in the long run the *quantity* of products and services that humanity can afford without destroying its natural livelihood depends on their *quality*: Where does our energy come from? Which technologies, substances and materials do we use? How sustainable are our production processes and products? The sustainability of an economy is fundamentally tied to its mode of production. Instead of making people feel guilty about their supposed excesses, we must find intelligent solutions for the aspirations and ambitions of the soon to be nine billion people on earth. We can learn a lot from nature in this regard. Its organic factory survives on solar power, water and carbon dioxide—the components of photosynthesis, which is ultimately the basis for the magnificent wealth of plants and animals that populate the globe. They consume many times more food and energy than humans without causing climatic catastrophes or contaminating soil, air and water. The chemist Michael Braungart tells a nice story about this: The biomass of ants is many times greater than that of humans. Their calorie consumption corresponds to that of 30 billion people. Most ants are not vegetarians, yet they do not pose an environmental problem. On the contrary, they are extremely useful; the tropical rain forest would not exist without them. Why is that? It all comes down to mass throughput. Ants live off organic matter and everything they use is turned back into nutrients for reuse in biological cycles.[2] They provide the blueprint for an environmentally friendly economy in which all residual matter flows back into either technological or biological cycles.

The great transformation has already begun. We have a tendency to focus on approaching danger. But we only have to open our eyes to see the promise of a better future everywhere: in millions of laboratories and engineering firms, in the various movements campaigning for fair trade and a just global economy, in the global rise of renewable energy sources and in the growing market for green products. It is being described in countless books and discussed at conferences, industrial fairs, trade union conventions and church congresses.

Empty illusions? Naive faith in progress? No, merely confidence that humanity will find ways out of its environmental predicament: as the danger grows, so too does the chance of salvation. We will have to exert all our strength and mobilize all our inventiveness if we are to completely reform industrial society within only a few decades, shifting from fossil fuels to renewable energy sources, from finite to infinite raw materials, from the waste of scarce resources to maximum efficiency, from throwaway society to a recycling-based economy, and from the plunder of nature to collaboration with it. For the foreseeable future the all-important question will not be *whether* GWP growth is going to continue, but *how*. The nature of growth has to change.

This is not an empty appeal. In fact the environmental restructuring process began a long time ago and is now gathering pace. The world's largest industrial fair, which takes place every spring in Hanover, is a good measure of this. What happens there gives us some idea of the topics, trends and technologies that will shape the future of industrial society. In 2012 the general theme of the fair was "greentelligence." Climate protection, the reduction of CO_2 emissions, gentler resource usage, reduced energy consumption, renewable energy and environmentally friendly production have become principles of technological development with respect to both one-off innovations and integrated solutions. Progress in measurement and control technology is facilitating increasingly efficient process engineering. Energy and material usage can be optimized, emissions and waste minimized. The spatial and temporal coordination of multistage production processes and the corresponding transport chains is saving energy and resources. Commodity flows can be better combined, transportation provision streamlined and dead freight avoided. A study conducted by the consulting firm Roland Berger predicts that until 2020 worldwide demand for innovative environmental technology will grow at an annual rate of 5.4 percent. The annual growth of the German environmental sector is expected to reach 8 percent, taking its share of the national economy as a whole to 16 percent.[3]

Even much maligned multinational corporations began moving toward sustainability long ago—not all of them and not at the necessary pace, but plenty of globally active companies are going green. Siemens, for example, is being systematically rebuilt as a pioneer for sustainable industrial technology. In 2011 as much as €30 billion of its revenue—40 percent of its total business—came from green products such as highly efficient gas turbines, block heat power plants, high-voltage electricity networks that suffer only minimal transport losses, train cars and electric motors, resource-efficient industrial plants, electricity-saving lighting, intelligent buildings engineering, water management and offshore wind power. Within a short period of time the company has become a global market leader for maritime wind power. Siemens invests approximately 5 percent of its revenue in research and development. In 2011 that was around four billion euros. A considerable part of that investment is being poured into green solutions. Around the world, 29,000 scientists and engineers are working on new products and processes. Like all research and development, environmental innovation proceeds according to a pattern of trial and error. Not every promising idea is economically successful in the end. For instance, the group invested hundreds of millions of euros in solar thermal technology, which converts sunlight into storable heat. Steam produced via a heat exchanger is used to drive an electricity generator. Siemens wanted to secure a place at the forefront of this technology, but a drop in the price of solar cells and progress in the development of photovoltaic storage technology thwarted its plans. In October 2012 the management announced the company's withdrawal from solar thermal research. It evidently did not believe there was any prospect of making a profit with the technology in the foreseeable future, although the timing of the decision was extremely surprising. It came at a point when the first major solar thermal energy projects in Morocco and Tunisia were taking concrete shape. This is not an isolated example. In an industry as young as environmental technology, competition between various technological paths is particularly intense. Only once implemented does their long-term feasibility become clear. Unless we intend to rely solely on public authorities to advance research and development, we need large companies. They have the financial capacity and cumulative engineering knowledge to expedite innovations whose profitability cannot be foretold.

Philips, the second-largest European energy concern, is also restructuring. Its goal is to generate half its revenue with green products by 2015. According to the company's own data it had already reached 39 percent by 2011. Such self-reporting should of course be taken with a big pinch of salt: all too often there are significant discrepancies between appearance and reality. But the fact that Philips received a top rating from the Carbon Disclosure Project (CDP, an organization that assesses companies' CO_2 emissions) at least indicates that its figures are not merely hot air (or what is sometimes referred to as greenwashing). Its investments in environmentally friendly innovation amounted to €479 million, €291 million of which went into optimized lighting, including a light management system that allows precise regulation of a city's outdoor lighting according to incidence of light and required brightness. In combination with LED lamps, City Touch uses up to 70 percent less energy than conventional lighting. By 2015 two billion euros are to be invested in the company's EcoVision program, which is divided into three strategic divisions: health care, energy efficiency and closed-loop material cycles. The goal is to increase the energy efficiency of the entire product portfolio by 50 percent as well as to double recycling of old appliances and implementation of secondary raw materials. If nothing else the program will save on energy and material costs. Another of the company's stated goals is to eliminate environmentally harmful substances such as PVC and bromine from its production.[4]

There is some truth to the claim that small is beautiful: Often the impetus for innovation comes from outsiders, while established companies generally try to defend their old business models for as long as possible. The energy sector is notorious for this. But the environmental reform of industrial society demands a combination of big and small. Corporations that have invested billions in particular product lines and systems will always try to squeeze a profit from them for as long as they can, but we should not underestimate the strategic intelligence of global players such as Siemens, Philips or General Electric. Quarterly profits are not their only concern; they reflect intensively on the future of their companies in a world where natural resources are becoming scarcer and people more environmentally conscious. More and more companies are recognizing that environmental responsibility and climate protection are key to future economic success. More efficient handling of resources and energy lowers costs, reductions in CO_2 emissions increase company value, developing environmentally friendly products generates pioneer profits and a credible green image raises reputation capital. As citizens, consumers and politically engaged individuals, we too have a role to play in pushing the economy toward environmental innovation.

Growing with Nature

In his magnum opus *The Principle of Hope* Ernst Bloch formulates ideas on a cooperative relationship between humans and nature that anticipate the thrust of the green industrial revolution. Until now, Bloch writes, technology has operated in nature like an army in enemy territory. It nourishes itself by plundering natural resources. Forests, oceans and soil are used as store cupboards from which industry serves itself freely. They are viewed as nothing more than material for the creation of value and added value. The richer industrial societies have grown, the poorer our natural surroundings have become. Industrialization has been conducted as a campaign against the environment in the course of which landscapes have been plowed up, forests chopped down, oceans fished until empty, the air poisoned and the atmosphere filled with greenhouse gases. All this is currently being repeated with the rapid industrialization of the Third World. Bloch proposes an appealing alternative: a technology of alliance (German: Allianz-Technik) under which symbiotic collaboration with nature, rather than exploitation, would be the guiding principle of future industrial society. The starting point for an environmentally friendly economy is not scarcity of natural resources but the infinite wealth of nature. In the words of Michael Braungart: "Nature does not live by the principles of frugality, self-denial and avoidance—nature is wasteful. Look at cherry trees in spring!"[5] From this perspective nature is not a hostile entity that must be conquered, but a great nourisher and teacher of humanity. Our task is not to wrest its treasures away from it but to make intelligent use of biological productivity. In order to do so we must first learn to understand it: How do plants transform sunlight into starch? How do migratory birds orient themselves? How do polar bears stay warm in spite of the Arctic cold? How do bacteria break down noxious substances? What makes spider silk stronger and more elastic than steel? How does the metabolic cycle work in symbiotic plant communities?

Above all else, growing with nature means learning from nature. This is the scope of *bionics*, a scientific discipline that aims to translate biological processes into technology and to learn from the amazing solutions that evolution has developed over long periods of time. From fish, for example, we can learn how to minimize drag on ships and vehicles. Or from lotus flowers how they keep their white leaves spotless—dirt simply rolls off them. The principle of closed-loop material cycles, in which every end product becomes the point of departure for new processes, is copied from nature. Waste-free production cycles, artificial photosynthesis and the enrichment of organic soil life for the purposes of soil recultivation are all concrete examples of learning from nature and all within the realm of possibility.

Sooner or later anyone searching for material to illustrate the concept of a green revolution will come across the Blue Economy project—a global platform for environmental innovation based on the principle of learning from nature.[6] By now more than three thousand innovative ideas have been collected, many of which are already in commercial use. The general idea of the project is to make use of synergy. Whether in the use of coffee grounds to breed mushrooms or the use of plant fibers accrued in growing and processing rice, coconuts, bamboo, sugarcane and bananas to make paper—the central idea is always to think in systems. Downsizing the economy is not the way to escape environmental crisis. The solution is to establish production cycles in which every waste product becomes the point of departure for new value chains, allowing for the multiplication of resource productivity. This means eliminating from the production process any material that cannot be reused. The zero-waste approach is already generating new business models and a new corporate culture. Entrepreneurship is an important impetus for the Blue Economy. True entrepreneurs recognize opportunities for sustainable growth instead of fixating on cost reduction and risk evasion. The spiritual leader and mastermind of the movement is Gunter Pauli, himself a successful entrepreneur and a proponent of the idea that the answer to environmental crisis lies in a second green revolution rather than in bans and self-denial.[7] Like all revolutions, this one is beginning in the mind: with ideas about linear production chains and eventually designs for material cycles. It is characterized by close cooperation between agriculture and industry, regional production clusters, cascade usage of raw materials and energy, and diversity rather than monostructures. Companies are organizing themselves as networks, with management structures akin to the human nervous system: "Decentralization with direct access to all information."[8] Departments are being combined in order to achieve optimal synergy at the research and development level: biology, economics, engineering, chemistry and physics are coalescing into a new generative science. This all sounds a bit new age, but it is based on an impressive fund of technological knowledge and proven management competence.

Until now the development of industrial society has primarily been based on excessive consumption of natural resources. In the future growth will be *synergetic*—the result of a new symbiosis between industrial society and the ecosystem. In contrast with symbiotic systems in nature, the process of human coevolution with nature must be consciously designed. That is the idea behind talk of the Anthropocene as a new stage of evolution. We have embarked on an age in which the human race wields great geological power with far-reaching consequences for the cycles of nature. In theory we have had this power since human civilization began. Now, however, the impact of humanity on global ecosystems has reached a level that compels us to take responsibility for the stability of the ecosphere. We can no longer tinker with nature like sorcerer's apprentices, unaware of the consequences of our actions. The impact of our intervention is too great for that. At the same time, the path back to a so-called natural way of life is closed to us. We must instead come to see ourselves as coproducers of nature who consciously intervene in its evolution without destabilizing it. Our task is to shape the metabolic relation between society and nature in such a way that the unintended side effects do not get out of control and destroy the existential basis of human civilization. That is what it means to grow with nature.

A Green Kondratiev Cycle

The capitalist global economy has not developed in a linear fashion, but rather in dynamic surges that have always been triggered by groundbreaking innovation: the mechanical loom and industrial iron production—the steam engine, railways and steel—electrification, chemistry and the combustion engine—petrochemistry, television, airplanes and space travel—computers, the Internet, cell phones and biotechnology. There were approximately fifty to sixty years between each of these innovation surges, during which time the impetus provided by the relevant basic technologies declined until they were replaced by new kinds. The first person to describe these long waves of economic activity was the Russian economist Nikolai D. Kondratiev in the 1920s. Joseph A. Schumpeter, one of the leading economists of the interwar period, went a crucial step further. He concluded that every period of growth begins with a reorganization of the economy driven by technological innovation. Leading industries are replaced by new ones, previously dominant production processes become obsolete and antiquated capital assets are destroyed. The energy revolution currently taking place in Germany is an example of a similar process. Nuclear power plants are being shut down, while coal-fired plants are being ousted by solar and wind power. The "creative destruction" of the old releases a wave of investment in new processes and products, leading to greater employment and higher incomes until the economy begins to slow down again, which in turn accelerates the search for new inventions.[9] In his groundbreaking study on the Industrial Revolution, the American economist David S. Landes likewise arrives at a cyclical view of economic activity: "Technological progress is not a smooth, balanced process. Each innovation process seems to have a life span of its own, comprising periods of tentative youth, vigorous maturity, and declining old age," during which the rise of new technologies begins.[10]

The next long wave of growth will be triggered by environmental innovation, and in particular by the transition to renewable energy sources, resource-efficient technologies and biotechnological processes. These are the fundamental innovations of our time. As soon as they become cost effective in certain key areas and a critical mass of research, development and political support has been reached, they will generate a self-sustaining process of change. As Landes puts it, change begets change. Ernst Ulrich von Weizsäcker speaks of "technological breakthroughs [...] spurring growth and creating a sense of excitement," and appeals for "confidence [...] in the opportunities lying in a new green technological revolution."[11]

Inspiring enthusiasm for a green industrial revolution is precisely the aim of this book, yet such appeals are regarded as rather odd in Germany, where the editors of feature sections vie to outdo each other with warnings about worshipping technology. Harald Welzer, a hero of the postgrowth movement in Germany, exemplifies this attitude with classic simplicity: "Global warming has come about because of the thoughtless use of technology, so any attempt to fix things through more and 'better' technology is part of the problem and not the solution."[12] By this logic we might claim that as democracy has led us into misery it is therefore an unsuitable means by which to overcome it.

The German attitude to science and technology verges on schizophrenic. There is a gaping divide between the success the country owes to its position as a leader in technology and the deep skepticism that broad sections of the public maintain toward technological innovation. The dominant attitude is one of aversion to danger. Avoiding risk is considered more important than opportunity. The struggle against nuclear power defined an entire (my!) generation: what some regarded as the epitome of technological progress seemed like a looming catastrophe to us. And while we were campaigning against nuclear power, the peace movement was fighting for nuclear disarmament. The atom bomb was the ultimate perversion of science and technology. It brought the very concept into disrepute. Climate change is likewise being interpreted as a warning that technological progress always turns on humanity in the end: "The end will be annihilation." In fact we need to redefine technological progress rather than renounce it.

It is a truism to say that the solution to humanity's problems does not lie in technological innovation alone. But neither the sublimation—whether voluntary or otherwise—of old, insatiable Adam, nor the vision of a postgrowth economy can replace the green industrial revolution. This revolution is about more than just technology. A new *mode of production*—Marx's term for the entirety of a historical epoch's dominant forces and relations of production—is at stake. Anyone who comes to the revolution with enthusiasm will find it a broad, rewarding sphere of activity: from campaigning for global public property to urban farming. The release of a new wave of inventiveness, enthusiasm and entrepreneurship will do more to change the world than any conference on the revival of communism.

Investment drives innovation and growth, and the ecological reform of industrial society requires an enormous investment program. The research institute Trend Research estimates that within a decade (2011–2020) investment of €250 billion will be needed for the implementation of energy reform in Germany alone. And that only covers the supply side, i.e. the production, storage and distribution of electricity. While approximately two-thirds of the investment will be spent on plants that produce electricity from renewable sources, the remaining third is to be divided equally between the development of electricity grids and repositories, and the provision of gas-fired power plants as a buffer for renewable energy supplies. But there will also be huge investment on the consumption side, primarily in the continued improvement of energy efficiency in industry and in private households.

The same applies to the heating market: the energy-related renovation of building stock is the most effective investment and employment program politicians could push for. In no other sector is there a more favorable correlation between public funding, private investment and jobs than that which accompanies the insulation of buildings, the fitting of energy-efficient windows, the modernization of heating systems and air conditioning systems, the installation of heat pumps etc.

Investments initially mean costs. They have to be financed from national income and thus lead to a reduction in consumption spending. But investments in environmental innovation also increase potential for economic growth and lay the foundation for future jobs and income. We may balk at the cost of environmental protection today, but we risk having to pay two or three times as much tomorrow, when climate change and resource crises are undermining nations' prosperity. According to a UNEP model, the growth potential of a green growth scenario in which 2 percent of annual GWP was invested in environmental protection would surpass the global growth rate of a business-as-usual scenario after as little as seven years, with the margin widening over time.[13]

The new green Kondratiev cycle is feeding off four fundamental innovations:

- A radical increase in *resource productivity* that allows for increased prosperity alongside minimized resource consumption. Increased energy efficiency is playing a key role here, both with respect to energy production, where there is still much room for improvement, and to the energy consumption of companies, the transportation sector and private households. Action must be taken to improve the efficiency of buildings, appliances and vehicles, reclaim heat and develop intelligent control systems that optimize the reconciliation of supply and demand and minimize energy losses.
- *Renewable energy sources* are replacing fossil fuels as the basis of social metabolism. While the aim of energy efficiency is to lower energy consumption, the issue here is meeting the remaining demand for electricity, heat and fuel from renewable sources. The goal is a CO_2-neutral energy supply.
- Rather than focusing exclusively on the perfection of individual products or production processes, *system design* is optimizing whole production cycles and supply systems. The transportation sector is a classic field for the application of system design, not only with regard to environmentally friendly cars or fuel-efficient airplanes, but an integrated concept of mobility that also encompasses urban planning, public transport, freight etc.
- *Biomimicry*, i.e. the development of products and technological processes in accordance with the principles of nature. A common example of this is the Velcro fastener, which was developed based on the example of the burdock plant. Related concepts

include bionics (a term we will encounter again below) and biomimetics. The aim of Biomimicry is not only to come up with new products and processes but to establish a new, symbiotic relationship between technology and nature.

Fundamental innovation is already underway in all these areas.

The green industrial revolution has already begun. Now the task is to blaze a political trail for it and inspire the younger generation to get involved. In pursuing these goals it is helpful to emphasize the big picture behind the tens of thousands of individual innovations taking place.

Revolutionizing Efficiency: The Bridge to the Solar Age

Revolutionizing efficiency means making more from less. It means multiplying the yield from every ton of oil, copper, bauxite and ore and from every kilowatt of electricity: greater prosperity from less material. It means extending the lifetime of scarce resources and buying time for the development of breakthrough innovations to replace them. Ernst Ulrich von Weizsäcker describes increased resource productivity as the "melody of the new wave of technological progress that is supporting a major new cycle of growth." Up to now the history of industry has primarily been a story of growing labor productivity. Today labor productivity is approximately twenty times higher than it was two hundred years ago. This trend has accelerated significantly since the 1950s (somewhat earlier in the US). Without the GNP growth that has taken place over the same period, the enormous increase in labor productivity would have created a constantly swelling reserve army of superfluous people for whom society no longer had any productive use—a fear that has arisen every time old technologies have been replaced by new ones. For instance, large numbers of home weavers lost their bread and butter when the mechanical loom was introduced. Gerhart Hauptmann gives a vivid account of this drama in his play *The Weavers*. Comparably bleak prognoses of increased unemployment accompanied the rise of computer technology. In fact, however, the continuous emergence of new products, services and branches of the economy has provided work for an ever-growing workforce, and in the long term real wages have risen.

While in this country skilled labor is becoming scarce, in populous nations there is a shortage of opportunities to earn money. In large sections of the world there will be no lack of manpower for a long time to come—very much in contrast with natural resources like arable land and freshwater. The International Labour Organization calculates that we are approximately eight hundred million jobs away from full global employment, and all the while the global resource crisis is intensifying—all the signs indicate that the dynamics of technological innovation must be steered toward resource productivity. Instead of extracting more and more from an hour of work, the primary objective now is to generate ever-greater prosperity from each cubic meter of gas, every kilowatt-hour of electricity, every ton of iron ore or bauxite, every hectare of farmland and every cubic meter of water. In other words, we must change the direction of technological progress: resource productivity must become the leitmotif of our time.[14]

Excursus: The Rebound Effect

Anyone who, like Weizsäcker and Lovins, advocates "doubling wealth, halving resource use" can expect to be accused of spreading false hope. The key phrase here is "rebound effect," which denotes the phenomenon of rising consumption brought about as the result of improved efficiency. The first person to describe the rebound effect was the British economist and philosopher William Stanley Jevons in his 1865 book *The Coal Question*: "It is wholly a confusion of ideas to suppose that the economical use of fuel is equivalent to a diminished consumption. The very contrary is the truth."[15] For example, when improved power plant technology leads to reduced coal consumption, production costs fall. The demand for electricity grows, providing an economic incentive to build new coal-fired power plants. As a result more coal is consumed than before. If engines become more efficient and use less gasoline, people may drive more. This is what is known as a direct rebound effect. Like a chameleon, however, the rebound effect has many faces. For instance, when private households experience a reduction in their heat consumption thanks to more efficient heating technology and better insulation they can spend the savings elsewhere. Energy consumption then rises in other areas. Furthermore, energy and raw materials are still required to manufacture condensing boilers and insulation.[16]

It sounds like an inescapable dilemma, doesn't it? No matter how much we invest in more efficient technology designed to relieve the burden on the environment, the savings will ultimately be gobbled up by increased consumption. Putting an end to growth is the only solution. National income must shrink if the demand for energy and resource-guzzling products is ever to fall. But there are many catches to this triumphant argument. One of the reasons why the rebound effect argument is so popular is that the effect is barely possible to quantify. The link between prices and demand (what economists call price elasticity) is not linear. For example, most people do not heat their apartments to 25 degrees just because heating costs drop. Falling prices for environmentally friendly energy sources can also trigger positive substitution effects: in the US, for instance, coal is largely being replaced by natural gas and CO_2 emissions are falling as a result. Increasingly efficient solar and wind power plants are having a similar effect. Ultimately we have a whole box of tools at our disposal to stem the rebound effect. Resource taxes can be tailored to compensate for falling prices and thus stop demand from rising. On the roads, speed limits lower gas consumption independently of gas prices. Gradually rising efficiency standards for cars, electronic devices and buildings keep the pace of innovation high. With regard to climate protection, the hard limits the EU puts on the CO_2 emissions of power plants and industry prevent emissions rising as the result of efficiency gains.

In order to eliminate rebound effects completely it would be necessary to compensate for every gain in resource efficiency by depriving the economy of a corresponding amount of purchasing power, thereby putting an end to any economic growth. But falling income and shrinking investments serve as brakes on innovation. Instead of accelerating the efficiency revolution they would choke it. The German example is proof that an absolute separation of economic value creation and environmental consumption is entirely possible, especially with respect to the classic ecosystems (soil, air, water and forests), whose quality has improved considerably since the 1970s, but also when it comes to reducing CO_2 emissions. Renewable energy sources have just begun to gather momentum. The energy efficiency of the building restoration and transportation sectors is still far behind where it needs to be. The really big leaps of innovation have not even taken place yet.

Taking 1990 as a reference point, by the end of 2010 Germany's total greenhouse gas emissions had fallen by almost 25 percent; that corresponds to a drop of 295 million tons, meaning that the country has exceeded its Kyoto obligations. This achievement is no mean feat, even though the numbers are skewed somewhat by the high number of pollution-spewing plants that have been shut down in the former East Germany. Approximately two-thirds of the nation's CO_2 savings have been achieved since 1995. During the same period GDP has risen by a third in real terms and German industry has continued to expand its exports. This separation of economic growth from greenhouse gas emissions has been achieved thanks to a strong environmental movement and an ambitious energy policy that is increasingly rubbing off on German industry. It is no coincidence that in 2011 we consumed less energy than in any year since reunification. We have continuously improving energy efficiency—the average rate of increase is 1.8 percent per year—and the ongoing transition to renewable energy sources to thank for this result. These two factors combined add up to an effective reduction in carbon dioxide emissions. As noted in the introduction to this book, CO_2 emissions in Germany rose again slightly in 2013–14, primarily as a result of the move to shut down half the country's nuclear power plants following the Fukushima catastrophe as well as rising exports of coal-fired electricity to neighboring European countries. But they will fall again in the coming years. Even the current Christian Democrat-led coalition government is committed to a reduction of at least 30 percent (in comparison with 1990) by 2020 and 40 percent by 2030.

In the European Union greenhouse gas emissions fell by 17.3 percent between 1990 and 2009. Per capita CO_2 emissions fell from 11.1 to 8.4 tons. In part these numbers are due to the relocation of CO_2-intensive branches of industry to Asia, particularly from countries like Britain, which have allowed their manufacturing industries to shrink in favor of the financial sector. The production-related CO_2 emissions of these countries have fallen as a result, but not their consumption-related emissions. As is well known, Germany has taken a different path. While the share of Britain's GDP accounted for by industry dropped from 13.9 to 10.8 percent between 2002 and 2011 (in France the numbers are even more dismal), in Germany this figure climbed from 21.5 to 22.6 percent, making the country's separation of carbon dioxide emissions from economic growth all the more remarkable. The decarbonization of our national economy has already begun. Now it must be accelerated across the board.

German industry reduced its energy consumption by a sixth between 1990 and 2010, while its revenue rose from €1 billion to €1.7 billion.[17] Even greater savings were made in commerce, trade and the service sector. In contrast, in 2010 the consumption of private households and the transportation sector was slightly higher than in 1990.[18] If we only take into account CO_2 emissions, there has also been a slight decrease in road traffic emissions, despite considerably higher traffic flow. In 2010 total carbon dioxide emissions were around five million tons lower than in 1990, mostly thanks to a 50 percent reduction in energy consumption per hundred passenger kilometers.[19] That sounds impressive, but it was only just enough to compensate for the increase in traffic. A whole host of further efficiency improvements, new types of vehicles and a move toward greater rail and water transportation are necessary in order to significantly lower greenhouse gas emissions from road traffic. Beyond that we must reduce the amount of traffic caused by subsidized transport prices or misguided land use policy. Classic examples of this include commuter traffic between suburban developments and cities, which is promoted by tax relief for commuters, or the transportation of crabs back and forth over thousands of kilometers because wage costs in Morocco are lower than the freight costs.

The chemical industry has been a pioneer in matters of efficiency. In the period from 1990 to 2009 its production grew by 42 percent, while it energy consumption fell by 33 percent and its greenhouse gas emissions by as much as 47 percent: an impressive example of the separation of economic growth from environmental consumption.[20] With energy costs accounting for around 28 percent of its gross value creation, the reduction of this key industry's energy requirements is also of considerable importance for its competitiveness on the world stage. Bayer, one of the two German chemical giants, reduced its greenhouse gas emissions by 12 percent (from 9.3 to 8.15 million tons) in the years between 2007 and 2011 alone.[21]

These numbers can either be interpreted as an encouraging beginning or as a mere drop in the ocean, but they don't allow us to deduce the potential for future energy and emissions savings. Up to now efficiency gains have tended to result from improvements to existing products, processes and facilities, such as the use of process heat and the combination of heat and power production in industry. The switch from oil to natural gas is also having a positive impact. In future more new technologies, processes, materials and products will result from a combination of gradual improvements and major innovations. The switch to renewable energy sources in electricity and heat production is generating CO_2 savings on an entirely new scale. Even on the basis of today's technology there is enormous scope for improving resource efficiency.

A wealth of concrete examples of how material consumption, energy expenditure and water consumption can be drastically reduced in every conceivable sector—even the resource-intensive basic materials industry—can be found in *Factor Five*. A switch to geopolymer cement in cement production, for instance, could reduce energy expenditure by approximately four-fifths.[22] There is an urgent need to reduce the amount of energy used to produce a ton of cement because demand for the building material is growing rapidly, especially in the southern continents. It is the raw material of urbanization. When mixed into cement as an organic supplement, plant fibers such as bamboo, wood fibers or sugarcane residue increase its durability and resistance to moisture.[23] With a combination of many small steps and big leaps in environmental innovation, environmental relief of 80 percent and more is possible almost everywhere: in residential and commercial buildings, in the transportation sector, in agriculture and in the energy industry. Exploiting this potential will allow us to make room for the rising demands of a growing global population without destroying the environmental basis of our existence.

How quickly and to what extent such potential is exploited will depend on two decisive factors: the development of raw material and energy prices and the political framework put in place for corporations and consumers. Investments made by industry to improve its energy and material efficiency usually pay for themselves within very short periods of two to five years. Stronger taxation of resource consumption accompanied by a reduction in income tax would trigger additional efficiency investments. Auctioning allowances for CO_2 emissions has the same effect, as long as they are continually reduced and exceptions for energy-intensive sectors are severely limited. There is a need for adjustments to the current distribution policy, under which large amounts of certificates are given out gratuitously. If the EU could finally get its act together and raise its CO_2 reduction goal for the year 2020 from 20 to 30 percent, the price of emissions certificates would rise accordingly. There should likewise be limits on companies substituting climate-friendly projects in developing countries for CO_2 reduction at home. As plausible as the prospect of achieving greater savings (with lower investments) in these countries initially sounds, the supposed benefits of such measures are difficult to monitor.

Up to now the EU's emissions trading system has proved to be a toothless tiger, providing grist to the mill of critics who do not rate market-like control mechanisms and would prefer to return to pure regulatory law. Intelligent regulatory policy uses both: price-based controls, which have the potential to trigger greater dynamism and have a broader impact than pure regulation, and control based on legal requirements for major product lines. There is no reason not to establish norms for the efficiency of vehicles, refrigerators and buildings in accordance with the highest technological standards at any given time. Such measures bring about a process of technological adaptation and improvement, while continually making resource consumption and emissions more expensive creates competition to develop the most efficient technologies—a systemic advantage over bureaucratic regulation. Furthermore, regulatory legislation can never cover the whole gamut of products and technologies, while a change in relative prices pervades entire production chains and also affects consumers.

Take-back obligations for trade and industry provide further leverage for reducing resource consumption. Anyone who brings a product onto the market is responsible for recycling it at the end of its usage cycle. Applying this principle to cars, electronic devices, computers etc. causes manufacturers to develop a strong sense of self-interest when it comes to selecting materials and designing products for optimal recyclability. The coming efficiency revolution, then, is not only a question of technology; its pace and scope will depend to a large degree on the courses set by politicians, particularly if the pace of ecological innovation is to be substantially accelerated. As Martin Jänicke has shown, incremental improvements in efficiency occur largely autonomously, but proactive public policy is required to speed up innovation.[24] Internalization of the costs of environmental damage, as economists call it, is the best way to achieve this. If soil, air and water pollution are not prohibited by law they must be given a prohibitive price tag. Prices only have the necessary effect when they tell the environmental truth. That is why taxes and fees for resource consumption and emissions as well as an efficient trading system for CO_2 allowances are indispensable to the acceleration of environmental reform. Together these measures are the most effective antidote to the rebound effect: as energy and raw materials costs fall due to more efficient technology the relevant fees should rise by a corresponding amount, counteracting any expansion in demand and simultaneously keeping the pressure to innovate high.

In political terms the rebound-effect apologists are caught in an inextricable contradiction. While on the one hand they claim that economic growth cannot be divorced from environmental destruction, on the other they demand drastic reductions in emissions and resource consumption. If their premises were accurate, such reductions would only be possible on the basis of a massive drop in the standard of living of modern societies—something that is simply not enforceable, at least by democratic means. Any serious demand for Europe and the US to reduce CO_2 emissions by 80 to 90 percent before the middle of the century must be accompanied by a push to divorce value creation from the consumption of natural resources rather than by declarations of impossibility.

Chapter 5

Bioeconomics

Increasing resource efficiency will buy us time for a second major operation: the transition to renewable energy sources and materials. Solar power, wind, wave power, hydrogen and geothermal must become the basis of our future energy supply, sustainable raw materials and biotechnological processes the basis of future industrial production. The blueprint for the economy of the future lies in the productivity of nature itself: in the conversion of sunlight into plant and chemical energy, in the as yet barely explored productivity of microbiological processes and in the process chains of organic life, which knows no waste.

The finite nature of fossil and mineral raw materials as well as the energy expenditure and environmental damage connected with their use point to the need for a gradual transition to a bioeconomy founded on a material basis of organic matter. Ultimately this means making sunlight the primary source of all production and consumption. We do not necessarily need to expand the area of agricultural land available to us in order to expand our biological raw materials basis, nor is it imperative that crop yields are increased. The UN Food and Agriculture Organization calculates that around a third of the food produced for human consumption worldwide is lost or thrown away. According to recent University of Stuttgart study, in Germany alone approximately eleven million tons of food end up in the trash. More than half this waste occurs in private households.[1]

The greatest potential for the future bioeconomy lies in using as much as possible of the biomass available to us. Up to now we have generally exploited only a fraction of the organic matter of plants and trees used in the manufacture of food or high-value industrial products such as chemicals, medicines, cosmetics, alcohol and paper. The remainder is burnt or ends up in the trash. For instance, at most 30 percent of the biomass of trees is used in the production of cellulose. The remainder—what is referred to as black liquor—is generally burnt, although the lignin and hemicellulose it contains could be used as basic materials for other biochemical products. In the processing of sugarcane only 17 percent of its biomass is used for sugar production. Here too the remaining 83 percent is usually burnt, although the fibers can be further processed to make biochemical products and used as an organic cement supplement or in the manufacture of gypsum fiberboard. In the manufacture of biological cleaning products with a palm oil base only 5 percent of the plant biomass is used, with the rest lost as waste. In the fishing industry 30 percent of fish caught are considered worthless bycatch and thrown back into the sea dead.[2] In general further biochemical and procedural research into the complete use of residual plant and animal matter is required. In some cases, however, cascade usage of biological resources is simply not considered because usage chains are organized in a linear fashion and not connected with one another. We only discover the potential for synergetic solutions when we make waste-free production our first principle.

Broadly speaking, transitioning to a bioeconomy means making nature's power usable for human purposes without depleting it. Technology becomes ecodesign or the "technological use of natural systems."[3] This formulation ties in with Frederic Vester's groundbreaking work on biocybernetics.[4] Vester was and is one of the great masterminds of environmentally friendly economics, even though he hardly plays a role in the debate today, just as the very concept of production in collaboration with nature has been supplanted by a purely quantitative outlook. To focus primarily on the question of growth is to reduce the ecological question to a crude quantitative problem: the restriction of production and consumption as the only way to stabilize the ecosystem. In doing so a crucial point is missed—the fact that, when it comes to production processes and products, the issue is less one of quantity than of quality. Ecosystems theory is not concerned with individual technological innovations, but with applying principles of biological evolution to the industrial mode of production: the development of symbiotic systems, cascade usage of energy and materials and closed-loop recycling. Today these principles are being most fully implemented in integrated chemical facilities. The new energy industry taking shape before our eyes is another example of the interconnectedness of decentralized units within complex systems: it links hundreds of thousands of local solar plants, wind parks, block heat power plants, electric cars, storage power stations etc. in an extensive grid that ensures stability and availability.

According to a 2010 report on innovative bioeconomics published by the Germany Bioeconomy Council, "bioeconomics encompasses every sector of the economy that produces, processes and uses biological resources."[5] Even this definition reduces biological systems to resources for the provision of biomass. This narrow outlook seems to me to be no coincidence. It corresponds to the strong industrial bias of the council. And industry is still dominated by a view of nature as a repository of raw materials. The fact that there is now a more intense focus on biological resources—i.e. on the world of animals, plants and microorganisms—does not change the instrumental nature of our relationship to nature. There is nothing wrong with searching for new products and procedures founded on biological materials and processes. It is where the future lies. But the only sustainable mode of production is one that conceives of nonhuman nature as a living system with which the human race cooperates and whose point of departure is the preservation of biological diversity. This applies to the entire wealth of plants and animals whose interaction accounts for the marvelous productivity of nature. In a broad sense, the purpose of bioeconomics is to use the potential of biological systems for human purposes without depleting it. Organic farming is a paradigmatic example of this kind of synergy. Bionics, i.e. the technological translation of biological processes and structures into new products and processes, is likewise based on learning from nature. We will deal with this subject in more detail below.

According to the Bioeconomy Council's definition,"the millennia-old processes used to cultivate agricultural crops, manage forests and domesticate farm animals in addition to simple biotechnological conversions of matter are the cornerstone of bioeconomics. Photosynthesis, which plants use to convert carbon dioxide, among other substances, into biomass, represents the foundation of life on earth. The biomass formed in this process provides the primary raw materials for bioeconomics." Its central players include agriculture, forestry and the fishing industry as providers of animal and plant products as well as users of these products such as the energy sector and the food, pharma, chemical and textile industries. In the long-term the resource basis of industrial society is going to shift away from fossil fuels toward biobased raw materials. Biochemical products today make up approximately 5 percent (and rising) of global chemical sales. Amino acids and antibiotics are classic biochemical products. Nowadays other standard products such as polyethylene made from sugarcane or corn are also making the leap into the mass market. Substituting biomass for 25 to 30 percent of the crude oil used by the chemical industry by 2025 is a realistic goal.

Resource efficiency has a central role to play in bioeconomic development going forward. The key concept here is synergy. Waste products generated in agriculture and forestry, in oil mills and breweries and in food production can be refined into high-value biological products: chemical raw materials, food and animal feed, basic materials for use in medication and cosmetics, fiber products and fuels. One example is the antibacterial biopolymer chitosan, which is reclaimed from the shells of shrimp and other crustaceans. Chitosan is used to preserve food and manufacture cosmetics, medical products and paper. It can also be used as a filter material. Integrated biological refineries that use straw, waste wood, grass, alfalfa or clover to produce a whole range of basic chemicals and fuels represent the next stage in this development. The principle of combined production allows the entire contents of organic matter to be used, though we still need to find ways to break down plant biomass in order to make use of the carbohydrates stored within.[6] The lignocellulose contained in cell walls must be broken down into its components: the pulp lignin and the sugars cellulose and hemicellulose. Lignin can be made into wood pellets, while the sugar mix extracted can be converted into basic chemical materials using enzymes. Diverse pilot facilities are currently in operation. For instance, the specialty chemical company Süd-Chemie in Straubing, Bavaria is operating a bioreactor for the manufacture of cellulose ethanol made from wheat straw. One thousand tons of ethanol are being produced from 4,500 tons of wheat straw each year.[7]

Land as a Scarce Commodity

The limit to the growth of the conventional bioeconomy lies in the fact that "availability of sustainable biomass will become a limiting factor in the foreseeable future," as stated in the Bioeconomy Council's study. Even just to meet the growing demand for food and animal feed crop yields must increase considerably in the coming decades. In a prognosis formulated in 2006, the FAO calculated that global grain production needs to be raised by as much as 70 percent by the middle of the century—and that under difficult climatic conditions. However, projections like this—which focus solely on the growth of agricultural production—neglect to consider the possibilities for reducing food waste on the way from the field to the consumer. They also extrapolate from current dietary behavior, and growing meat consumption in particular, to reach their conclusions about the expansion of animal feed production in future.

It is nevertheless beyond reasonable doubt that demand for all kinds of food products is going to rise considerably. The future access of industry and the energy sector to raw materials thus depends on agricultural productivity, which must be raised at every level of the agricultural system: from cropping systems, irrigation and land management geared toward breeding higher-yield, climate-robust species to harvesting, storage and processing. No matter how you look at it, if agricultural raw materials are increasingly to replace fossil fuels, an increase in sustainable biomass production is needed too. And that is the crux of the matter. As the sobering results of the biofuel hype of recent years have shown, the sustainability of agricultural raw materials depends on two crucial factors: they must not detract from food production and they must not ruthlessly exploit nature.

All around the world there is growing competition for the scarce resource that is land. The land area available to us cannot be expanded indefinitely. Only 29 percent of the earth's surface is made up of land and only around a third of that is suitable for farming; the other two-thirds are covered with ice or consist of deserts, forests and mountains. Altogether, then, only about 10 percent of the earth's surface fulfils the climatic and topographical criteria for food production. Moreover, due to the expansion of urban spaces as well as the extension of industrial parks, transport infrastructure, recreation areas etc. that land is being continuously decimated. Statistically speaking there are still considerable reserves for the expansion of agricultural land, but there are limits to what can be done with them. The crop yields of some of this land are insufficient, while in other cases a great deal of effort is required to cultivate it. Another issue is the loss of large amounts of arable and grazing land to erosion, salinization and advancing desertification. Given the growing need for agricultural production, the recultivation of lost land must be expedited. Numerous examples show that erosion and desertification can be reversed by planting trees and dung plants, adapting animal breeding and improving irrigation.

The land question is also politically explosive. Competition for fertile land is already well underway. Land grabbing—the purchase or leasing of large agricultural areas in developing countries by private or government-controlled investors from wealthy countries—is becoming more common around the world. According to the development organization Oxfam, since 2001 it has been used to acquire land corresponding to the area of Western Europe in Africa, Latin America and Asia.[8] The motivation for this new form of agricultural colonialism is above all the need to secure high-yield land for the production of food and agricultural fuels. We are thus already witnessing a concrete conflict between global bioeconomics and food production for domestic needs. There has been a particularly sizeable expansion in the amount of land used for energy plants like sugarcane, corn, palm oil and rapeseed. Approximately 7 percent of the grain harvested in the world at present is processed to make ethanol. Even putting industrial hunger for new resources to one side, demand for agricultural land is growing due to the food requirements of a growing global population. Changes in dietary habits are further heightening this effect. Meat consumption is growing in line with prosperity, particularly in the emerging nations. Demand for animal feed is also rising disproportionately as a result, its cultivation coming into competition with the production of plant-based foods. Even without taking other demands for biomass into account, we can consequently expect land and agricultural prices to rise in the long term. Land is becoming a lucrative capital asset. The poorer sections of the population are being particularly hard hit by this state of affairs.

An effective strategy for countering the scarcity and increasing cost of agricultural products is to significantly raise investment in *agricultural research* and thus increase agricultural productivity. Investigations show that there is a clear positive correlation between research efforts and agricultural yields. Increased crop yields in turn lead to price cuts. Both political measures (land reform, training, investment in agrarian infrastructure, microloans) and improved land management can substantially intensify this effect, as can the expansion of private and/or state storage facilities for agricultural products as a measure to counteract growing price volatility. Reserve supplies can be stocked up in times of excess, while in times of significant price rises market supply can be increased, stabilizing prices and revenue in the agricultural sector. We can substantially increase the amount we get out of available agricultural products by using them more efficiently. Here too resource efficiency has a key role to play in determining how narrowly or broadly the limits to growth are drawn. The requirement for improved efficiency is that all parts of plants (and animals) are fully exploited in combined usage chains. The bottom line, however, is that the use of agricultural products as materials or energy must remain secondary to the food security of a growing global population. First food, then bioeconomics—this principle is inviolable.

Next to agricultural land, *forests* are a biological economy's most important resource. Germany's woodland areas are growing by approximately twenty thousand hectares annually. Around 43 percent of felled wood goes into energy production. Wood, fruit, plants, nuts, mushrooms, medicinal herbs, cork, resin—the reservoir of valuable forest products is inexhaustible as long as woodland ecosystems have the capacity to regenerate. And that is precisely the problem. In February 2011 the FAO presented a report on state of forests around the world. The results are alarming. Despite various international declarations on forest protection, woodland corresponding to the size of England is still disappearing every year. It is being cut or burnt down in order to satisfy growing hunger for land, energy, raw materials, animal feed and meat, with demand from Europe, North America, Japan and the rapidly growing emerging nations playing a crucial role. Admittedly there are also encouraging countertrends. In Asia as well as Europe woodland areas are growing again. In China millions of hectares of new forest are planted each year. In the Philippines, which is still experiencing strong population growth, forests are also recovering. Having fallen to 21 percent, the land area covered by forests in Costa Rica is now up to 45 percent.[9] But the destruction of forests still surpasses reforestation by around five million hectares annually—in the 1990s as many as eight million hectares were lost per year. The expansion of the land area used to cultivate soy and palm oil is partly responsible for this. Deforestation for the production of animal feed and energy makes a farce of bioeconomics.

Excursus: Palm Oil

Palm oil is extracted from the fruits of the tropical oil palm, which is mainly grown in Indonesia and Malaysia. Growing demand for cheap plant fats has sparked a genuine palm oil boom. The multifaceted raw material is now found in every other supermarket product, from lipsticks and frozen pizzas to toothpaste, detergent and chocolate bars. The implementation of palm oil in the manufacture of biofuels and as fuel for power plants has also contributed to rising demand. Production has doubled in the last decade, with a corresponding rise in the amount of land dedicated to growing oil palms—at the cost of the tropical rain forests of Southeast Asia. The environmental impact of this kind of raw material extraction is negative in various respects. In many cases tropical forests stand on peat soil that contains huge amounts of carbon. Vast quantities of CO_2 are released as a result of fire clearing and the drying out of peat soil. Diverse vegetation is being replaced by monocultures that are intensively fertilized and treated with pesticides. Producers frequently run roughshod over the land rights of resident populations.

Nowadays there are various initiatives campaigning for greater sustainability in the production of palm oil. In 2004 the conservation organization World Wide Fund for Nature (WWF) initiated the Roundtable on Sustainable Palm Oil (RSPO), which involves palm oil producers, retailers, consumer goods manufacturers and NGOs.[10] The stated goal of the project is to hold producers and importers to minimum environmental and social standards: no clearing of old-growth forests; water, soil and forest protection; respect for the land rights of local communities; no child labor; support for peasant farmers; and independent inspections. The initiative has been criticized by other environmental and development organizations as a sham—the claim is that its criteria are too lax, there is no guarantee they will be adhered to and that the RSPO certificate merely provides an alibi for continued exploitation. The self-presentation of the multistakeholder initiative certainly seems excessively slick. There are no shortcuts when it comes to the arduous task of balancing environmental, social and economic interests. Import companies and consumer goods manufacturers in Europe can make an important contribution in this area by only introducing palm oil that satisfies verifiable environmental and social standards. Similarly, both the European Union and the German government must establish stricter criteria for the use of imported agricultural raw materials. Otherwise the EU's proclaimed goal of fueling at least 10 percent of road traffic with renewable sources by 2020 will be a nonstarter.

Energy from the Fields?

Not all biological innovations are good for the environment. If this is true of supermarket produce, it is particularly applicable to biogenic fuels sailing under green colors. The two most significant biofuels are bioethanol, which is extracted by fermenting and then distilling biogenic raw material, and biodiesel, which is produced from plant oils. Biofuels are environmentally problematic in at least three areas. Firstly, they compete with food production for land use. Secondly—see palm oil—environmentally valuable land is frequently sacrificed to grow energy plants. And thirdly, oilseeds and corn are generally produced as monocultures using large amounts of artificial fertilizer and pesticides. These three factors tip the environmental balance of many agricultural fuels into the red.

Biological energy sources, and especially the expanding agricultural fuels sector (ethanol, agricultural diesel), are playing a growing role in the energy mix worldwide. Brazil in particular is pioneering the switch from conventional to agricultural fuels. More than 90 percent of new cars sold there now run on a mixture of gasoline and ethanol. After oil, ethanol—which is primarily extracted from sugarcane—is the second most important energy source for the South American raw materials giant. Ten percent of its ethanol is exported. The manufacture of agricultural diesel from soybeans is also playing a growing role and is to be significantly expanded in future, with the European Union providing a lucrative export market. While this might initially sound positive, it is at best ambivalent. Although sugarcane is not grown in the Amazon region, the increasing conversion of grazing land into sugarcane plantations for use by the agricultural fuel industry is helping to displace cattle breeding toward the Amazon, where tropical rain forests are being cleared on a large scale to make way for meat production.

Given the Brazilian government's ambitious plans for a massive increase in the production of agricultural fuels, there is a danger that this displacement effect will continue to intensify. A team made up of German scientists and experts from the UN Environment Programme in Nairobi has projected that additional agricultural land corresponding to half the size of Germany would be needed to realize the targeted expansion of biogenic fuel production. Soy cultivation—for which forests are being specifically cleared—is particularly land intensive. Incidentally, clearing a hectare of rain forest releases approximately three hundred times more carbon dioxide than the so-called biofuels extracted from it save in a year (in comparison with conventional fuels). At that level of emissions it would take three hundred years to generate any climate relief—while pollution occurs abruptly and immediately. In order to limit these negative effects, researchers suggest shifting the basis of biodiesel production from soy to palm oil, which has a higher yield. Oil palms only need around 4 percent of the area required by soy to produce a corresponding amount of fuel.[11] As discussed above, however, the environmental impact of palm oil is dependent on land availability and cultivation methods. The extraction of ethanol from sugarcane can be increased without expanding the area of land used. Until now only the juice of the sugarcane plant has been used in fuel production. Using the rest of the plant as an additional energy source would increase its yield dramatically. Intensive research is currently being carried out on manufacturing processes for second-generation biofuels such as this.

If biofuels have become a controversial issue in Brazil, where the conditions for agricultural fuel production are relatively favorable, the matter is even more contentious in Europe and the US. Approximately forty-five billion liters of ethanol were produced in the United States in 2010, making it the world's leading producer (even ahead of Brazil). Measures introduced under President George W. Bush and thus far continued by the Obama administration are responsible for stimulating the biofuel boom. The US Environmental Protection Agency (EPA) has approved the sale of the biofuel blend E15 (15 percent ethanol) at gas stations. The primary ingredient in American ethanol production is corn. The environmental impact of corn is significantly worse than that of Brazilian sugarcane (particularly that grown on fallow land), especially when it is grown in huge monocultures, as in the Midwest of the US. Forty percent of the American corn harvest—a larger share than that used for animal feed—now goes into fuel production. This is bad news for the security of global grain production. If the American harvest slumps due to extended drought, as happened in the summer of 2012, corn prices in Latin America and Africa shoot up and the number of people starving rises. What improves US energy independence intensifies food crises in other countries—a fact that led FAO director general José Graziano da Silva, writing in an editorial for the *Financial Times*, to call for the

American government to suspend ethanol production: it is perverse to pursue large-scale biofuel production when food and animal feed are running low. The interests of both hundreds of thousands of farmers and an expansive processing industry make a short-term change of course problematic, but against the background of great drought, debate over the sense and nonsense of agricultural fuel production has broken out again in America too. Not only the usual suspects are criticizing the misappropriation of grain; in response to the acute shortage and increased cost of animal feed experienced during the summer of 2012 a broad coalition of milk farmers, cattle breeders and poultry producers called for the mixing of bioethanol and gasoline to be suspended.

In Germany approximately fifty-three million tons of biomass is harvested from fields and meadows every year. Over 90 percent is used in food, animal feed and industrial products.

Biogenic energy sources currently account for around 8.5 percent of agricultural production. They account for less than 1.5 percent of primary energy consumption, though the cultivation of energy plants for the production of fuels and biogas has steadily increased in recent years.[12] The German Agency for Renewable Resources estimates that in 2011 a land area of approximately 2.28 million hectares was devoted to growing energy plants—a 6 percent increase on the previous year. According to one energy scenario developed by the German government, biomass could meet up to 23 percent of the country's primary energy demands by 2050.[13] One of the main arguments in favor of biogenic energy sources is that burning them releases no more carbon dioxide than is bound during the growth of the biomass. However, this ignores the energy expenditure and emissions associated with growing and processing agricultural raw materials. Further arguments include reduced dependence on energy imports and new income sources for domestic agriculture and industry. Originally the European Union had set itself the goal of meeting 10 percent of its fuel demand with plant-based fuels by 2020. The percentage for conventional biofuels has since been limited to 5.5 percent due to growing criticism of the negative effects of biofuel production. Future expansion up to 10 percent is to be achieved with second-generation biofuels produced from algae, agricultural waste products or effluent sludge.

At present the environmental balance of agricultural fuel is not in good order. A study conducted by Paul Crutzen came to the conclusion that biodiesel from rapeseed is up to 1.7 times as harmful to the climate as normal fuel and bioethanol from corn up to 1.5 times as harmful, mainly due to the release of laughing gas, which is produced when nitrogen is used as a fertilizer. The effect of laughing gas on the temperature of the atmosphere is three hundred times stronger than that of carbon dioxide.[14] While not as disastrous, a report for the European Commission also came to the negative assessment that fuel production using rapeseed releases 4.5 percent more CO_2 than conventional fuel production and that soy-based fuel production releases 11.7 percent more.[15] This undermines the standards set by the European Union renewable energy directive passed in April 2009, which stipulates that the use of biofuel may only be applied to member states' CO_2 reduction targets if its carbon balance is at least 35 percent below the pollution levels of conventional fuels. This regulation applies regardless of whether the agricultural raw materials used are grown inside or outside the EU. Only sustainably grown raw materials may be used, and there are detailed specifications for what counts as sustainable. For instance, raw materials from old-growth forests (such as rain forest regions) are not allowed.[16] What they fail to take into account, however, are the indirect climatic consequences triggered by agricultural displacement. If the lucrative growth of energy plants displaces cattle breeding and arable farming from their traditional homes and new areas have to be cleared for them, the indirect effect on land use has a negative impact on the environmental balance of agricultural fuels.

The use of plants to produce *biogas* is likewise proving problematic. Around 7,300 facilities have sprung up in Germany thanks to the country's Renewable Energy Act. Most run on corn, which is converted into gas by microbes. This has led to considerable expansion in the growth of corn. Corn for energy production is now being grown on approximately 6 percent of German agricultural land. In Lower Saxony it is grown on almost every third hectare—an abhorrence to conservationists. In this part of the world corn requires a lot of fertilizer; nitrogen fertilization releases gases that have a major impact on the environment, while nitrates harm soil and groundwater. Corn is predominantly grown in monocultures, leaving barely any space for the habitats of other plants and animals.[17]

On top of all this, agricultural fuels have also come under fire for indirectly driving up the cost of food. There is some dispute as to what extent the growth of energy plants contributes to rising food prices. But there can be no reasonable doubt that repurposing arable land for biofuel production causes food supplies to run low and prices to rise, particularly in years with below-average harvests. This is exactly what happened in 2012. According to Detlev Virchow, head of the Food Security Center at the University of Hohenheim, corn consumption for the production of agricultural fuels has more than doubled since 2006. In 2010 approximately 6 percent of global corn production was turned into fuel.[18] Other sources indicate that around 2 percent of arable land worldwide is used to grow energy plants—a significant amount when you take into account increasing land shortages and the growing demand for food. In fact, the World Bank believes that rising food prices are predominantly due to agricultural fuel production. Biofuels have unintentionally become an example of how something expected to be a blessing can turn into a curse. Agricultural fuels once seemed to be a win-win undertaking, from which the environment would profit just as much as farmers, investors and equipment manufacturers.

In July 2012 scientists from the German National Academy of Sciences presented an assessment of the overall environmental balance of bioenergy. They came to the conclusion that "with the exception of the use of biogenic waste, the large-scale use of biomass as an energy source is not a real option for countries like Germany."[19] This recommendation is based on a comprehensive examination of the environmental and climatic costs of using biomass as energy, taking into account all the direct and indirect effects of production and processing. These include

- the energy expenditure and high-impact greenhouse gas emissions associated with nitrogen fertilization,
- the soil and groundwater pollution caused by phosphate fertilization,
- the amount of water required to grow energy plants,
- the effort required to sow, plow, harvest and transport the crops,
- the energy consumption and emissions involved in converting biomass into gaseous or liquid energy sources and

- the displacement of food, animal feed and industrial raw material production. The authors expect competition for land use to further intensify given the rising demand for food. It is for this reason that the production of ethanol or butanol from edible, sugary or amylaceous plants is forbidden in China.

Considered objectively, the report concludes, Germany's goal of meeting 23 percent of its primary energy needs with biological resources by the middle of the century is not achievable by environmentally sustainable means. The authors instead suggest accelerating the expansion of renewable energy sources that yield more while requiring less land. They do however consider the combination of food production, industrial processing and the use of residual plant materials for energy to be expedient.

Ultimately, they write, increasing the portion of our diet that comes from plants offers greater potential for relief than biogenic energy sources: "A shift toward a more vegetarian diet would result in less biomass being devoted to animal feed, allowing land to be farmed less intensively—as a consequence, GHG emissions would decline. A reduction of climate-relevant GHG emissions associated with less intense agriculture could contribute more to climate-change mitigation than the production of bioenergy." The problem with this recommendation is its moralistic formulation—should, would, could. There are a hundred good reasons to eat less meat and among the younger generation the number of vegetarians is growing. We must nevertheless expect the global demand for meat to rise in the coming decades. It is also unlikely that biomass giants such as Brazil, the US and the Southeast Asian palm oil exporters will abandon the production of agricultural fuel. We will thus continue to struggle with conflicting goals.

Completely abandoning the extraction of gas, electricity and fuel from biomass is not a realistic option, but we must aim to defuse the conflict with food security and seriously improve the environmental balance of agricultural fuels. That will require technological innovation, legal standards and international conventions. The IPCC, the United Nations' panel of experts on climate change, has come to a significantly more positive assessment of global bioenergy production. In the spring of 2012 it presented a comprehensive *Special Report on Renewable Energy Sources and Climate Change Mitigation* that the scientists of the German National Academy describe as overly optimistic.[20]

The upshot of all this is that despite various criticisms of current practices we should not condemn energy production from agricultural raw materials outright. Here as elsewhere the nature of the production is decisive: Which raw materials are being used as energy sources? How are they produced? What effort is involved in processing them? The goal should be to avoid generating energy from products that could be better used as food or animal feed. Subsidizing biofuel and biogas made from corn sends the wrong message. The primary function of arable land must be to serve food production. The second priority is raw plant material for the pharmaceutical, chemical and textile industries. The use of biomass to produce energy should come only at the end of a complex usage chain. Its environmental balance must be unambiguously positive. Based on these considerations many of the bioenergy production techniques currently in use are not sustainable, but that does not have to be the last word on the matter. If our aim is to eliminate fossil fuels from electricity production, the heating market and the transportation sector as quickly as possible in order to lower CO_2 emissions, it would be risky to count on solar and wind power alone. Energy from biomass can be easily stored in any physical state—as a solid, liquid or gas. The capacity of decentralized power plants that run on biomass or biogas can be easily adjusted in line with demand. In this regard they are an optimal supplement to fluctuating levels of solar and wind power. Their ability to stabilize supply and distribution networks will remain an advantage at least until efficient storage technologies for ecofriendly electricity are ready for implementation and a wide-ranging grid of renewable energy sources can guarantee a balanced supply.

Biofuels also have a lot to offer when it comes to reducing the carbon dioxide emissions of air travel. Given the substantial growth of the aviation industry (for many years air travel has been expanding at an average annual rate of 5 percent), this matter is extremely relevant to climate policy. It is intended that fossil fuels will eventually be replaced by biokerosene. Plant oils like rapeseed, palm and purging nut oil can provide the basis for this. The purging nut tree can be grown on scraggy and dry savannas. It requires little water and as it is poisonous, no chemical pesticides are necessary. Algae with a high oil content is another option for the production of kerosene. Experts anticipate that it will be possible to implement biokerosene as a standard fuel from 2015 at the earliest; a first test flight with biodiesel was carried out by Air New Zealand in January 2009. The airlines Lufthansa and KLM have implemented a 50 percent biokerosene mixture on some passenger flights. The Brazilian airplane manufacturer Embraer is making planes that run on second-generation bioethanol.[21] Airbus, leading European airlines, the European Commission and European biofuel producers have agreed that from 2020 two million tons of biofuel per year are to be produced for air travel.[22] Here too it is essential to consider the environmental impact of manufacturing these fuels. To clear rain forests and grow soy and corn on an agroindustrial scale in order to produce airplane fuel would be to jump from the frying pan into the fire. Given the limited potential for sustainable production of agricultural fuels it might make sense to reserve them for air travel in the medium term, while road traffic is largely switched to electromobility.

In order to avoid the diverse negative effects associated with the manufacture of fuels and biogas from agricultural crops, intensive experiments are being done with *second-generation biofuels* including cellulosic ethanol, biomethane and biokerosene. While first-generation biofuels use only a small part of plants (fruits or seeds), the next generation uses almost their entire mass, making the production process much more effective. Significantly less land, water, fertilizer etc. are needed to produce a certain quantity of biofuel. The fact that the required biomass either comes from residual agricultural and industrial materials or can be grown on low-maintenance land that is not in competition with food production is a further advantage. Suitable raw materials for the manufacture of cellulosic ethanol include small-diameter wood from forests, waste from the wood processing industry and fast-growing plantation woods like cottonwood or eucalyptus, straw or reeds. Cellulose makes up the major part of plant biomass but it has to be broken down in a laborious process using a special cocktail of microorganisms and enzymes. If this process can be implemented on an industrial scale, cellulose-based fuels could attain a climate balance 10 times better than that of previous and current agricultural fuels.[23] Relevant processes are already being tested at pilot facilities. The raw materials for these fuels come from organic waste, residual material from the agricultural and forestry sectors or grass grown on degraded land, easing the conflict between plate and tank.

A third option, one that still seems futuristic at this point, is the use of algae to produce fuels, biogas or hydrogen. Algae exhibit significantly higher biomass growth per area than plant energy sources. They can be cultivated in open aquacultures or closed bioreactors; the CO_2 required for this could be diverted from power plants or industrial facilities. Well-known companies are already investing in the development of algae-based fuels. For instance, ExxonMobil and Synthetic Genomics Incorporated are collaborating on plans for a 600-million-dollar project in this area. The US aviation group Boeing has announced test flights with fuels produced from algae. In a pilot facility at its lignite-fired power plant in Niederaußem RWE is researching the use of microalgae to purify exhaust fumes. Desulfurized exhaust gases are fed into a 600-square-meter facility where algae swim in saltwater. The microalgae convert the CO_2 into organic growth and oxygen using photosynthesis.[24] The carbohydrates stored in the algae can be converted into ethanol or oil by microbes. As of yet, however, there are no commercial facilities in operation. The costs are still too high, particularly given the expense involved in purifying the fuels.

Bionics: Learning from Nature

Why did evolution equip the zebras of the African savanna with a black and white coat? One naturally assumes that it was not just an aesthetic flight of fancy on nature's part. Indeed the zebra's coat is a cooling system that is simple and effective in equal measure. While the dark sections absorb sunlight, the white stripes reflect it. The resulting temperature difference (up to twenty degrees Celsius) causes air to circulate in a cooling fashion. The striped pattern also serves as camouflage and protection from insects, but the important thing for our purposes here is the principle of passive air conditioning. The Swedish architect Anders Nyquist, a pioneer of environmentally friendly architecture, has used the same black and white pattern on facades and roofs in the construction of self-regulating buildings that operate without artificial heating and cooling, allowing for considerable savings in domestic utility energy and costs. This is just one example of learning from nature, the basic principle of bionics. Leonardo da Vinci—who applied knowledge gained from analysis of avian flight to his flying machines—was an early precursor of this discipline. More recently, bionics has received a major boost from computerized processes and interdisciplinary collaboration. Its diverse applications have long been part of our daily lives: Velcro on clothes and shoes, self-cleaning surfaces and coatings, aerodynamic chassis, lightweight construction in the aviation and automobile industries and structural frames based on the construction of bones are all copied from nature.

Bionics is the combination of biology and technology. A semiofficial definition published by the Association of German Engineers in 1993 reads: "Bionics as a scientific discipline is concerned with converting the structures, processes and developmental principles of biological systems into technology." More and more universities and corporations are working on translating biological solutions into new products and technologies. In Germany alone more than seventy universities, research institutes and individuals working in the field have come together under the auspices of the research group Biokon.[25] We are only on the threshold of a world of discoveries gained from a better understanding of biological organisms and systems. In this respect bionics is in a race against the massive disappearance of animals and plants due to mankind's brutal interventions in nature. All in all, more than one hundred largely unexplored species are dying out every day. Nobody knows what medicinal, nutritional and material promise is being lost in the process. Thus far only a fraction of the biological riches of the earth has been scientifically surveyed. Its diversity holds immeasurable potential for a future mode of production based on the harmonious synergy of man and nature. Over billions of years evolution has developed materials, structures and metabolic processes designed for optimal functionality under specific circumstances. We must not only observe individual organisms but develop a deeper understanding of the systematic processes at work in the biological world: the optimization of expenditure and yields, high adaptability to changing environmental conditions, the self-organization of complex systems and the symbiotic relationship between individual life forms and their environment.

People have always borrowed from nature. Wearing fur for protection from the cold is a classic example of this. Modern bionics systemizes the process of learning from nature. It investigates how the results of biological specialization can be applied to the world of technology. It is not about simply copying nature but about identifying functional analogies, a process that begins with the question of how animals and plants achieve the astounding things they do. The following are some examples of bionic discoveries:

- In 1976 the biologist Wilhelm Barthlott noticed that the leaves of certain plants were astonishingly clean. He found the explanation for this phenomenon under the microscope—coarse surfaces that repelled dirt particles and water droplets—and thus deciphered what is known as the lotus effect. The implementation of this principle led to the development of colors and coatings for self-cleaning surfaces, which have long been state of the art. By now over two hundred new applications have been found for Barthlott's groundbreaking discovery, one of the pioneering acts of modern bionics.[26]

- The reason flies can walk up smooth walls is that their feet are covered in countless tiny little hairs that are subject to a strong molecular attraction. These hairs enable them to defy gravity. A particularly incredible exponent of this kind of adhesive force is the gecko: even holding onto a roof with a single finger it could still hold an entire bucket of water without falling. The translation of these capabilities into bionic designs is opening up new solutions for materials and adhesive technology.
- Adding a bulge resembling a dolphin's nose to the bow of a transport ship can reduce fuel consumption by up to 10 percent. The bulge reduces drag.
- The coarse, scaly skin of sharks serves as a paradigm for the coating on ships' hulls that prevents encrustation with barnacles and aquatic plants and reduces resistance. Applying this coating can reduce fuel costs by up to thirty thousand dollars per day while decreasing emissions of CO_2 and other air pollutants.
- Aviation also frequently borrows from nature—the very fact that man has learned to fly is itself a classic case of bionics. For instance, devices called winglets, angled edges on wings, reduce the kerosene consumption of airplanes. Here as elsewhere cost-effectiveness and environmental protection go hand in hand.
- Polar bear hairs have a transparent core that lets warming sunlight penetrate to the skin before trapping

its heat for a long time. Applied to the insulating layers of buildings, this model facilitates improvements in the use of passive solar power.
- Although bones—as porous hollow bodies—exhibit low density, their structure makes them very stable. This paradigm can be applied to the manufacture of highly resilient, low-weight materials.

Biological methods of pest control can be used to replace chemical insecticides in agriculture, keeping harmful insects away from fields with the aid of repellant substances (deterrent technology). One particularly artful (or perfidious) example is the process used in viniculture to inhibit the reproduction of the European grape berry moth: when special dispensers are used to distribute the artificially manufactured pheromone of the female insect throughout vineyards the males become so confused that they can no longer find the females and the mating cycle is interrupted. In Switzerland this technology is used to protect 60 percent of vines and half of fruit plantations.[27]

The application of biological processes to technical procedures also promises much for the energy production of the future. Photosynthesis will be discussed in detail below. The production of hydrogen from cellulose is another example. Termites are our teachers in this process. They live off a diet predominantly made up of cellulose. When they digest their food with the help of symbiotic microorganisms, hydrogen is formed. According to Professor Andreas Vilcinskas, head of the Fraunhofer research project Bioresources, termites can produce around two liters of hydrogen from the cellulose contained in a sheet of A4 paper.[28] A fuel cell car can drive approximately ten kilometers on that amount of cellulose—without exhaust fumes or CO_2 emissions. If this process could be reproduced on an industrial scale it would make fuel cell technology considerably more effective.

Biorobotics

Biorobotics is a new direction in bionics that applies technology adapted from nature to the construction of robots. A research team at the University of California, for example, has succeeded in building a six-legged robot that can walk, climb and negotiate surface edges—capabilities that are particularly in demand in the implementation of rescue robots. Their research was inspired by an extraordinary characteristic of cockroaches. Cockroaches may not be the most pleasant creatures, but have the remarkable ability to take off at speeds of up to fifty times their body length per second and swing themselves onto the underside of tables in the process. With the help of high-speed cameras researchers have now been able to analyze this acrobatic procedure. The recordings show how the insects cling to the edges of surfaces with tiny hooks on their hind feet, triggering a 180-degree pendulum motion that catapults them onto the underside. In doing so they are subjected to a force three to five times the earth's gravitational pull. Other animal acrobats—namely geckos—use this technique too. They can disappear under large leaves, for instance, at the speed of lightning. Together with robotics experts, researchers have set about applying this clever mobility technique to a robot called DASH (Dynamic Autonomous Sprawled Hexapod). They equipped the robot with Velcro-like structures on its hind legs and programmed its motion sequence to mimic the behavior of its natural prototypes.[29] Researchers at Osaka

University have developed a similar system: a mechanical spider that can scale slopes or stairs and crawl underneath flat obstacles. The possible uses of the Arachnobot include searching for survivors in rubble after an earthquake. The Fraunhofer Institute for Manufacturing Engineering and Automation also produces this type of spider robot.[30]

With the rapid progress of sensory technology and information processing, biorobotics is becoming more and more successful at constructing robots based on real creatures—robots that can recognize colors, process chemical information, sense smells and orient themselves in impassable terrain. They can be implemented in scenarios ranging from industrial manufacturing to domestic service and military technology. One helpful application is the exploration of contaminated industrial facilities or sunken shipwrecks. For instance, a team at the University of Essex in the UK has developed a swimming robot modeled on a fish, with a tail and fins. It is significantly more maneuverable than conventional floating bodies powered by propellers. The mechanical fish, which is equipped with chemical sensors, can inspect bodies of water or damaged ships for noxious substances.

The latest trend is for robots capable of acting autonomously on the basis of complex sensory information—they make their own decisions about what is to be done in a given situation. As so often, military technology is pioneering this development, which raises entirely new ethical and legal questions: Is it right, for instance, to let fighting robots decide when and on whom they open fire? And who is legally responsible for the mistakes made by such machines? The unmanned weapons systems that have been in use up to now are programmed to attack set targets. Future fighter drones and armed robots programmed to select targets for themselves would put us in new territory. As fascinating as the wonderland of biorobotics is, the time has come for science, politics and the public to address how the development of artificially intelligent systems, which are becoming subjects with their own decision-making power, should (and can) be regulated.

Biotechnology

The Greek word "bios" means "life". Biotechnology is the technological use of biological substances and processes for human purposes. Over the last few decades, biotechnological research and applications have become more and more specialized. They can be divided into three main groups:

- *Red biotechnology* takes its name from the color of blood. It deals with applications in medical diagnostics and treatment, such as the cultivation of mesh for skin transplants or the development of pinpointed medications that only release their active ingredients into sick organs. The production of medications using biotechnological processes also comes under the heading of red genetic engineering. A familiar example is the production of insulin (a hormone previously obtained from the pancreases of pigs) using genetically modified bacteria. Antibiotics, vaccines, proteins and vitamins are likewise manufactured using biotechnological methods.
- *White biotechnology* is the generic term for the application of biotechnological processes in industry, especially in process engineering. A time-honored method of industrial biotechnology is beer brewing;

the implementation of enzymes as biocatalysts in the chemical, pharmaceutical and food industries is a newer one. Catalysts slow down or speed up biochemical reactions. They allow processes that have traditionally taken place under high pressure or at high temperatures to be conducted with much lower energy expenditure. The conversion of biomass into basic chemical materials, industrial fibers or fuels comes under this heading too.

- *Green biotechnology* aims to improve the characteristics of plants. It encompasses green genetic engineering, the most controversial member of the extended biotechnological family.

Over time various subgroups have been added to the categories listed above. Blue biotechnology, for instance, deals with maritime organisms, such as ocean bacteria or algae, as sources of useful substances. Grey biotechnology refers to the application of biological processes to soil rehabilitation, sewage purification and waste treatment. The implementation of microorganisms to decontaminate soil or treat effluent in fact has a relatively long history. Sewage treatment plants were working with bacteria a long time before the concept of biotechnology emerged. The use of microorganisms to rehabilitate contaminated soil around refineries or chemical plants is likewise a tried and tested technique. In Germany there are more than seventy fixed facilities for biological soil treatment capable of purifying around four million tons of earth each year. The best thing about this process is that toxic substances are taken in by microbes as nutrients and converted into carbon dioxide and water. An overview of the various different processes and areas of application can be found in the *Leistungsbuch Altlasten und Flächenentwicklung 2004/2005* (Inventory of

Contaminated Zones and Land Development 2004/2005) published by the Environmental Agency of North Rhine-Westphalia.[31]

Contaminated wastewater from industrial facilities or dumps can also be treated using microbiological processes. A pilot project currently ongoing in Saxony is using microorganisms and heavy-metal-absorbing plants to detoxify contaminated slurry from the riverbed of the White Elster to the point where it can be used as topsoil.[32]

Grey biotechnology is a classic end-of-pipe technology applied at the end of long process chains in order to neutralize toxic substances. It is not elegant, but it is necessary if we are to wipe out the pollution legacy of industrial society. In future we should be aiming to stop such pollutants getting into the biosphere at all. The best avoidance strategy is to replace them with environmentally friendly materials and production processes. That is precisely why biotechnology is important. It has the potential to reduce material expenditure and energy consumption, to substitute renewable substances for fossil fuels and, wherever possible, to replace the old triad of raw materials, processing and waste with biological cycles.

Biogenetics

Medical bionics explores the effectiveness of biological substances and processes for the art of healing. For example, it can reconnect severed nerves using spider silk. The silk serves as a bridge, along which nerve cells grow together again. It works antibacterially and the human body tolerates it well. It can be used to sew up wounds during surgery. Spider silk can also be used to make artificial ligaments and tendons, while researchers at Hanover Medical School have succeeded in cultivating human skin cells on a mesh made out of it. Among other applications this technology could provide natural skin for the treatment of extensive injuries or burns.[33]

The astonishing characteristics of spider silk also make it useful in areas other than medicine. It is both tear resistant and highly flexible, stronger than steel and more elastic than rubber. The secret of this miracle material lies in a complex structure of protein molecules. Long chains of stably interconnected proteins alternate with loosely connected sections that provide high elasticity. Computer simulations have shown that it could even be used to build guard nets for airplanes that overshoot runways. In many cases it could replace steel or artificial fibers. But where are we to get the quantities needed for industrial application? In contrast with silkworms, spiders cannot be bred in large quantities. They fight over territory and eat each other. This is where *biogenetics* comes into play. A research group led by Florence Teulé at the University of Wyoming has managed to alter the genetic make-up of silkworms so that the characteristics of their silk resemble those of spider silk. The researchers introduced genes from the golden silk spider (Nephila clavipes) into the silk ducts of the worms, whereupon their silk fibers took on some characteristics of the spider silk proteins. Their durability corresponded to that of the spider silk.[34] Alongside biotechnological attempts to produce spider silk researchers are working to develop an artificial spinning apparatus that reproduces the complex biochemical procedures involved in manufacturing it naturally.

Anyone who opposes the genetic manipulation of animals and plants on principle may cringe at the thought of mankind intervening in evolution like this. From the perspective of many scientists, however, there is little distinction between experimental cultivation in laboratories, which likewise aims to alter the characteristics of biological organisms, and biogenetics, which takes a direct approach to altering DNA. The line is particularly fine when it comes to reprogramming specific segments of DNA without introducing genes from foreign species into the genome of an organism. The human race has long since passed the point of actively intervening in biological evolution. Moreover, any critique of biogenetic processes must reflect on the fact that we are not only responsible for what we do but also for what we choose not to do, although we have the capacity to. Given the resource requirements of a growing population, it is by no means obvious which decision is the ethically correct one: to make use of biogenetic methods or to abandon them.

One of the most recent developments in biotechnology is the emergence of *synthetic biology*, which deals with the construction of new organisms. Of course, building completely new complex life forms in laboratories is still the stuff of science fiction, but for the time being researchers are working on implanting synthetically produced genes into already existing organisms in order to give them new characteristics and capabilities. The demiurgic turn of scientific inquiry is thus complete. It has gone beyond recombining previously existing genes—as green genetic engineering does—and begun building new life forms. Like all other living things, these creatures are subject to mutation, though we are assured that, at least to a certain degree, they are to be made resistant to it.[35] Just as synthetic biology is still in its experimental phase, the ethical, social and political implications of the technology have not yet been resolved. Critical objections range from concern about the threat of bioterrorism to the question of ownership rights over living organisms and outright opposition. In 2007 the EU started a project named SYNBIOSAFE intended to highlight safety-related and ethical aspects of the discipline.[36]

Artificial Photosynthesis

By now the notion that there can be no limited growth on an unlimited planet has become commonplace. But the earth is only limited in geographic terms. From a thermodynamic perspective it is an open system, rather than a closed one.[37] All life on earth is ultimately dependent on the permanent supply of external energy provided by the sun. The amount of energy that strikes the earth in an hour of sunlight is enough to meet the needs of the entire human race for just under a year. Sunlight facilitates the permanent renewal of organic life on our planet. The point of departure for this is *photosynthesis*: the conversion of sunlight and water into energy in the form of carbon compounds. The photosynthetic process has two parts. Sunlight provides the energy required to split water into the elements oxygen and hydrogen; in the next step hydrogen and carbon dioxide, which is absorbed from the air, are used to build complex carbons like sugar and oil. Plants divide this process into two phases, with one taking place during the day and the other at night. During the day sunlight and water are converted into energy-rich chemical compounds; at night plants take carbon dioxide from the air and use it to build sugar molecules. Photosynthesis not only produces food for plants and microorganisms; it also removes carbon dioxide from the air and enriches it with oxygen. Without photosynthesis there would be no human life on earth.

Aside from plants, agents of photosynthesis include algae, bacteria and the microbes that live in the sea. A liter of seawater contains approximately one hundred million of these protozoans—the smallest known organism capable of photosynthesis. Using sunlight, water and CO_2 they make approximately a quarter of the oxygen we breathe.[38] Every year this giant solar power plant of living organisms converts approximately one thousand three hundred and fifty terawatts of solar power into biomass. For the purposes of comparison, the human race needs approximately sixteen terawatts of energy per year. As enormous as this number seems in isolation, in comparison with the potential of solar radiation it is rather modest. As Hanno Charisius puts it, "Artificial photosynthesis has what it takes to relieve a few of our energy worries."[39] Even the fossil fuels coal, oil and gas are ultimately nothing more than condensed solar power. They formed from plant matter over millions of years.

Artificial photosynthesis is the collective term for diverse methods of converting solar power into energy sources like methane, ethanol or hydrogen. In contrast to solar electricity, these can be used as basic materials in the chemical industry. They can also be easily stored. Methane can be fed into the existing natural gas grid, ethanol can be used within the infrastructure for liquid fuels and the energy density of hydrogen is three times that of gasoline—it can either be used directly as an energy source or converted into electricity using fuel cells. Numerous research projects around the globe are already working in these areas. Britain has launched an entire program of research and Japanese teams are developing new kinds of solar cells. The US Department of Energy has undertaken to invest $122 million over five years in a center for artificial photosynthesis in California.[40]

At MIT a research group led by the chemist Daniel Nocera has developed an artificial leaf that can split water into hydrogen and oxygen. The leaf, which is the size of a playing card, is made of silicon; a cobalt-phosphate mixture acts as a catalyst for the acceleration of the photochemical process. The amount of electricity required for the electrolysis is low. If the catalyst is applied to the back of commercial solar cells and the flat unit put in a container of water, hydrogen can be obtained without an external electricity source. Nocera's next goal is to develop a stand-alone system that households can use to produce their own energy from sunlight and a few liters of water. This technology would primarily be of use to the populations of rural regions still not connected to a national energy supply. Nocera's invention is still a long way from commercial use, but that was also the case with the first photovoltaic systems.

The German start-up Sunfire has developed a process for making synthetic fuels from carbon dioxide and water. Electrolysis is used to split water into oxygen and hydrogen, which reacts with CO_2 in several steps to produce gasoline, diesel, kerosene or methane. The carbon dioxide is extracted from the air with a filter. Using high-temperature steam electrolysis, 70 percent efficiency is achieved. This percentage of the electrical energy used is stored as calories in the fuels produced, making the process well suited as a storage technology for surplus wind or solar power. The first laboratory-scale test facility was set up in 2010. The first preindustrial prototypes are to follow by 2016. This process is of particular interest to the aviation industry and long-distance freight carriers, which cannot operate with electric engines due to the low energy density of electric batteries.[41]

The American physicist Freeman J. Dyson—famous for his unorthodox ideas—believes that the key to the development of rural regions all around the world lies in the combination of solar power, photosynthesis and the Internet, with solar power delivering electricity wherever it is needed, photosynthesis powering transportation and the Internet putting an end to the isolation of village communities and opening up access to information and markets.[42]

A second main strand of research into photosynthesis builds on the capacity of natural organisms to convert sunlight and carbon dioxide into carbon compounds. Algae and bacteria cultivated in bioreactors can take up CO_2 and use it to make substances that can be synthesized into biodiesel or ethanol. Scientists at the University of California, for example, have developed a promising process for making butanol out of carbon dioxide. James Liao and his colleagues cultivated genetically modified variants of the bacteria Ralstonia eutropha in a water tank through which they fed carbon dioxide gas. Electricity provided by a commercial solar cell caused the carbon dioxide to react with water and produce formic acid that was in turn taken up by the microbes and converted into butanol. The alcohol, which exhibits a relatively high energy density, can be used to synthesize biofuels. The process is not yet efficient enough, but it provides an interesting indication of how carbon hydrides could be used to store solar electricity in future.[43] Processes like this are already being implemented on an industrial scale. One of the pioneers of fuel production using biological organisms is the American military—not out of concern for the climate, but because it sees this kind of production as a way to become oil independent and reduce long transport chains. The first test flights with biokerosene have already taken place.[44]

A third approach involves attempts to optimize the process of photosynthesis in plants in order to stimulate their growth and increase crop yields. In this case optimizing nature means using solar power more effectively to produce nutrients. The amount of solar power taken up and converted into carbon compounds by a plant has a significant influence on the growth and volume of its leaves, roots, fruits and seeds. In general green plants use at most 3 percent of the sunlight that falls on them. The efficiency of the conversion process differs from plant to plant. Corn, millet, sugarcane and miscanthus, for example, have developed specialized cell apparatuses for the conversion of sunlight into hydrogen as well as for building sugar compounds out of CO_2. This division of labor makes the whole process significantly more efficient than in rice, for instance, which has not developed in the same way, although it is genetically capable of doing so. If targeted genetic modifications could be introduced to set this mechanism in motion, crop yields could be improved considerably. An international research consortium coordinated by the International Rice Research Institute (IRRI) in the Philippines is working on this.[45] The project is funded by the Bill & Melinda Gates Foundation. The Institute for Developmental and Molecular Plant Biology at the University of Düsseldorf in Germany is involved in the alliance. If rice were capable of high-performance photosynthesis (C4 photosynthesis), researchers believe, crop yields would increase by around 50 percent while water consumption would be substantially reduced.

It is important to note that rice is the staple food for approximately half the world's population. In Asia at present a hectare of rice fields feeds approximately twenty-seven people. By the middle of the century the same amount of land will likely have to feed 43. Population size is growing while land and water are in short supply. Rice is an irrigation-intensive grain. Around 30 percent of the available freshwater is used to grow it.[46] The foreseeable consequences of climate change will put added strain on agriculture. It is vital for food security in Asia that we find a way to increase crop yields and improve the resistance of rice to drought and heat. Various possible methods and approaches must be tried out in practice in order to determine the best way of achieving these goals. In *Factor Five* Ernst Ulrich von Weizsäcker reports on a new type of rice called Hardy, which is apparently capable of high crop yields under dry conditions. Scientists at the Virginia Bioinformatics Institute introduced into rice plants a gene originally responsible for highly efficient water usage in rock cress. It reduced water loss in the rice plants and boosted photosynthesis. The crop yield of the new type of rice under dry conditions increased by 50 percent.[47]

An increase in photosynthetic bioproduction would in its turn increase the potential of biomass as a material and an energy source and lead to more CO_2 being extracted from the atmosphere. The opportunities and risks associated with this process must be soberly evaluated in a dialogue between politics, science, industry and civil society.

CO_2: The Climate Killer as a Raw Material

Carbon dioxide, a chemical compound of carbon and oxygen, is an incombustible, colorless and odorless gas. It is generated by the cellular respiration of living beings and the fermentation of organic matter. To this extent it is a natural component of air. In the atmosphere carbon dioxide absorbs part of the solar radiation reflected by the earth, producing the famous greenhouse effect, which raises the average temperature on earth from minus 18 to plus 15 degrees and makes organic life possible. It only came to be viewed as a climate killer when the human race began burning massive amounts of coal and oil, thus releasing additional carbon dioxide into the atmosphere. When the concentration of heat absorbers in the atmosphere rises, the greenhouse effect is intensified and average global temperatures rise. Natural phenomena such as cyclical fluctuations in solar radiation can intensify or subdue this mechanism but it shapes the long-term developmental trends of the earth's climate. Since industrialization began the CO_2 concentration of the atmosphere has risen from 280 to 380 parts per million. Between 1880 and 2010 the average global temperature rose by 0.9 degrees, with the pace of the increase speeding up throughout that period. The decade from 2000 to 2009 was the warmest ever recorded by some distance, followed by the 1990s. If this development continues, it risks getting out of control, for global warming is not a continuous, linear process. Were the rise in the global temperature to exceed two degrees Celsius it could start to increase exponentially. Scientists talk of climatic tipping points. These include the release of huge amounts of methane due to thawing permafrost soil in Canada and Russia and the melting of the polar and Himalayan ice caps—events that would be followed by a further rise in the amount of solar heat absorbed by the earth. There is also a threat that the sea level could rise by several meters due to the collapse of the Greenland or Antarctic ice sheets.[48]

In order to stabilize the earth's climate, then, carbon dioxide emissions caused by mankind must be reduced to a level the biosphere can absorb. Our economic system must become CO_2 neutral by the middle of the century at the latest in order to avoid climatic chaos. The greatest potential for reduction lies in substituting renewable energy sources for fossil fuels: sun, wind and biomass instead of coal and oil. Given that at present greenhouse gas emissions are still rapidly rising, we must also look for ways to reduce the CO_2 concentration of the atmosphere again. The most effective way of doing this is to raise the intake capacity of natural carbon sinks, for example through reforestation and soil recultivation. In recent years intensive research has been conducted into a second approach to CO_2 reduction: CO_2 recycling or the use of carbon dioxide as a raw material. If CO_2 is extracted from the atmosphere in this way over time or fossil fuels are replaced by carbon dioxide we will see some relief of the pressure on the climate. It presents an interesting alternative to CCS technology: why go to the expense of injecting carbon dioxide into subterranean dumps when it can be used as a resource? The German magazine *Wirtschaftswoche* compiled a list of current research projects in this area.49 When you see who is already involved it becomes clear that it is more than just a lofty idea. For instance, in 2010 the US Department of Energy invested more than one hundred million dollars in research and development. The German Federal Ministry of Education and Research has likewise invested one hundred million euros. Then there is the potential of chemical and technology companies like Bayer, BASF, Evonik and Siemens. Energy companies such as RWE and EnBW are also involved. Alessandra Quadrelli, head of the faculty of sustainability at CPE Lyon, calculates that up to 10 percent of the required reduction in greenhouse gases could be achieved using CO_2 recycling methods. That is an ambitious amount, but it also shows that CO_2 recycling is no alternative to avoiding carbon emissions in the first place. The *Wirtschaftswoche* authors wildly exaggerate when they say that it "could make the climate killer less frightening." Avoidance must take priority over reuse. The use of CO_2 as a material is a supplementary method of climate protection—no more and no less.

Carbon is the cornerstone of the chemical industry. That is what makes the idea of using carbon dioxide as a resource so appealing. Even today it is already being synthesized on a large scale in the production of basic chemical materials. Fifty million tons are being used in the manufacture of urea alone, which is further processed to make fertilizers or synthetic resin.[50] CO_2-based solvents are also being implemented in the decaffeination of coffee. Prior to now high energy expenditure has stood in the way of broader use. Carbon dioxide is low in energy and inert. Its conversion takes place at high temperatures and under high pressure. The development of biochemical catalysts and processes capable of speeding up its reaction with other substances is thus vital to reducing energy requirements and costs. Carbon dioxide can serve as a raw material for chalk or soda, for building materials, bulk chemicals, medications, synthetic coatings, foam plastics and compostable packaging. It replaces oil and gas in the manufacture of these products. A number of these processes are already operational on an industrial scale. A research team at the Freiburg Materials Research Center has developed a process that makes it possible to obtain pure methane from the synthesis of hydrogen and carbon dioxide. Special catalysts can be used to improve the reactivity of CO_2 and thus reduce the energy expenditure of the process. Ten percent of Germany's current carbon dioxide emissions would be enough to meet the country's fuel needs for a whole year.[51]

Another option is to use carbon dioxide as a fertilizer in greenhouses. CO_2 is indispensable for plant growth. Plants use it in combination with sunlight and water to form sugar molecules for energy and nutrients. The CO_2

concentration of the air in densely occupied greenhouses is often insufficient. As long as there is enough light available additional doses speed up plant growth.

The use of carbon dioxide as food for the cultivation of algae is a further exciting application. It can be used to produce up to one hundred tons of dry matter per hectare, with up to two hundred tons of CO_2 being bound in the process—up to twenty times more than when rapeseed is grown on the same area. Algae make very effective use of CO_2. They are already being used today as a protein-rich supplement for animal feed and as a basic material in the chemical and pharmaceutical industries as well as in the manufacture of biofuels. The process systems provider GEA is developing a process that uses CO_2 as the raw material for an entire value chain. First it serves as a nutrient in the large-scale cultivation of algae. Yeast cells convert the sugar contained in the algae substrate into alcohol, which is then separated and processed into biofuels. The yeast cells as well as the algae can be reused as animal feed or fertilizer, resulting in an almost waste-free product cycle. A trial using the CO_2 emissions of a cement factory is currently underway in Spain. Whether this process proves to be commercially viable will depend for one thing on the sales prices of the end products and for another on the future cost of CO_2 emissions. The higher their price, the more lucrative investing in carbon recycling will be.[52]

As so often, there is a danger here that a new, promising technology will be used to cover up the harm old industries do to the environment. Energy companies like RWE or Vattenfall installing pilot systems at lignite-fired power plants in order to divert a tiny fraction of the carbon dioxide emissions into algae cultivation is far from enough to constitute climate-friendly carbon-based electricity provision. CO_2 recycling is an attractive option for industrial facilities that are going to remain dependent on fossil fuels for the foreseeable future. In combination with biomass power plants and biogas facilities, the recycling of CO_2 might even lead to a net reduction in carbon dioxide. But it is certainly not an excuse to build more coal-fired power stations.

Chapter 6

The Future of Agriculture

The language in which the Bioeconomy Council's report is written leaves no room for romantic notions of peasant agriculture conducted in harmony with nature. Despite all its references to the diversity of agricultural structures and practices around the world, it consistently portrays agriculture as a scientifically operated industry whose aim is to optimize the cultivation of soil, plants and farm animals—which are roughly treated as mere resources—in order to deliver as much biomass as possible. Ultimately it regards the biological world as a means to an end—as matter from which maximum utility must be extracted for the human diet, for industry and for the energy supply. Plants and breeding animals are perceived as biological machines whose performance must be maximized using all the means of modern biotechnology. Everything is geared toward growth: crop yields, plant growth, the milk output of cows and poultry production.

This attitude is only consistent with the logic of contemporary agricultural economics—according to every available prognosis the demand for all kinds of agricultural products is going to rise steeply in future, while at the same time we are suffering from a shortage of land. In 1970 there were 3,800 square meters of agricultural land available to feed each member of the global population. By 2005 that number had already fallen to 2,500 square meters. By 2050 the area of agricultural land available per person will have shrunk to approximately one thousand eight hundred square meters.[1] There only seems to be one answer to this: a rise in agricultural productivity with constant increases in per hectare crop yields. In fact this logic is not quite so iron clad as it first appears. The number of calories being produced around the world today—approximately four thousand six hundred per capita—is sufficient to feed even a future global population of nine billion people. However, a third of that amount (according to some estimates as much as half) is lost on the way from the field to the consumer—food rots on fields, goes off during transport or ends up in the trash. Approximately eight hundred calories are diverted into animal feed for meat production. The effects of increased meat consumption on the global food supply can be illustrated using the example of the US. Due to high demand for animal feed, the 5 percent of the global population that lives there consumes almost a third of global corn production and a fifth of soy crops. Add the conversion of grain into biofuels and in the final analysis 80 percent of American corn production is diverted into animal feed and agricultural fuels. Only 11 percent is actually used as food.[2] In Germany only 28 percent of agricultural land serves the production of food. Twelve percent is used for bioenergy. In contrast, the cultivation of animal feed accounts for an enormous 57 percent. The rest is used for miscellaneous purposes. Reducing crop wastage and changing our eating habits could thus significantly improve the global food situation.

It does not follow, however, that the agricultural industry can otherwise continue as before. The intensive brand of agriculture prevalent today in the US and Europe is not sustainable, nor is the productivity of peasant farming in the developing countries sufficient to meet the increased demands of a growing global population. Those who have risen from bitter poverty to modest prosperity will no longer be satisfied with a bowl of rice or a handful of millet. Food is becoming more plentiful and varied. Meat and fish are being added to menus. At the same time there is growing demand for a whole plethora of agricultural raw materials: cotton, plant oils, starch, plant fibers, wood etc. The UN Food and Agriculture Organization predicts that food production will increase by 70 percent before the middle of the century. We may or may not accept this, but even if crop losses are reduced and less food is thrown away, agriculture still has to become more productive. The contentious issue is how to achieve this. Here as elsewhere the big question is not *whether* agricultural production needs to grow but *how* it should grow.

Industrial agriculture has a bad reputation among the green movement. It is true that it is energy intensive and harmful to groundwater, that it leaches soil and advances erosion, turns animals into production machinery, decimates species diversity and transforms vivid landscapes into monotone wastelands. Nevertheless, the development of modern agriculture cannot be reduced to a continuation of the fall of man. Reality is more complicated than that. The first big scientific and technological revolution in agriculture had four pillars: fertilization using industrially produced nitrogen, chemical pest management, continuous improvements in the productivity of animal and plant breeding methods, and the implementation of modern agricultural machinery. This combination of science, technology and practical agriculture made possible the enormous yields required to feed a steeply growing global population. If we had had to produce the food volumes of 1998 with the per hectare yield of 1961, 82 percent of the earth's land area would have been required, rather than the 38 percent actually used.[3] The enormous increase in productivity was accompanied by a strong concentration of production activity among progressively fewer companies that grew larger and larger in size, constantly increasing their yields. In Germany the number of farms shrank from 1.65 million to 300,000 between 1949 and 2010. The number of workers employed in the agricultural sector dropped from 4.8 million to 648,000. During the same period the number of people fed by each farmer rose from 10 to 132.[4]

As the yields from arable and livestock farming rose, so too did the resource and energy consumption of the agricultural industry: the growing output was made possible by growing input. This equation is not sustainable. Like other sectors, the agricultural industry needs to revolutionize efficiency. Its transformation into an industrially operated branch of production was founded on a cheap, plentiful supply of oil—a necessary ingredient in the production of fertilizer and the operation of increasingly comprehensive machinery. Now phosphorus, nitrogen fertilizer and diesel are becoming increasingly expensive, while the rising energy expenditure of the agricultural sector has driven up its CO_2 emissions. If we add the carbon dioxide, methane and laughing gas emissions of the sector and its feeder industries to the effects of expanded land use at the cost of forests and wetland, agriculture causes almost a third of global greenhouse gas emissions.[5] A good portion of its value creation (and the related energy expenditure) has migrated to feeder industries: the fertilizer and seed industry, pest control and agricultural machinery. Then there are the enormous freight volumes of a globally interconnected food industry that circulates animal feed, raw materials and finished goods worldwide. Cheap freight tariffs have lengthened the distances traveled by food between harvesting, processing and consumption. In the five years between 1995 and 2000 alone the volume of animal feed and food transported in Germany grew by 30 percent. The example of the crabs taken from the North Sea to Morocco to be shelled—2,500 kilometers there and back—is notorious. This is the kind of absurdity that arises when the differences in wage costs between countries are significantly larger than transport costs. Over 95 percent of the groceries supermarket customers pack into their trollies today have traveled more than one hundred kilometers. Many have traveled halfway around the earth.[6]

Agriculture is the world's largest water consumer, accounting for 70 percent of freshwater use. This makes it extremely vulnerable to climate change, which in many areas of the world is connected with rising temperatures and drought. Agricultural monocultures leach soil and aid erosion. They are susceptible to pests and require lots of chemical pesticides. Heat waves and drought have a particularly severe impact on regions where they are grown—where the land is covered with nothing but corn, soy or cotton as far as the eye can see. Furthermore, the tendency to concentrate on a few high-yield breeds has drastically decimated crop diversity. In India the number of rice varieties fell from around fifty thousand in the 1960s to around fifty at the end of the 1990s. Admittedly, industrial agriculture has considerably increased it yields, but at a high price: approximately two billion hectares—almost 40 percent of the world's agricultural land—is affected by soil degradation. The industry is thus undermining the foundations of its own long-term existence. Many more sins could be added to this list. The need for change is clear. But the way in which global agricultural production is changing is not straightforward.

Organic Farming

One alternative to the energy- and water-intensive practices of conventional agriculture is *organic farming*, which makes use of a combination of traditional and modern methods, practical knowledge and new scientific findings. This new direction in agricultural production regards nature as a living system instead of as a mere resource from which as large a yield as possible must be extracted. Its methods, which are based around the principles of cycles, aim to increase the fertility of land and make use of biological synergy. They include

- abandoning synthetic chemical products such fungicide, herbicide, synthetic fertilizer and antibiotics,
- the use of residual animal and plant matter and natural minerals as fertilizers,
- the reintroduction of crop rotation in order to boost soil regeneration,
- the periodic cultivation of green manure crops that loosen up the soil and enrich it with nutrients,
- biological pest control (the use of microorganisms and plant or mineral substances to combat pests),
- gentle soil cultivation that does not compact farmland and maintains the biological activity of soil,
- the integration of arable farming and livestock breeding in accordance with the principle of closed-loop recycling (fields provide cattle feed, animals provide fertilizer for arable farming) and

- the combination of arable farming and forestry (agroforestry): trees improve microclimates, provide shade, offer protection against soil erosion, bind water in soil and fertilize it with their leaves.

Organic farming aims to work in harmony with nature. Chemical pesticides, mineral fertilizers and green genetic engineering are forbidden. Livestock is farmed extensively rather than intensively, the acquisition of animal feed is regulated, animals are bred using methods appropriate to their species and their natural need for movement accommodated. The climate balance of organic farming is far superior to that of industrialized animal breeding and conventional forms of arable farming, which use large amounts of fertilizers and pesticides. A study conducted by the Berlin Institute for Ecological Economy Research concluded that a switch to organic farming could reduce global greenhouse gas emissions by 15 to 20 percent.[7] Whereas green genetic engineering focuses primarily on the optimization of plant characteristics, organic farming addresses soil improvement. Targeted enrichment of organic soil matter allows more carbon to be stored—it is one of the most promising ways to reduce the CO_2 concentration of the atmosphere. Many organic farming methods can also have a beneficial impact within conventional agriculture. For instance, periodically fertilizing soil by growing lupines, alfalfa or certain types of clover enriches it with nitrogen and improves its biological activity. Lupines can also be used as food or animal feed; their seeds can be made into milk and tofu. They contain all the essential amino acids and are cholesterol free. The protein-rich seeds of sweet lupine can be turned into gluten-free flour with a high fiber content. When it comes to plant protection there are also biological alternatives that could largely replace pesticides. Take the push–pull technique—a method of strategically combining plants that repel or attract pests. For example, planting desmodium in corn fields keeps unwelcome insects away, while Napier grass is planted at the edges of fields to attract them. A related method is the implementation of plant-based repellents and bait.

The Research Institute of Organic Agriculture valued the global market for organic food at $59.1 billion (€49 billion) in 2010, with Europe accounting for $28 billion. The biggest organic markets are the US, with $20.2 billion, and Germany, with around six billion.[8] But many of the benefits of multifunctional organic farming cannot be expressed in monetary terms, in particular its contribution to maintaining species diversity and the cultivated landscapes of peasant farming.

Although organic farming is in growing demand, from a global perspective it is still a marginal pursuit. In 2008 35.1 million hectares were organically cultivated by 1.4 million producers. Around two-thirds of this area is grassland. Organic farming accounts for approximately 0.3 percent of agricultural land use (pastures and arable land) around the world. Of course, many millions of peasant farmers in developing countries practice agriculture that is close to nature without being officially labeled as organic. Helping them to increase their crop yields using the methods of organic farming is the most promising way to overcome poverty and hunger. In Germany organic farming has a 6 percent market share, in Austria almost 16 percent. Its popularity is growing, among other reasons due to increased demand for organic produce among the urban middle classes.

The main objection to organic farming invoked by advocates of industrialized agriculture is the relatively small size of its yields in comparison with conventional farming. According to a review of 362 studies comparing organic and conventional cropping systems recently published by scientists at Wageningen University, the yield deficit of organic farming amounts to an average of 20 percent per hectare. Next to its limited use of pesticides, the main reason for this is its rejection of mineral fertilizers.[9] The greater land requirements of organic farming call its environmental advantages into question. The results of an American study published in the spring of 2012 in *Nature* came to similar conclusions.[10] According to that research the main discrepancy is in grain production, whereas organic farming is capable of similar yields when it comes to fruit, vegetables and legumes. Given that productivity varies depending on the types of crops grown, soil conditions, climate, irrigation techniques etc., sweeping statements should be treated with caution. An earlier study from 2007, which was likewise based on analysis of a range of field studies but took regional differences into account, came to a much more positive conclusion: when compared with high-input agriculture in industrial nations, the yields of organic farming methods were shown to be 9 percent lower on average. In contrast, in southern countries they attained yields that were up to 74 percent greater.[11]

There is considerable evidence that organic farming is particularly well suited to the small-scale farming structures prevalent in Africa, Asia and Latin America: it requires less capital than conventional agriculture, extracts diverse products from small land areas and facilitates closed-loop recycling that delivers organic matter back to the land. With a combination of practical knowledge handed down from previous generations and modern agricultural research the productivity of environmentally friendly agriculture can be substantially increased. Up to now peasant farming has been chronically neglected in most countries, while large farms, which often produce for export, have been supported. With land reform, better training and advice and more efficient irrigation systems, storage options and market access, the productivity of environmentally sustainable peasant farming structures can still be significantly increased. There is a lot of room to improve soil cultivation, crop selection, pest control and fertilization as well as to breed higher yield and stress-resistant species. Against the background of around a billion underfed people, a population that is continuing to grow and rising demand for a high-quality diet, the FAO and the International Fund for Agricultural Development (IFAD) calculate that food production in the developing nations must be increased by as much as two-thirds by 2030. The reduction of crop wastage is a key priority: in many developing countries a third of the crops produced are lost due to a lack of warehouses, transportation options and processing capabilities.

The Dispute over Green Genetic Engineering

Genetic engineering is a subject that polarizes people. A broad and stable majority of the population in Germany is opposed to genetically modified (GM or GMO) food. On the other side of the debate a relatively small group of proponents warn against Europe falling behind in GMO research and development. In this context, the modifier "green" refers to the use of modern genetics in plant breeding. Specific genes are introduced into the genetic makeup of plants with the intention of improving their resistance to pests and resilience to drought, raising their nutritional value and increasing crop yields. At this point there is actually little evidence that green genetic engineering can make a relevant contribution to food security in times of climate change. The genetically engineered development of stress-resistant plants that can be grown in dry or extremely saliferous soil has so far not progressed beyond the experimental stage. A few years ago Monsanto announced its intention to plant a drought-tolerant variety of corn (Mon 87460) on 250 experimental fields in the US. Green genetic engineering also has competition from alternative processes of precision breeding (smart breeding) that likewise aim to develop more resilient species capable of higher yields. The company Pioneer, for instance, has bred a type of corn that it claims will increase crop yields under hot conditions by 7 percent.[12] The International Rice Research Institute has succeeded in breeding a variety that can endure flooding for several weeks.

While plant breeding based on selection and crossbreeding accelerates the natural processes of mutation and genetic recombination in order to create new varieties, green genetic engineering has so far relied on the introduction of foreign genes into plants. Jumping over species boundaries like this verges on the taboo. Mixing species seems like a crime against nature to many people. For thousands of years, mythology—the collective unconscious of humanity—has been populated by chimeras and monsters: ugly, terrifying or sympathy-inducing half-breeds. There is also a well-founded public skepticism toward the kind of genetic reductionism that establishes linear causality between genetic complexes and specific capabilities. It is clear to even an interested layperson that the features and characteristics of organisms are "not a willful translation of genetic information into proteins, anatomical structures and behavioral patterns," as the science journalist Bernhard Kegel writes with reference to the biologists Scott Gilbert and David Epel: "The phenotype is not an essential consequence of the genotype."[13] There is complex interplay between individual sections of DNA and other genetic information. Furthermore, the translation of genetic material into concrete characteristics depends to a large extent on environmental influences. We cannot be sure what unforeseen metabolic modifications the introduction of foreign genes into organisms will trigger, especially as gene transplantation methods have thus far been highly imprecise: when foreign genes were injected into the genetic makeup of the first generation of transgenic plants it was not known which sections of the DNA they would attach themselves to.[14] When outcomes are uncertain there is an increased risk of unwelcome side effects such as resistance to antibiotics or the activation of allergies.

Since then there have been various developments in genetic research. Using synthetically manufactured amino acids it is possible to activate any sequence desired in the genetic makeup of an organism. In combination with what are known as genetic scissors (nucleases), individual base pairs can be inserted into or removed from DNA and genes activated or shut down. "Adding to, deleting, exchanging and revising the material of genetic texts has become almost like child's play as a result."[15] What sounds like science fiction is in fact already being practiced in numerous laboratories around the globe. The field is developing rapidly. New techniques have enabled scientists to make targeted changes to genetic information from within, instead of embedding foreign genes as carriers of particular characteristics. The TALEN (Transcriptional Activator-Like Effector Nucleases) method makes is possible to breed organisms whose DNA cannot be distinguished from that of plants, though they have developed as a result of crossbreeding or mutation. Food produced from such products no longer exhibits any trace of genetic modification. The first test plants to be modified using noninvasive methods are already being cultivated in the greenhouses of the seed industry. This is new territory for the regulatory authorities—should cisgenic plants developed using selective gene modifications be subject to the same stipulations as transgenic organisms? The genetic engineering debate is entering a new phase.

Up to now the application of green genetic engineering around the world has concentrated on four agrarian plants: 77 percent of soy is now genetically modified, as is 49 percent of cotton, 26 percent of corn and 21 percent of rapeseed. In North America, sugar beets—95 percent of which are genetically modified—also feature prominently.[16] Herbicide and insect resistance are the two most frequently modified characteristics. The immunization of soy, corn and cotton against herbicides is a controversial subject. It encourages the implementation of nonspecific, blanket herbicides that kill other plants and can also poison animals. That is precisely what the seed giant Monsanto is aiming to achieve by selling transgenic seeds in a bundle with its superherbicide Roundup. Proponents of this approach point out that the growth of herbicide-resistant plants in the US and Brazil has led to the expansion of plowless agriculture and thus reduced soil erosion, fuel consumption and greenhouse gas emissions. It is still up for debate whether growing transgenic crops ultimately leads to sustainable crop increases while decreasing pesticide use. The results differ depending on methods of application, climate conditions and environmental circumstances.

One of the negative side effects of green genetic engineering is that by concentrating on a few mass products it contributes to the increasing prevalence of extensive monocultures. Sustainable agriculture relies on a diversity of crops and cultivation methods that are optimally suited to the soil and climatic conditions of the areas in which they are implemented. Given the varying impacts of climate change in different regions, global standardization of seeds and cultivation methods is counterproductive. Instead, stronger regional differentiation is called for.[17] Owing to high research and development costs, the market for genetically modified seeds is dominated by a few large corporations. Development is concentrated on a few product lines that are sold globally. One of the main criticisms of green genetic engineering is thus that it further reduces species diversity, while the business models of these companies are another major cause of protest around the world. The market leader Monsanto has come into disrepute for rigidly enforcing its patent rights and taking brutal measures against farmers whom it accuses of breaching their contracts. License contracts and the sale of hybrid plants ensure than seeds must be bought over and over again, suppressing the traditional agricultural practice whereby part of a harvest is sown anew. This produces a structural dependency that can ruin peasant farmers. In 2012 the Indian government declared a 10-year moratorium on genetically modified seeds in order to protect peasant farming from insolvency. It noted that the cultivation of genetically manipulated plants promotes agricultural concentration; the horrific suicide rate among ruined farmers is also frequently connected with the business model of the genetic engineering industry.

In Europe the stalling tactics of environmental groups and consumers opposed to green genetic engineering have thus far been successful. In other areas of the world it is seen more positively. Agrochemical companies like BASF and Bayer have consequently relocated their genetic engineering divisions to America and Asia. In 2010 there were approximately fifteen million farmers (90 percent of them in developing and emerging countries) growing genetically modified plants on 148 million hectares of land. That corresponds to around 10.7 percent of global agricultural land. In Argentina 72 percent of agricultural land was given over to genetically modified crops (soy, corn, cotton), in Brazil 42 percent and in the US 39 percent. China, however, provides an interesting counterexample: only 3 percent of the agricultural land there was planted with transgenic crops, yet the productivity of Chinese agriculture is above average. In China a hectare of land has to feed approximately ten people, more than twice the global average. This is made possible by a very labor and irrigation-intensive farming culture and the use of large amounts of fertilizers, which if nothing else shows that high-yield agriculture is possible without genetically modified organisms.

Even besides genetic engineering modern agriculture is being operated more and more in accordance with scientific and industrial methods. Laboratory-based precision cultivation (smart breeding), for example, now has little in common with traditional breeding processes. Advanced technology is being used to speed up and select the changes that occur in genetic material due to reproduction and natural mutation. Numerous plant varieties have resulted from mutations triggered by bombarding genetic material with radiation—a method that was widespread until the 1970s. Nowadays the genetic makeup of plants is analyzed using genetic markers in order to determine the best crossbreeding combinations.

Here too the aim is to cultivate new breeds or modify genetic characteristics—albeit with the difference that no foreign genes are introduced into the DNA of the new organisms. The desired characteristics must already be present in the genetic makeup of a plant in order to be transferred via crossbreeding.[18]

Modern agriculture is an enormous, global business. In 2009 the revenue of the seed industry alone was $36.5 billion—an amount surpassed by sales of pesticides ($40.5 billion) and fertilizers ($85 billion). All three sectors are highly research intensive—the two German pesticide giants Bayer and BASF each invest approximately one billion euros in research and development every year. In 2009 a total of around four thousand billion dollars were spent on food and demand will continue to rise substantially in the coming decades. Given that there is a limit to the amount by which agricultural land area can be expanded, there is growing pressure to generate much higher yields on every hectare of arable land and from every animal. This will remain the case as long as the production of animal feed continues to occupy large amounts of land that could be used for the direct cultivation of plant-based foods. Modern, scientifically conducted plant and animal breeding is just one example of the diverse ways in which biotechnological methods can be applied. Rapid progress in the decoding and recombination of genomes is constantly providing new possibilities for generating new types of crops.

Food First?

Food is the first thing. Morals follow on.[19]

—Bertolt Brecht, *The Threepenny Opera*

How far the intensification of agriculture will be driven depends not least on the dietary habits of a growing global population. The more meat we consume, the more the pressure on agricultural land grows. Currently as much as 50 percent of global plant production is used to make meat and dairy products—a number that is likely to continue rising. According to a prognosis made by the FAO in 2009, demand for animal-based foodstuffs will rise by approximately 70 percent by 2050, i.e. by more than double the growth of the global population. The reason for this is clear: consumption of meat, fish and dairy products rises in line with rising income, at least up to a certain saturation point. As overall environmental consciousness also increases in line with prosperity levels, the educated classes of the highly industrialized nations are taking an increasingly unfavorable view of excessive meat consumption, but their concern is not shared by less affluent populations. While in Germany, for example, annual meat consumption per capita fell from 97.4 to 88.5 kilograms between 1991 and 2008, it is rising steeply elsewhere, and particularly in the emerging nations. In this matter, as in others, China, India and Brazil are leading the way. In 2005 they accounted for around two-thirds of the total meat production outside the industrial nations. In the period between 1980 and 2002 per capita meat consumption in the developing nations doubled from 14 to 28 kilograms.[20] As a result, demand for animal feed is also rising. This development is taking place at the cost of staple food production and thus having a negative impact on the calorie supply to poorer sections of the global population.

The loss of calories caused by feeding grain to animals—instead of using it directly as food for humans—corresponds to the annual needs of 3.5 billion people. In Germany an average of approximately seven plant calories are needed to produce one calorie of meat. Depending on production conditions, the energy expenditure of beef production is between 6 and 20 plant calories and that of poultry production between two and four. A meat-intensive diet thus requires much more agricultural land than a vegetarian one, while meat production also increases the water and energy consumption and greenhouse gas emissions of the agricultural industry. As the bulk of the grazing land available today is already being used to excess, forests are being cleared to facilitate the expansion of cattle breeding. At the same time, more and more is being demanded from breeding animals: if limited land prevents an increase in the farm-animal population, individual animals must deliver more meat or milk. Their transformation into four-legged biomachines is simply the consequence of rising production pressure.

Whereas a dairy cow in the 1950s provided approximately six hundred and forty liters per year, by 2011 the average had risen to an unbelievable 8,173 liters. Peak performers deliver around ten thousand liters or more. That is an average of almost thirty liters per day—an amount that pushes cows' bodies to the absolute limit. Pasture-based breeding is unusual nowadays. The overwhelming majority of the at least four million dairy cows in Germany are kept in box stalls. Instead of standing on grass they stand on concrete. The animals are systematically groomed for high performance, and that has its price. They are more susceptible to disease, exhibit reduced fertility and die earlier. A quarter of them are slaughtered prematurely due to chronic udder inflammation. Statistics show that dairy cows generally live for five years. It takes two years to breed them, then they have an average of three calves, after which they are sent to the slaughterhouse, worn out. A modern cow stall with a thousand animals is essentially an automated factory. Robots perform the milking and the animals are monitored using sensors and cameras. Chicken coops now hold up to one hundred thousand animals, while pigs are bred in megastalls of tens of thousands where any breakdown in the ventilation system leads to mass death. In order to avoid the spread of disease, antibiotics are mixed into the animals' feed. In the breeding of laying hens approximately fifty million male chicks are disposed of as useless waste each year. There is no use trying to fatten them up for the table since laying hens are not bred to put on flesh.[21]

Over one hundred years ago Upton Sinclair described the conditions in Chicago's slaughterhouses in his famous novel *The Jungle*. At that time around 80 percent of the meat consumed in America was produced on the production lines of Union Stockyards. Twenty-five thousand workers were employed in this earthly inferno. During each year of the 1920s 13 million pigs and cows were slaughtered in Chicago. The meat was processed to make conserves or transported all over the country in refrigerated trucks. Cattle breeding, meat processing and consumption were strictly divided worlds. It was possible to enjoy your steak or corned beef without thinking about how the animals they came from had been bred, transported and slaughtered. Since then hygiene regulations have been sharpened and minimum standards introduced for animal breeding, but nothing in the basic structure of industrialized meat production has changed. Animals have become mere factors of production that are required to yield maximum output at as low a cost as possible. It would of course be rather hypocritical to put all the blame for this on the meat industry, while ignoring consumer complicity. People who want a frequent, plentiful and cheap supply of meat and sausage on their plates have no right to complain about mass animal breeding. There is no other way to meet the demands of the billions of urban consumers who regularly eat chicken, hamburgers and steaks. Anyone who believes in animal dignity must change his or her diet. That does not necessarily mean we have to renounce all animal products. If animals are bred using species-appropriate methods and treated respectfully we may eat them. But the supply of sausage and meat will be scarcer and more expensive.

Ultimately there are many benefits to a diet based on more grain, legumes, vegetables and fruit. It contributes to food security in developing countries, helps to limit climate change, is less hard on soil and allows for species-appropriate animal breeding. Seldom has a change in our everyday behavior made so much sense. But eating less meat is not a purely altruistic act: it is also good for us. In America and Europe excessive meat consumption has become a public health problem of the first order. Medical research connects lifestyle diseases like cancer, diabetes and heart attacks with the copious consumption of meat and sausage. In this case the saying "less is more" is actually true. For a growing number of people Bertolt Brecht's claim that moral sermons cannot fill us up no longer applies. We can afford to reflect on the morality of our diet.

Excursus: Vitamins for the Poor

Given the growing demands on farming as a provider of food, agricultural raw materials and energy crops, increased agricultural productivity is a top priority for the German Bioeconomy Council. It hopes for innovations including "the cultivation of high-yield plants and animals that, in addition to certain other characteristics, contain the ingredients for a healthy diet." This means both the breeding of plants that are naturally rich in protein, vitamins and trace elements (like iron and zinc) and the fortification of food by the food industry in order to provide better nutrition for the approximately three billion people in the world suffering from starvation or malnourishment. These people are not starving because of an absolute shortage of food but because they are poor. For the most part they cannot afford the blessings of industrial food technology. The prosperous middle classes of the world rather than its favelas, slums and townships are the target market for enriched yogurts, smoothies and dietary supplements. In an attempt to redress the balance, Nobel Peace Prize-winning social entrepreneur Muhammad Yunus, who became famous for his microloan bank, established a joint venture with the French food giant Danone. Together they developed an affordable yogurt fortified with iron, vitamins, calcium, iodine and zinc. Yunus hoped the project would help combat the malnourishment suffered by half the children in Bangladesh. The results have been mixed. According to a report in the German business news magazine *Wirtschaftswoche*, Grameen Danone erected a factory in Bogra, to the west of Dhaka, developed a distribution network and trained saleswomen who went door to door with the yogurt Shokti Doi. At first everything seemed to be going well. But when in 2006 milk prices around the world began to rise, the costs of the project went up too. Yunus pushed through a price increase—after all, a social enterprise is not a charity— but this caused sales to plummet (by as much as 80 percent in rural regions). Grameen Danone dropped the price again in many of these areas but also made the yogurt cartons smaller. Four years later the venture was at least close to breaking even.[22] What can we learn from this? Even charitable companies that reinvest their profits in the expansion or improvement of production infrastructure are not immune from upheaval on the global market. Even they cannot avoid passing on the rising cost of agricultural raw materials and energy to their customers. Nevertheless, this business model has the potential to create job opportunities for the poor and improve their diet by reducing the cost of packaging, advertising and distribution as well as the profits paid to shareholders in order to lower prices. Social and cooperative enterprise is an important element in the fight against malnutrition.

Water, Water!

Water shortages are one of the big challenges facing agriculture in the coming decades. Agricultural production is water intensive, intensive agriculture even more so. In dry locations artificial irrigation is needed to increase crop yields, while in many areas groundwater levels are falling due to decades of overuse. A research project featured in the renowned scientific journal *Nature* inspected eight hundred groundwater aquifers worldwide and found that 20 percent of them had already been greatly overused. The affected regions include the Nile Delta, northern India, Pakistan and California.[23] Dwindling water supplies are a threat to the livelihood of 1.7 billion people and climate change will continue to intensify the water shortages in many regions. Aridity and drought are spreading. America was given a foretaste of this future in the summer of 2012 when it experienced its highest temperatures since weather records began in 1895. In the grain belt of the Midwest crops withered in record time. Monocultures are particularly susceptible to extreme weather. The losses in the US, which accounts for a quarter of global grain exports, led to an unparalleled rise in wheat prices on the world market—from $5.60 per bushel (approximately thirty-six liters) in May to $8.60 in July, further limiting the already meagre rations of millions of people.

It is essential that future increases in agricultural production are not accompanied by a proportional increase in water consumption. We are simply not equipped to cope with that, especially given competition from rising urban water consumption. Agricultural water use must thus be made significantly more efficient in future, with a higher yield being obtained from every cubic meter of freshwater. Ernst Ulrich von Weizsäcker and his coauthors list numerous examples of how freshwater consumption can be lowered by 50 to 80 percent: more efficient irrigation technology, drainage designed to improve rainwater storage and the improved treatment and recycling of greywater are among the main ideas.[24] According to the WWF, Indian pilot projects involving several thousands of peasant farmers have managed to reduce water consumption by half.[25]

A study conducted jointly by the FAO and the OECD identified Israel as the global leader in water-saving technologies for dry areas. Thirty years ago Israel's agricultural industry accounted for 70 percent of the country's water consumption. Today, in spite of rising production, that number has fallen to 52 percent, with a large share coming from reprocessed greywater. A very efficient irrigation technique that is now practiced worldwide originated in Israel with an observation made by the engineer Simcha Blass: Blass noticed a tree in the Negev Desert that was stronger than its neighbors. When he investigated more closely, he established that the tree was getting water drop by drop from a leaky water pipe. Today the company Netafim, which was founded in 1965 on the basis of this concept, is globally recognized as the pioneer of drip irrigation. It has 2,400 employees and operates irrigation systems in 112 countries—a real environmental and economic success story.[26] Drip irrigation reduces the amount of water lost to evaporation and deep drainage. It also avoids the leaching of soil nutrients. Practical experience shows that it can reduce water requirements by 30 to 70 percent and increase crop yields by up to 90 percent. It exists both in high-tech, computer-controlled formats and in cheap versions using the simplest of components that even poor farmers in developing countries can afford. Paradoxically, the subsidization of water prices that takes place in many countries is a disincentive to introducing this kind of water-saving technology. In order to make the required investments cost-effective, water prices must be brought in line with real costs and structured on a sliding scale, as they already are in Israel. This is the only way to incentivize efficient use of what is a scarce resource—a further example of the extent to which political and economic frameworks determine resource efficiency.[27]

Recultivation

Compared with the billions that are being invested in breeding high-yield plant varieties, up to now inadequate research has been conducted into soil. Yet, next to looming water shortages, the continual loss of fertile land is the greatest threat to global food security. Conversely, the most likely way to increase in crop yields is to improve soil quality. Arable land is literally the foundation of human civilization. Its fertility depends largely on the soil organic matter of the earth (Latin: humus). According to the United Nations Convention to Combat Desertification (UNCCD), approximately twenty-four billion tons of fertile earth are lost in the struggle against desertification each year, while 12 million hectares of land are transformed into desert. This poses a danger to the livelihood of around 1.5 billion people. The three main factors contributing to the loss of fertile land are rapid urbanization, the salinization of artificially irrigated soil and the creeping soil erosion caused by intensive mechanical processing. Given the rapidly rising demand for agricultural products, it is not enough to slow the rate at which land is being lost. We must aim to recultivate arable and grazing land and to improve the quality of farmland in order to increase soil yields. The regeneration of biological activity in the humus layer is likewise crucial to the struggle against climate change: if the American physicist Freeman J. Dyson is correct in his assessment, a millimeter of growth in the humus layer would bind three times the amount of CO_2 emitted by the human race in 2010.[28]

Reforestation has a key role to play in the recultivation of land. Trees are a blessing for the planet. They bind carbon dioxide, produce oxygen, store rainwater, counteract soil erosion and provide natural fertilizer for the regeneration of the humus layer. They are also of the utmost economic importance, providing wood for building materials and energy, materials like cork and resin, fruits, herbs and medicinal plants.[29] A study on the environmental services European forests provide found that they bind around eight hundred and seventy million tons of carbon dioxide annually—10 percent of the greenhouse gas emissions of the countries in which they are located. In 2010 alone they provided 578 million cubic meters of wood at a value of €21.1 billion.[30]

Agroforestry, i.e. the combination of forestry and agriculture, has a lot to offer when it comes to improving soil quality. In the tropics, multilevel agriculture involving bushes, shrubs and trees is already widespread. Now farmers in Germany are discovering it too. Rows of trees planted in the middle of fields provide shelter from the wind; bind water; attract birds, bugs and microorganisms; provide shade and produce fruit and wood. In the autumn falling leaves fertilize the soil.[31] The so-called African fertilizer tree (Faidherbia albida), whose leaves are particularly rich in nitrogen, is being planted in large numbers in the Sahel. The roots of the tree are over twenty meters long and collect nutrients and water from deep beneath the surface of the earth. It is thanks to it that the continent's agricultural land area is growing again—by approximately two hundred and fifty thousand hectares per year in Niger alone. Over the past 20 years five million hectares have been reforested. Tony Rinaudo, an agricultural expert at the aid organization World Vision, describes this as the most important positive environmental change taking place in West Africa, if not all of Africa.[32] Trees can replace mineral fertilizer, which many farmers cannot afford. They improve soil fertility and increase crop yields. For this reason the World Agroforestry Centre in Nairobi has set up major training programs in Malawi, Tanzania, Mozambique, Zimbabwe and Zambia. The courses are reaching four hundred thousand farmers. The combination of coffee plants and trees has also proven successful on coffee plantations, while trees planted on grazing land increase the amount of milk produced by dairy cows.

The way in which soil is cultivated can advance or prohibit erosion. One particularly controversial practice is deep plowing, the process of tilling and substantially loosening up the uppermost level of soil, burying plant remains and weeds at a depth of approximately twenty-five centimeters. Soil torn up in this way dries out more easily and becomes susceptible to erosion, while over the years the soil organic matter decreases. An alternative practice is *conservative soil cultivation*, where rather than being plowed the soil is merely loosened up. *Direct sowing* is a method that avoids loosening up the soil at all. Special seed drills are used to make narrow insertions and deposit seeds a few centimeters below the surface.[33] Over a period of several years annual increases in soil organic matter of up to a ton of carbon per hectare and year have been measured on experimental sites using conservative soil cultivation, showing that these methods lead to additional CO_2 being bound in the soil. The volume of earthworms in soil is a sure sign of improved quality. Thirty to forty specimens are found per square meter of plowed field, whereas directly sown fields contain up to two hundred. Earthworms mix plant remains into subsoil, increasing moisture penetration and cultivating a higher density of microorganisms. They create tunnel systems of up to two meters in depth, which allows rainwater to percolate through soil more easily. They also enable plant roots to penetrate deeper into soil and access deeper-lying water stores, making them more resilient to drought. Greater biological activity in soil leads to higher yields. While conservative soil cultivation has thus far been slow to catch on in Germany, Brazil is a pioneer in this area. Just under half the country's agricultural land is now directly sown; the rest is largely tilled using field cultivators and other conservative methods.[34] *Growing multiyear crops* also improves the biological activity of soil and enriches it with nitrogen and carbon, though many more years of intensive breeding will be required before multiyear varieties of grain are available.

Another way to increase soil fertility is to use organic waste as fertilizer. A particularly interesting variant of this practice is the manufacture of terra preta (black earth). The name comes from an especially humus-rich type of soil found in the Amazon region—the legacy of an ancient Indian civilization that mixed biological waste, excrement, bones and other organic matter with charcoal and fermented it in large clay jugs using lactic acid bacteria to produce one of the most fertile types of soil on earth. Reproducing this process using modern methods would allow us to create extremely humus-rich earth, recultivate depleted soil and achieve significantly increased crop yields. Organic waste from the restaurant industry, food processing and private households is suitable for use in the production of terra preta, meaning that black earth can be produced close to cities and used on gardens and farms in urban environments—an interesting prospect for urban farming, which is growing in popularity around the world.

Agroparks

Alongside the developments described above, industrially organized agriculture is being taken to a new level. Key developments include agroparks and metropolitan food clusters—urban agroindustrial centers that integrate a broad range of agricultural processes with the aim of maximizing synergy and minimizing transport requirements. The spatial and functional integration of plant production, horticulture, animal breeding and processing reduces water and energy consumption, lowers land use and cuts emissions. It could help to reverse the equation of industrial agriculture with increased pressure on the environment. Nowadays agroparks are garnering interest around the world, but especially in developing countries with rapidly growing cities that require as effective a supply of agricultural products as possible. An agricultural center that will create jobs for ten thousand people has been planned as part of a major port and industrial development project in Caofeidian, China. The center will combine greenhouses, animal breeding, dairies, fish farms, processing plants and logistics facilities with research and training.[35]

The advantages of combining plant breeding, aquaculture and animal production in agroparks close to cities are obvious: the use of waste to produce fertilizer or bioenergy, integrated energy and water supplies, professional wastewater treatment, consolidated marketing and shorter transport distances. It also increases demand for skilled workers—while manual labor is still required, technicians and engineers, biologists, vets and economists are also needed. As skill and earnings levels rise, jobs in agricultural production are becoming prestigious again. The concentration of various areas of production in agroindustrial centers takes up less land than traditional agriculture, allowing for the protection (or creation) of relatively unspoiled landscapes not dominated by human use. It also facilitates higher yields per unit area, providing an answer to the dilemma of increasing agricultural production without plowing the last remaining undisturbed areas of land.

Greenhouses are a traditional form of location-independent plant and vegetable production. In Holland they have long since been operated like factories. Prior to now they have had a less than stellar reputation among environmentalists—they are seen as the epitome of energy-intensive agriculture—but now a new generation of greenhouses are leading the way in technology-driven resource efficiency. They make use of closed-loop water cycles, treating and recycling greywater. Temperature and humidity are controlled by computer. Surplus solar power is stored in the soil and used for heat in winter. Solar thermal and geothermal energy replace fossil fuels. All in all these new production methods are considerably more resource efficient than conventional crop growing. Compared with the 60 liters of water required to produce a kilogram of tomatoes on tomato fields, for instance, modern Dutch greenhouses with closed-loop water and energy cycles only need three to four liters.[36]

Urban Farming

In a disused meat factory in Chicago, John Edel and a group of largely volunteer enthusiasts are working on a futuristic-sounding project: the production of organic food in the middle of the city. The goal of The Plant is to grow fresh, *emission-neutral* fruit and vegetables. Not in kitchen gardens or free-standing greenhouses but on four floors of a factory building. The Plant is only one of many pilot projects pioneering the implementation of what is referred to as vertical farming. Vertical farming is the use of multilevel buildings for agricultural production. In the future, office and apartment blocks will be found alongside high-rise buildings housing food production and fish breeding. We are used to thinking of soil as the necessary foundation for food production. In fact plants only need three things: water, light and nutrients. If water is used to supply nutrients, arable land becomes superfluous. Crops can be planted in durable and reusable natural or artificial substrates that allow water and air to circulate and facilitate healthy root growth.

The technical term for plant breeding without soil is hydroponics—a form of vegetable production where plants receive nutrients from an inorganic substrate rather than from the earth. Its advantages are obvious: Hydroponic systems facilitate controlled nutrient delivery and irrigation. Temperature and light conditions can be adjusted for optimal results. Vegetation cycles become shorter; multiple harvests are possible. Pesticides and herbicides become superfluous; organic waste can be used on site for energy production or as fertilizer.[37] Water consumption is reduced tenfold or more thanks to closed-loop greywater recycling. Proximity to consumers saves energy and costs. Production is unaffected by extreme weather—droughts and storms are no longer a threat. In greenhouses crops can be grown and harvested regardless of the season; rather than being limited to one harvest per year, production is continual. Productivity per unit area improves in leaps and bounds as a result. The amount of soil required to meet the food requirements of a growing urban population falls. According to Dickson Despommier, professor of public health at Columbia University in New York and author of *The Vertical Farm*, 30 times as many strawberries can be produced on an acre (0.4 hectares) of greenhouses than on a field.[38]

Excursus: The Tomatofish Project

The Tomatofish project is a nice example of the synergistic effects of combined production processes. A research team at the Leibniz Institute of Freshwater Ecology and Inland Fisheries in Berlin has developed a facility for breeding tilapia and tomatoes in an integrated biological cycle. The technical term for this kind of breeding is aquaponics, a combination of the words "aquaculture" (fish breeding) and "hydroponics." The exciting thing about the combination is the significant increase in resource efficiency it generates. Water from the fish tanks is used to irrigate the plants, while water vapor produced in the greenhouse is cooled and fed back into the fish tanks. The water savings are astounding: traditional fish breeding systems require a thousand liters of water to produce one kilo of fish; a conventional hydroponic facility needs six hundred liters of water for one kilo of tomatoes. The Tomatofish facility makes do with 220 liters for a kilo of fish and 1.6 kilos of tomatoes—a saving of almost 90 percent. Only 3 percent of the daily water requirement has to come from freshwater; 97 percent is recycled. Rather than ending up in the shared purification plant, the metabolic products of the fish serve as phosphorus- and phosphate-rich plant fertilizer. The CO_2 exhaled by the fish is taken up by the tomato plants and converted into oxygen. The facility is emissions free, with its energy coming from a biogas system and a photovoltaic plant.[39] A further advantage is that production can take place in any location with space for a substantial greenhouse, giving customers access to fresh fish and freshly picked tomatoes regardless of location. This makes the project a perfect fit with the new trend for urban farming. A small demonstration facility is already in operation on the Malzfabrik compound, the site of an old malt factory in Berlin, and two larger facilities—including a roof farm with an area of seven thousand square meters—are in planning.[40]

At this point in time conventional agriculture is still less expensive to operate than farming in buildings, primarily because arable land is cheaper than real estate. The need to partially replace sunlight with artificial light also has an impact on costs. The more successfully solar power is implemented and the more the internal material cycles of urban farms are optimized, the more cost-effective and environmentally friendly the facilities will become. Floating greenhouses anchored on lakes or rivers near cities are a promising prospect for the future. Roof gardens growing tomatoes and cucumbers are no longer unusual. The next step will be to install greenhouses of the flat roofs of supermarkets and office buildings. These facilities will be heated with waste heat from the buildings, use filtered wastewater for irrigation and maximize the capture of solar energy. According to the Fraunhofer Institute for Environmental, Safety and Energy Technology there are around 1.2 billion square meters of flat roofs in Germany, not including residential buildings. Around a quarter of them are suitable for growing herbs and vegetables. The plants would bind almost twenty-eight million tons of CO_2 annually. That corresponds to a full 80 percent of the CO_2 emissions from German industrial operations.[41] Studies into the construction of high-rise agricultural buildings equipped with the latest in modern energy, water and buildings technology are being expedited around the world. The usable areas provided by these kinds of buildings—which can be up to several hectares depending on building height—facilitate vegetable and plant production on a grand scale, boosted by the fact that their crop yields per unit area are many times higher than those of conventional agriculture.[42]

Up to this point even environmentalists should be able to get on board. Red flags start to go up at the suggestion that chickens and pigs could be piled up in vertical farms—an idea advocated by the previously cited agropark expert Peter Smeets.[43] Smeets makes a forceful argument from the perspective of the Dutch agricultural industry: when nowadays as much as 80 percent of pork is being exported and demand is still increasing, why not concentrate pig fattening in agroindustrial complexes near ports? Imported animal feed could be delivered directly from ships to silos, with the animals being slaughtered on site and loaded onto refrigerator ships. This idea takes the transformation of living creatures into mere material for meat production to extremes. A perversion, certainly, but entirely logical in the context of globally rising meat consumption. Species-appropriate animal breeding is only possible if we eat less meat. We cannot have both a clear conscience toward animals and our daily meat ration.

It should be noted that urban farming is not an attempt to make cities more rural but rather to urbanize agriculture. It provides entirely new ways for densely populated urban areas to supply themselves with fresh food. At present we can only speculate to what extent city farms might one day replace traditional agriculture. But the more cities are able to supply their own food, the less pressure there will be to expand agricultural land areas irrespective of the costs and increase crop yields by any means possible. As a side effect urban farms create jobs and generate income for growing urban populations. Planting on roofs improves microclimates and binds carbon. The storage life of fruits and vegetables and the ease with which they can be transported is not an issue; they are delivered fresh to the table. And if nothing else, agricultural cooperatives, neighborhood gardens and local markets improve the social cohesion of cities.

A Provisional Conclusion

There is no cookie-cutter solution to the food problems of the twenty-first century—only a range of interconnected approaches. Over the coming decades agricultural production will continue to evolve on a broad spectrum between peasant subsistence farming and agroindustrial centers, organic farming and urban agriculture. Organic farming will change too. Growing food organically does not mean renouncing the findings of modern plant biology, soil science and agricultural engineering. On the contrary, it involves making optimal use of nature's productivity, which requires an ever better understanding of biological processes. Agriculture is a system of direct exchange between humans and nature. The more we know about the biological activity of soil and biological metabolic processes, the more sustainable we can make this exchange. In this regard scientific approaches to food production are the continuation of a development that began with the laying out of fields, the enclosure of pastures and the breeding of animals and plants. The aim has always been to cultivate nature, to emancipate ourselves little by little from its constraints: whether by implementing artificial irrigation systems, terracing landscapes, increasing soil fertility or breeding high-yield plants and farm animals. Thanks to an unprecedented breadth and depth of agricultural research our conscious efforts to shape nature will continue to accelerate in the twenty-first century.

It would of course be wrong to seek salvation in high-performance agriculture alone. The vast majority of the world's agricultural producers are peasant farmers; 75 percent of them own less than two hectares of land. Establishing food security in developing countries primarily means increasing the crop yields of peasant agriculture. Land rights, transport options, warehouses, favorable loans and a secure energy supply are thus just as important as improved cultivation methods. Education and training are key to higher yields and a better life for peasant farmers. When it comes to meeting rising demand for agricultural products, applied science is growing in significance across the agricultural spectrum.

Chapter 7

An Energy Revolution

In June 1993 Germany's energy companies took out newspaper adverts bleakly predicting that even in the long term sun, wind and water were incapable of meeting more than 4 percent of the country's electricity needs. Within less than twenty years renewable energy sources accounted for a quarter of German energy consumption. The country is in the middle of an energy revolution. It started with the Renewable Energy Act—introduced by the Social Democrat–Green coalition government—that came into effect in 2000. The act contained two guarantees that turned out to be crucial to driving energy reform: firstly, it guaranteed feed-in tariffs for green electricity for a period of 20 years; secondly, it required network operators to feed electricity from renewable sources into the energy grid ahead of electricity from conventional sources. The extra costs arising from these provisions are applied to the general electricity tariff. In other words, the law indirectly displaced the cost of renewable energy onto coal and nuclear power. It created long-term yield stability for investors, triggering a genuine investment boom. Germany became a pioneer for wind and solar power. By 2012 the share of energy provided by renewable sources in five of its federal states had already exceeded 35 percent.

Mecklenburg-Vorpommern leads the pack in this regard with 84 percent, followed by Schleswig-Holstein and Brandenburg, each with around 75 percent—the big wind power locations in Germany are already close to meeting all their electricity needs with environmentally friendly sources.[1]

The rise of renewable energy sources has become a motor for job growth: according to a study carried out by Germany's Federal Environment Agency, in 2011 around three hundred and eighty thousand people were employed in the renewable energy (electricity and heat) sector—twice the number there had been seven years previously. Approximately a quarter of these jobs can be traced back to the Renewable Energy Act. With 125,000 workers (including tradespeople), the solar industry was the biggest employer, closely followed by the bioenergy and wind power sectors.[2] That said, employment in the German solar industry slumped massively the following year—the Solar Industry Association puts job losses for 2012 at thirty thousand—due to surplus capacity around the world, falling prices and unmatchably cheap competition from Chinese manufacturers aided by interest-free loans and other concessions from their government. While the Renewable Energy Act indirectly supported foreign solar companies, who massively increased their exports to Germany, Chinese policy is specifically designed to support Chinese companies. Only 15 percent of the solar cells installed on roofs in Germany were produced by German companies, while 60 percent come from China.[3] The share of German companies in the global market dropped from 20 percent to 6 percent (9 percent for solar panels, 35 for alternating-current converters). Installation costs fell by an unbelievable 64 percent within six years (2006 to 2012). Admittedly the German solar industry must take some responsibility for the crisis. According to the Federal Ministry for Economic Affairs it spends an average of only 2.5 percent of its revenue on research and development (as of 2009). This amount is quite frankly ridiculously low, particularly for a young industry with high innovation potential and strong international competition. In comparison, the research and development quota in the German car industry is 6 percent, in electrical engineering 7 percent and in pharmaceuticals 9 percent.

A Price Booster or a Model for Success?

This setback notwithstanding, the Renewable Energy Act has up to now been a real success story. Almost a hundred countries around the world are investing in similar schemes for the expansion of renewable energy production. Germany is thus by no means unique. In Europe the Scandinavian nations are leading the way. By 2020 Denmark will be using renewable energy sources to generate no less than 70 percent of its electricity, with the majority coming from land-based and offshore wind power. Sweden is aiming to meet half of its total energy needs (electricity, heat, transportation) with renewable sources by 2020. The efficiency of wind and solar plants is constantly improving while costs are falling. Renewable energy has become competitive.

Nevertheless, the future of energy remains contentious. In Germany calls to slow the expansion of wind and solar power have become louder, ostensibly on the grounds of rising electricity prices, which have been blamed on renewable energy. The surcharge for renewable energy rose to 5.27 cents per kilowatt-hour in 2013, an increase of 47 percent over the previous year. For a household that consumes 3,500 kilowatt-hours that equates to a rise from €125 to just under €185 per year.[4] The main reason for the increase is the rapid expansion of photovoltaics, which accounts for a growing portion of the renewables surcharge, although the guaranteed price for solar electricity has been drastically reduced.[5] But how accurate is the claim that the expansion of wind and solar power is sending electricity prices through the roof? Objection, your honors! On second glance the issue is in fact much more nuanced. Between 2000—when the Renewable Energy Act came into force—and 2012 the household electricity tariff increased from 14 to just under 26 cents. The renewables surcharge accounts for just 3.59 cents of that amount—less than a third of the additional cost. The main reason for rising electricity prices is in fact the rising cost of the conventional energy sources coal and natural gas. Without the growing availability of green electricity they would have an even stronger impact on prices. The development of photovoltaics in particular is dampening prices on the German Power Exchange, currently providing relief of just under a cent per kilowatt-hour. This benefits electricity-intensive businesses in particular.

Industrial corporations have less reason than anyone to whine about electricity prices rising due to the Renewable Energy Act. The Social Democrat–Green coalition that introduced the act largely exempted energy-intensive companies competing on the global market from the renewables surcharge. They only pay 10 percent of the total amount. This was problematic because it distributed the burden of the act unequally, but it was nonetheless the right thing to do: the aim is not to drive companies with higher electricity bills out of the country, but to support them in developing as energy-efficient a mode of production as possible. Germany's status as an integrated industrial center for the manufacture of steel, aluminum and basic chemical materials is fundamental to its manufacturing sector, from mechanical engineering to the automotive industry. However, under the more recent conservative–liberal coalition the circle of exempt companies was widened considerably.[6] Without these exceptions the renewables surcharge would be just under a cent lower. Industrial companies also pay less electricity tax, lower grid fees and significantly lower electricity tariffs, meaning that the main financial burden of energy reform is being borne by private households and small businesses. This imbalance must be reduced in order to avoid damaging public acceptance of energy reform.

The fact that certain branches of the economy are now trying to put a stick in the spokes of energy reform should come as no surprise. Up to now they have done rather well for themselves in an energy system whose true costs have been passed on to the general public. The price of coal does not come close to covering the costs associated with air pollution and climate change. The nuclear industry, too, has been propped up by high public subsidies since its inception. Thus far there have been relatively few complaints from the business world about these kinds of subventions; in fact it has profited from them. It is obvious why energy companies are unhappy with the Renewable Energy Act: their share in the market is constantly diminishing—the rise of solar and wind power has effected a fundamental change in the *structure* of the sector: photovoltaic installations and wind power plants are predominantly in the hands of individual citizens and farmers who are either providers themselves or involved in cooperatives that are. The business model of the former monopolists is being eroded. In 2010 the so-called big four (Eon, RWE, Vattenfall and EnBW) held only 6.5 percent of the facilities for renewable energy generation installed nationwide.

Nonetheless, the fact that the criticism of the Renewable Energy Act has a hysterical streak and is obviously motivated by special interests does not mean everything can stay as it is. The scheme to promote renewable energy must be reformed and the whole market reorganized—precisely because the act has been so successful. It was intended to mix up the energy market and kick start the expansion of alternative energy sources. In both respects it has been more successful than even the architects of the law expected. Renewable sources have made a considerable dent in the market share of nuclear power and fossil fuels. Now, with a market share of 27 percent (as of 2014) and the goal of meeting at least 40 percent of the country's electricity needs by 2020, the energy market must be rebuilt.[7] The old concept of an electrical base load generated predominately by nuclear and coal-fired power plants has become outdated. The last nuclear reactors are to be removed from the grid by 2022; coal has to be phased out for climatic reasons. On sunny and windy days renewable sources are already capable of providing all the energy we need. If their production is accelerated, coal-fired power plants will increasingly have to be shut down or export their electricity at prices that are not cost-effective. There are even some days when the German Power Exchange records negative prices—in other words, producers have to pay consumers. Under these circumstances it is not even worth building modern gas power plants whose production can be adjusted according to demand. But since renewable sources are still a long way from reliably meeting electricity needs 24 hours a day, 365 days a year, a flexible power plant reserve will still be needed for the next stage of their development.

There is ongoing discussion about capacity markets and the necessary structure of a future incentive system designed to compensate producers for supplying reserve capacities. The necessary magnitude of the reserve will not only depend on the efficiency of renewable energy sources. Progress on the demand side is just as important: the expansion of renewable energy and falling energy consumption are two sides of the same coin. The cheapest kilowatt-hour of electricity is always the one that isn't used: the negawatt rather than the megawatt.[8]

The New World of Energy

Energy reform must encompass both production and consumption. Using energy more intelligently is itself an answer to rising prices: higher costs for electricity, oil and gas need not entail a higher energy bill if price increases are neutralized by improvements in energy efficiency. This applies to the electricity, transportation and heating sectors alike. Energy-efficient appliances and buildings and optimal demand management obviate the need for new investments in expensive power plants. An energy supply built on renewable energy is like a jigsaw puzzle whose individual pieces must fit together seamlessly:

- A diverse production capacity, with respect to both energy sources and systems engineering as well as regional distribution.
- Flexible reserve power plants whose production levels can be adjusted—preferably decentralized block heat power plants.
- The expansion and modernization of the electricity network in order to connect the main production centers

for wind and solar power with major consumer centers and minimize transport losses. Efficient interregional electricity networks reduce the need for expensive storage.

- Energy storage facilities that capture fluctuating supplies of wind and solar power and distribute it again according to need. Surplus energy can be temporarily stored in decentralized battery systems, for example, or in pumped storage power plants; a further option is to convert it into methane or hydrogen.
- The use of intelligent energy grids that connect producer and consumer data in real time to better synchronize supply and demand and facilitate optimal management. Energy and data networks merge to form these smart grids.
- Better integration of the three major energy sectors: electricity, heat and transportation. Electric vehicles can contribute to load management; superfluous wind power can be converted into hydrogen or methane for the production of heat, fuels and electricity according to need.
- Pan-European integration of renewable energy sources in a network stretching from the wind-swept coasts of northern Europe to the sunbelt of the Mediterranean. Integrating a broad variety of energy sources and production centers increases supply security, meaning that fewer storage and reserve facilities are required. The old opposition of central and local is outdated. A power system based entirely on renewable energy must combine maximum local supply with a supraregional network of renewable energy sources.

It will soon no longer be possible to expand wind and solar power provision without implementing these changes. There is a need for stronger coordination of production, grid operations and demand. Given that we are talking about long-term investments, steps must be taken to provide investor security. That does not mean returning the energy industry to state control. In future a combination of political regulation, public infrastructure and private competition will be required to keep costs under control and speed up innovation. Any reform in the pricing system for renewable energy sources has to secure the investment necessary for their expansion in addition to promoting competition among innovators and linking prices more closely to the market. It should combine a guaranteed base price with a demand-oriented component.[9] This kind of compensation would also extend the allocation of solar power beyond midday and promote the development of virtual power plants combining solar power and wind engines with flexible biomass power plants and storage technologies.

Alongside these developments, the integration of European electricity markets on the basis of renewable energy sources must be expedited. Promotion schemes must be brought into line with one another and electricity grids across Europe connected.[10] In the long term energy reform in Germany will only succeed through cooperation with other nations. Every kilowatt-hour of solar electricity we can export is a kilowatt-hour that does not have to be stored at great expense. Conversely, integration with other countries helps to absorb demand peaks without having to maintain an oversized and expensive reserve of fossil-based power plants. Ultimately the law of comparative advantage applies as much to renewable energy as it does to anything else: investment in wind power, solar electricity and geothermal should be concentrated on the areas that promise the greatest yields after transport costs have been deducted. That will require a functioning intra-European market for renewable energy sources and a corresponding grid infrastructure.

When it comes to energy management, national autarchy is not a sensible goal, nor does it make sense politically. Indeed, there is no reason for a supranational renewable energy network to stop at the borders of the EU. We should both be cooperating with our eastern neighbors and building bridges toward North Africa and the Middle East. One promising concept is the idea of building large-scale solar and wind power facilities in the North African desert and transferring the overspill to Europe.[11] The potential here is enormous. A study conducted by the German Aerospace Center has shown that electricity generated in North African deserts could easily meet up to 15 percent of Europe's energy requirements. Investments of around four hundred billion euros would be required to realize its potential. Whether this vision remains a fata morgana or eventually leads to concrete projects is less a technological question than a political one. It is easier to build thermal solar power plants and lay electricity cables under the Mediterranean than to reconcile the numerous players needed to bring a multilateral project like this to fruition. The political instability of the Maghreb states presents a further obstacle. Nevertheless, it remains a fascinating idea that promises to create jobs and income for the areas in which it is implemented, provide professional training to younger members of a rapidly growing population, generate environmentally friendly electricity for the agricultural and industrial development of the region and safeguard the European energy supply. Against the current background of political and economic turmoil in the Arab world, generating green electricity in the desert could give North African countries a chance for sustainable development and deepen the region's connections to Europe. The potential is huge: the solar radiation that falls on the earth's deserts in six hours of a single day corresponds to the amount of electricity consumed worldwide in a whole year.

Excursus: A European Community for Renewable Energy

If the European Union really wants to set out its stall with regard to climate policy, it must set itself the ambitious goal of switching its entire energy supply to renewable sources by the middle of the century. Europe has the natural and industrial potential to meet most of its energy requirements using wind, sun, biomass, geothermal and hydropower. An energy revolution like this would also catapult the European economy onto a sustainable course. It would be an appropriate response to the deep economic crisis currently spreading across our continent—a project that would mobilize enthusiasm and investment across Europe and reinvigorate European integration. And it would provide a boost for European industry, which in most parts of the continent has been in steady decline for the last few decades. Renewable energy is on the rise around the world. The growth rates are enormous—on average almost 20 percent per year for the period 2008–13. That corresponds to a newly installed capacity of 142 gigawatts. China is now leading the way in this area. The People's Republic is home to six of the world's ten largest solar cell manufacturers and five of the ten largest windmill producers.[12] Unless Europe wakes up to the fact that energy policy is also industrial policy it will fall behind here too.

At this point European energy policy cannot exactly be described as a success story. Nor can we seriously talk of a common energy policy. Nuclear power is not the only issue where the member states diverge. They also differ in their coal policies and are notably still competing for Russian gas supplies. The EU really is like a bunch of headless chickens in this regard. New measures must be taken to advance the expansion of renewable energy on a European scale and promote cooperation within the EU. One such measure could be to found a European community for renewable energy.[13]

The roots of European unification can be traced back to the European Coal and Steel Committee, formally established in 1951, and to the subsequent foundation of Euratom, the European Atomic Energy Community, in 1957. Euratom was established to advance the use of nuclear power and thus reduce Europe's dependence on energy imports. Since then nuclear energy, once championed as the industry of the future, has proved to be a dead end: too dangerous, too expensive and incompatible with a growing market share for renewable energy sources. The European community for renewable energy would take a different path, making Europe a pioneer of twenty-first century energy provision.

In order to reach this goal, the new community would

- support European research in the field of renewable energy—in comparison with the amount invested in nuclear research and nuclear fusion, there is a considerable amount of catching up to be done here,
- support the establishment of pilot facilities for innovative technologies,
- work to advance the development of a pan-European renewable energy network combining a range of energy sources from a variety of countries,

- help to bring into line the various national promotion schemes for green energy production,
- guarantee fair competition conditions and
- promote joint projects with neighboring countries to the east and south of the EU.

Coal: The Climate Killer

The energy sector has a key role to play in the fight against climate change. Action we take here will do more than anything else to help us leave behind the fossil-powered industrial age and embark on a sustainable future. The two main courses of action we must take are to increase energy efficiency and transition to renewable energy sources. Even for Germany making the necessary changes will be a huge challenge. It will be even more difficult for the emerging nations, which are in the middle of a turbulent period of growth. In its *World Energy Outlook 2012* the International Energy Agency claims that global energy consumption will rise by more than two-thirds before 2035.[14] According to this forecast, 60 percent of the increase will take place in China, India and the Middle East—economies whose growth is largely dependent on fossil fuels. The enduring dominance of coal and oil in the global energy system is not least a result of massive public subsidies. The IEA calculates that in 2011 alone an unbelievable $523 billion were spent to make fossil fuels cheaper for industry and consumers. So far the expansion of renewable energy has not progressed quickly enough to supplant fossil fuels. Failure to fully exploit the savings potential of more efficient energy and buildings technology is a particular problem. If these trends continue, the IEA predicts, long-term global warming will reach an average of 3.6 degrees (other prognoses are significantly higher).

Committed environmentalists would like nothing more than to create a society capable of meeting all its energy needs with renewable sources. And they want nothing less than to spend their time thinking about the future of coal, given that—next to crude oil—the conversion of coal into electricity and process energy is the main cause of the growing carbon content of the atmosphere. Yet, in recent years we have seen a surge in coal-fired power generation, particularly due to the emerging nations' hunger for energy. Coal is still the cheapest and most readily available fuel. In 2010 it provided approximately 30 percent of the primary energy consumed worldwide, just behind oil with 34 percent. Accounting for 40 percent of electricity production, it was the most important energy source in that field by some distance.[15] Coal has been used to meet almost half the increase in the global energy demand over the last 10 years.[16] Up to now China's economic rise has primarily been powered by coal-fired plants. In 2007 it accounted for 81 percent of newly erected production facilities. In 2012 that figure dropped to 65 percent, but even taking into account the great efforts of the Chinese government to promote alternative energy sources (including nuclear power), the share of coal in the country's energy production is unlikely to drop below 50 percent before 2030, especially as all its newly built power plants will probably be in operation for another 40 years. The situation is similar in India. These two countries alone account for approximately 75 percent of the growing demand for coal.

The International Energy Agency estimates that coal consumption in the newly industrialized (non-OECD) nations will almost *double* by 2035 unless serious adjustments are made. A corresponding increase in CO_2 emissions would deal a heavy blow to the climate. We must hope that the community of nations manages to agree on a global climate treaty to avert this scenario. The IEA actually underestimates the pace at which renewable energy sources are becoming competitive. For the time being, however, growing coal consumption in Asia remains the most important cause for the rise in global CO_2 emissions. Alongside the expansion of renewable energy and the improvement of energy efficiency we must consequently do everything we can to lower coal-specific carbon emissions. We should avoid the misleading label "clean coal." Coal remains a dirty business. But there is significant scope to reduce environmental pollution caused by coal-fired power plants, and from the perspective of climate policy it would be negligent not to use it, particularly when it comes to the retrofitting of existing power plants. Relatively simple measures such as improvements in process management or exchanging turbine blades can lead to considerable CO_2 savings. Every 1 percent improvement in the efficiency of coal-fired power plants reduces their carbon dioxide emissions by 2 to 3 percent.

In contrast, the much publicized carbon capture and storage (CCS) technologies are not a realistic option. Based on today's technology, CCS reduces the effectiveness of coal-fired power plants by 20 to 25 percent, leading to a corresponding rise in fuel costs. More primary energy must be input in order to produce the same amount of electricity. Then there is the as yet unresolved question of how to dispose of the huge amounts of carbon dioxide that accumulate when coal is turned into electricity. It is thus far more worthwhile to invest in energy-saving measures and renewable energy. In contrast with coal-related technology costs, costs for renewable electricity will drop in the long term, particularly with respect to solar power. New installations are becoming ever cheaper, and there are no fuel costs for renewable energy sources. You do not have to be a mathematician to see that putting your money in a combination of coal and CCS for a period of 40 years is a bad investment. During that time quantum leaps in the development of alternative energy sources will make coal-fired power plants look like dinosaurs. The future use of CCS combined with biomass power plants to remove carbon from the atmosphere is a different matter. All the indications are that future generations will have to implement a mix of reforestation, soil recultivation and technological measures to bind CO_2. But that is another chapter.

The most effective way to put an end to the use of coal would be a climate protection convention establishing binding but differentiated limits on the CO_2 emissions of industrial and developing nations. Involving emerging nations in CO_2 emissions trading could also be an effective tool for accelerating the move away from carbon-intensive growth. CO_2 taxes serve a similar purpose. If the price of carbon dioxide emissions is gradually increased, renewable energy sources will become more competitive. Expensive emissions pricing provides an incentive to make existing power plants as efficient as possible, whereas it makes building new charcoal piles less cost-effective. Finally, it is up to the old industrial nations to demonstrate that the entire energy supply of a modern society can be switched to renewable energy sources. Ultimately action is required to make a radical transition to renewable energy the right economic choice as well as the right environmental one. Germany must do everything it can to make its ongoing energy revolution a model for success.

Chapter 8

The Postfossil City

Cities are one of the great achievements of human civilization. They are where the concepts of autonomy, the public and democracy were born. They are greenhouses for science, art and culture; laboratories for technical innovation; havens for refugees and outsiders; and stages for great political revolutions. At the same time, today's cities are ecological monsters that consume an immense amount of energy, water and raw materials; emit huge amounts of pollution; and produce avalanches of traffic, rivers of sewage and mountains of trash. In the early days of the environmental movement urban metropolises were considered the epitome of man's estrangement from nature. People moved to the country, away from the aberrations of consumer society and the bustle of the city, in search of an alternative way of life. Now the pendulum has swung the other way. Cities are environmental and social flash points, but they are also pioneers of change. They are at the heart of our problems, and yet these concentrated sites of human cohabitation, with all their social and cultural diversity, their wealth of knowledge, their democratic publics, their creativity and their capacity for innovation, also contain all the elements needed to solve them.[1]

The idea of disbanding big cities in favor of decentralized settlements not only runs counter to every real developmental trend indicated by accelerated urbanization all over the world. The land use required for such an undertaking would also be an environmental catastrophe. Today, for the first time in human history, more than half the global population lives in cities, and almost all of its continued growth over the coming decades will take place there. By the middle of the century around 80 percent of the world's inhabitants will live in densely populated urban areas. Asia, Africa and Latin America are in the middle of a huge urbanization process. Cities of millions are springing up almost overnight. Megacities with more than ten million inhabitants are smashing the paradigm of the European city. They are springboards for social mobility, miracles of public spirit and proactivity, and at the same time infernos of poverty, crime, drug addiction and violence. While many old European cities are dealing with demographic change and economic stagnation, cities in developing countries are coping with turbulent growth. For both groups, there is much to be gained from going green. It has the potential to make cities more attractive and yet more resilient at the same time—in both environmental and economic terms. Investment in education, science and a vital start-up culture are crucial to creating an environment conducive to innovation and improving the future prospects of the younger generation (particularly young immigrants).

At the same time, cities must act to overcome the kinds of social and spatial divisions that kill urban communities. Public institutions and the public space play a central role in the development of urban citizenship: community kindergartens and schools, libraries, cultural centers, public transport, market squares, parks, promenades and sports facilities are places where people from different backgrounds and social circumstances encounter and form relationships with one another. The significance of this kind of public property for the social cohesion of cities cannot be estimated highly enough.

Multiply the growth of the global population to around nine billion people by living space, jobs, mobility, communications technology, food, water and various consumer goods and you have a huge test for an already overstretched ecosystem. Our current construction methods, energy supplies and transportation systems are not up to this challenge. The cities of the future will be vastly different from today's metropolises. They are on the verge of a great structural change that will affect all spheres of urban living: domestic life and work, energy and transportation, communication and culture.

Architecture and urban planning have always been cosmopolitan professions. Even in antiquity master builders and tradesmen roamed from country to country, while at the beginning of the modern era European cities engaged in active economic and cultural exchange. Today cities around the world are networked with one another. They are partners and yet also competitors when it comes to attracting investment and talent from around the world. Even if the realities of urban life in old Europe, Asia and Latin America are different in many ways, cities continents apart can still learn from each other. Collectively they are also a global political player in their own right. The most important international urban alliance is ICLEI (Local Governments for Sustainability), which has more than one thousand two hundred members from 70 different countries. It represents around five hundred and seventy million city dwellers. ICLEI provides advice and training and facilitates information exchange in all fields of sustainable urban development, supports joint projects between its members and represents the collective voice of cities at international intergovernmental conferences.[2] Faced with the paralysis of international climate diplomacy, municipalities are taking on an avant-garde role. This was demonstrated during the Rio+20 conference that took place in early 2012. While governmental delegations were mired in fruitless negotiations over hollow compromises, a global town hall meeting involving over five thousand delegates took place. Concrete projects and ambitious goals were discussed. Most cities are ahead of their countries in matters of applied climate policy.

Green and Urban

Cities around the globe are reinventing themselves. They are pioneering reductions in greenhouse gas emissions, embracing renewable energy sources, modernizing public transport systems and returning to the original concept of cities as compact spaces comprising a mixture of apartments, businesses, shops, schools, kindergartens, cultural establishments, administrative authorities, public squares, restaurants, fitness centers and parks. The *Athens Charter*—perhaps the most disastrous urban planning doctrine of the modern age—which was adopted by an international architecture convention in 1933 and further developed by Le Corbusier in the years afterwards, is finally being consigned to architecture museums. Drafted with the aim of humanizing cities, after the Second World War it developed into a program of urban destruction. Its central idea was the spatial division of cities along functional lines, separating commerce, residential areas, shopping and culture. It resulted in wide thoroughfares cutting through urban landscapes, transporting mass man between monotonous residential quarters, incongruous commercial areas and sterile city centers. The devastation wreaked by the Second World War in the old, densely built cities of Germany provided the proponents of functionally divided cities with an ideal field on which to wreak their own brand of destruction.

The source of a city's energy also shapes its infrastructure. In this regard the footprints of spacious, decentralized and car-friendly cities are very much the product of an age with seemingly limitless access to cheap crude oil. Electricity from gigantic coal-fired power plants made possible the energy-intensive lifestyle of cities that never sleep. Electric elevators, lighting and air conditioning facilitated the construction of high-rise buildings. First mass modes of public transport powered by electricity were developed—trams, underground railways and high-speed commuter trains experienced their heyday in the 1920s and 1930s—then, from the 1950s onward, the car took over. Cheap oil was the lubricant of the automobile revolution that dramatically changed urban environments. The private car advanced suburbanization—the sprawling growth of city outskirts into open landscapes—further increasing the flow of traffic. With this development commuting times increased, tailbacks grew and the automobile came to dominate public space. What had been conceived as a positive contribution to the quality of human life turned into a loss. The spatial separation of different areas of life destroys the specific quality of cities that only comes with multifunctional land use, lively neighborhoods and public squares bustling with passersby. The large housing developments that came about in the 1960s and 1970s are a concrete relic of this antiurban way of thinking. The same goes for the no less sterile subdivisions of single-family homes to which the middle classes fled, not to mention all the barren commercial areas on the edges of cities.

The impending paradigm shift toward resource-efficient cities whose energy mostly come from renewable sources will alter these structures once again.[3] The city of the future will be more compact; it will reconnect things that belong together functionally; public spaces will be regenerated and traffic organized around a tightly woven network of public transportation, electric cars and bicycles. Types of housing that consume a lot of energy, including the once so popular detached single-family home, will gradually disappear. Energy provision will be decentralized, combining a variety of solar facilities, block heat power plants and wind turbines installed on roofs into networks linked to the pan-European renewable energy grid.

Making cities more environmentally friendly does not at all mean making them more rural. On the contrary: environmentally friendly urban planning intensifies the urban character of cities. Green cities are compact spaces with mixed-use neighborhoods of apartments, offices, schools, kindergartens, restaurants, service providers and a diverse range of retail outlets. They attract skilled professionals and young families who value traffic-calmed zones and a well-developed public transport network. Prioritizing renewable energy, public parks and green rooftops not only provides cleaner air but also creates a positive image; the conservation of recreation areas near cities improves microclimates and increases the value of free time.

The structural change taking place in urban economies likewise favors a return to compact cities with multifunctional land use. The age of the smoking chimney is coming to an end—not because industry is disappearing, but because factories can be made emissions neutral. At the same time, the structure of energy production is changing; the gigantic coal-fired power plants of the past are being replaced with renewable energy and environmentally friendly gas power plants. Thanks to solar power and decentralized block heat power plants, energy production is returning to cities. The distances between commercial and residential areas are being reduced once more. Old industrial wasteland, port areas and traffic thoroughfares are being transformed into sophisticated neighborhoods. The rediscovery of the city is being accompanied by the rise of a new creative economy made up of design firms, media companies, galleries, fashion studios, software developers, cultural promoters, consultancy firms, financial service providers and research institutes seeking a communicative environment. Proximity to culture, education, day care, restaurants and health food stores is becoming an important factor in determining the desirability of locations. Young urban professionals no longer regard the car as a status symbol. Nowadays they have no interest high-powered sedans. Renting a hybrid vehicle or electric car and only paying for the miles driven is just as good. Rather than an expensive set of wheels, people are buying fancy city bikes, membership in car sharing organizations and monthly tickets for regional public transport.

There is a social downside to the cultural and political dominance of an ecologically enlightened urban citizenry and the new love of affluent professionals for city life.[4] In all booming cities gentrification has become a point of contention. The term denotes the discovery of previously neglected residential areas by the so-called creative classes and the subsequent rent increases that little by little push out people who have lived there for years. Urban environmental projects—such as the conversion of industrial wasteland into parks—can become involuntary triggers for the commercial transformation of neighborhoods. Artists, students and alternative projects are often the harbingers of socioeconomic change. In the search for cheap apartments, studios and offices they move to neighborhoods that have previously not even been on the radar of the real estate industry. They are followed by bars and more studios, the self-employed and young academics. One street of houses after another is renovated, parks and playgrounds are spruced up, greenery is planted on roofs and bike racks are built. Real estate prices climb and the upper middle class moves in.

This development is advancing through the central districts of Berlin in waves. The results are ambivalent. On the one hand gentrification brings new life to cities: run-down buildings are renovated; restaurants and start-ups bring investment, jobs and purchasing power to neglected districts; young families move back; visitors flock from all around the world and the urban economy recovers. After decades of creeping erosion, buildings and public infrastructure are modernized. Beyond a certain point, however, it becomes impossible to overlook the negative effects of this development: renovation and construction almost only happens at the top end of the market, meaning that there is a lack of cheap lodging. The creative mix gives way to a new uniformity; cultivated boredom spreads. Small tradesmen, the independent art scene and low earners are driven into the outlying districts.

It is nevertheless strange to hear gentrification talked of as a kind of foreign infiltration. Big cities are dynamic organisms; their demographic, social and physical structure is permanently changing. Attempts to maintain the status quo in low-income districts can result in a downward spiral. Schools decline, specialty stores are ousted by cheap ones and anyone who can afford to moves away. Private investment, entrepreneurial spirit and a certain number of higher earners are needed to reverse the trend. That does not mean money must be given free rein. City politics must take the necessary countermeasures to defend cultural and social diversity: by reviving social housing and promoting cooperative models, making schools inclusive and establishing a real estate policy that secures space for noncommercial projects.

In recent years the scope for change of many cities has largely been nullified under the pressure of financial need. This trend must be reversed. Action must be taken to counter the displacement of inexpensive housing, small shops and businesses. Building and planning law provides various possibilities in this regard. The spread of expansive shopping centers through city centers is not a law of nature. Take a walk through Rome or Barcelona and you will be amazed at the compact, diverse mixture of apartments, shops and restaurants has survived in their historic centers. Urban greening and socially inclusive politics are not opposites; they are two sides of the same coin.

Ecocities

More and more cities have come to realize that sustainability is not only vital from an environmental perspective but also a clear economic advantage. Nowadays there is ambitious competition for the title of greenest city. Friedrich von Borries gives an informative overview of the kinds of measures cities are taking in his essay "Zehn Thesen für die Stadt von morgen" (Ten Theses for the City of Tomorrow).[5]

- In the near future Vancouver wants to renovate all its public buildings to make them CO_2 neutral.
- London wants to become the cleanest and greenest city in the world, Paris the most sustainable metropolis and Copenhagen, by 2025, the first CO_2-neutral capital city—a goal it is making concrete plans to meet.
- New York is also going green. The official plan NYC 2030 allots investments of $50 billion to the modernization of public transport alone. Buildings are to be made more energy efficient and new high-rises constructed in accordance with the LEED (Leadership in Energy and Environmental Design) standard. This increased capital investment will be money well spent. Certified environmentally friendly buildings cost less to run and command higher rents and sales prices. Improved climate control, better light conditions and the elimination of unhealthy building materials increase employee motivation and lead to a drop in sick leave.[6]

There are three big challenges when it comes to building a sustainable city: The first is to overcome dependence on fossil fuels, increase energy efficiency and meet the remaining demand for electricity, heat and transport energy using renewable sources instead of conventional ones. The second big issue is the reduction of car traffic and the subsequent reclamation of public space. This is an economic matter as well as an environmental one: money not spent on maintaining an oversized road network can be put into public transport and the expansion of bike paths. Thirdly, every forward-thinking plan must account for the degree of climate change that is already inevitable. Expanding and connecting urban green spaces is a vital part of this. Parks, roof gardens, trees planted along the sides of streets, plants along bike paths and sidewalks, water features and inner-city gardens dampen global warming, bind precipitation, supply fresh air and provide habitats for plants and various animals.

Parks are not only a place to get away from the everyday stresses of city life; they create a sense of community and identification. Central Park is no less a part of New York than Broadway or the Museum of Modern Art. Any self-respecting city must defend its green lungs against pressure from wealthy investors keen to get their hands on open spaces in downtown areas. In New York the plan is to create new green spaces, making it possible for every resident to reach a park on foot within 10 minutes, The High Line—a former railway high above the streets of Manhattan that was turned into a public park—has gained international fame. Typically for America, the park is maintained by a citizens' action group called Friends of the High Line.[7] A debate is now raging over the extent to which the project, which was initially greeted with enthusiasm, has become a catalyst for supergentrification.[8] The park has backfired on long-established residents and opened the floodgates to investors, who are now in the process of turning Manhattan's West Side upside down. Of the 3.7 million people who used the High Line in 2011 only half were locals. Tourists as a plague—this lament is often heard in the Kreuzberg district of Berlin. Evidently the same mentality is prevalent in the Big Apple, the biggest people magnet on the planet.

New York City Council has started a campaign called Million Trees NYC to get citizens involved in planting and caring for trees. The New York Urban Food Plan has been established to promote food production on rooftops and in open spaces. Urban agriculture is the latest trend. Its manifestations range from community gardens to the use of repurposed former factories for vegetable production and fish breeding. In New York there are bold plans for a 200,000-square-foot site with the goal of setting up the world's most productive urban farm.[9] In Europe, too, open-space planning is back on the agenda. At last the people responsible for promoting economic development have got the message that attractive parks, river banks and easily accessible recreation areas are among the factors that make a city appealing.

Green is the new urban trend. The old dichotomy between cities and nature is being broken down, though not in favor of the traditional garden city with its loose construction and expansive greenbelts. The new ideal is a compact city incorporating a high volume of parks, roof gardens, greenhouses, green facades and trees planted in the streets. Not only do these things please the human inhabitants of cities, but urban areas are an often underestimated habitat for plants and animals. Many urban landscapes exhibit greater species diversity than rural areas in which intensive agriculture has completely stripped the land. The biologist Josef H. Reichholf describes Berlin as "the city with the greatest species diversity in Germany." Creatures as varied as beavers, cranes, northern ravens and even sea eagles have been sighted in the metropolitan area.[10]

Environmentally Friendly Construction

In order to really tackle climate change we must address the way humans build. The energy consumption and CO_2 emissions of our man-made surroundings are higher than those of industry and the transportation sector put together. Around 40 percent of the greenhouse gas emissions of highly industrialized nations come from construction. Less than 10 percent of that amount is due to materials; more than 90 percent relates to how we use them. The potential for savings is thus enormous. In addition to experience with previous low-energy construction projects, numerous studies show that energy consumption can be reduced by 50 to 80 percent. In combination with renewable energy sources, zero emissions can be achieved. Even energy surpluses are possible. Houses become power plants that feed their surplus electricity into the grid. While demographic change in Europe means that the main focus there is on modernizing old buildings to make them more environmentally friendly, in other areas of the world new megacities are springing up. Existing metropolises are expanding at a rapid pace; whole areas of cities are being built from the ground up within short periods of time. Given the increase in urbanization taking place around the world, the way in which these cities are built is of crucial importance for climate change and resource consumption—not only with regard to their infrastructure (transportation, energy, water management) but also with respect to the buildings where the world's city dwellers live and work.

Nowadays innovative examples of green construction that consume hardly any external energy and minimize water consumption can be found around the world:

A prime example of environmentally friendly construction is Council House II in Melbourne. It uses 82 percent less energy and 72 percent less freshwater than the old council house, while producing only 13 percent of the greenhouse gas emissions.[11]

A second pilot project is the Pearl River Tower in Guangzhou (formerly Canton), China: a 310-meter-high skyscraper with a usable area of 214,000 square meters that opened its doors in 2012 after almost six years of construction work. Originally conceived as the first zero-emissions high-rise building in the world, the ambitious plans had to be scaled back during the construction phase for regulatory and economic reasons. It has nonetheless become a model of sustainable design. Its construction was based on four interconnected principles:

- Maximizing energy and water savings by means of an internally ventilated, double- and triple-glazed facade; a combination of passive and active ventilation/cooling; and a building management system that reacts to changing light and temperature conditions.
- Absorbing external energy, primarily using photovoltaic installations integrated in the facade and wind turbines with horizontal axes.
- Reusing internally circulating energy and water for tasks such as cooling or heating the fresh air brought in from outside.
- Using highly (80 percent) efficient microturbines that can be operated with various fuels (biogas, methane, natural gas, diesel) to meet any further energy requirements. The turbines are air cooled and the warm waste air they generate can be implemented for heating or cooling purposes. This fourth component had to be put on hold due to resistance from the regional energy supplier, which was not prepared to feed the fluctuating surplus electricity into its grid—an indication of how important regulatory issues are when it comes to expanding the use of alternative energy technologies.[12]

A third project that I would like to outline here is the Urban Forest Tower designed for the center of Chongqing by the Beijing architecture firm MAD: a stunning complex with 70 staggered horizontal floors of different shapes stacked in a tower of 385 meters. The building is filled with green spaces, gardens and trees: a vertical forest designed to compensate for what has been lost in the course of urbanization. If the aim—as the planners declare—is to integrate nature into a skyscraper, it is a thoroughly artificial kind of nature arranged by man. But it is nonetheless a fascinating example of what green architecture can look like in the ultramodern age, especially as the building is reported to be packed full of every environmentally friendly technology available.[13]

An example from Zurich demonstrates that modern solar architecture can be effective even in older buildings. During renovation work, the facades of two high-rise buildings containing 170 apartments were lined with solar panels, creating a 98-kilowatt solar installation designed to meet at least a third of the electricity needs of the circa five hundred residents. Thanks to thin-layer panels that can convert sunlight into electricity without direct radiation, the northern facades also contribute to the electricity production.[14]

New materials, technologies and construction methods enable contemporary architects to integrate functionality, aesthetics and ecology in their designs. The classic Bauhaus principle of "form follows function" is being replaced by the precept of "form follows energy." The best thing about this concept is the fact that facades and roofs are regarded as surfaces for energy generation. Thanks to increasing efficiency and the falling price of solar cells, the primary goal is no longer to minimize energy losses by making buildings as compact as possible but to maximize energy gains. In order to achieve this, buildings must be designed to exploit as much solar and thermal potential as possible. This requirement will change the architectural style of twenty-first century: it will be more strongly influenced by local circumstances and climatic conditions. Construction in Madrid must be different from construction in Berlin or Helsinki.[15]

Environmentally friendly construction combines various components into intelligent systems: building facades produce solar electricity and regulate temperature, horizontal wind power installations rotate on rooftops, decentralized combined heat and power stations cater to any remaining energy needs, surplus heat is stored in the earth, vertical gardens built into the shells of buildings serve as heat buffers and improve indoor climates, water recycling reduces freshwater consumption, air conditioning and lighting are managed according to the time of day/layout of buildings and all building materials can be recycled. These are not utopian ideas; state of the art technology makes them possible. But without government promotion schemes it will take decades for pioneering technologies like these to spread to existing buildings. The long lives and depreciation cycles of buildings are the main problem. The pace of innovation is likewise very slow in the construction sector. Yet there is enormous potential for heat savings in old buildings.[16] Environmentally friendly renovation can also function as an extremely cheap employment program and a major boost to local tradespeople. Insulation, the modernization of heating systems and the installation of heating pumps are jobs that cannot be outsourced to low-wage countries. Prior to now there has been a lack of economic incentives to accelerate the renovation of old buildings. The Renewable Energy Act and its guaranteed feed-in tariffs have led to rapid structural change in the energy industry. Comparable legislation is needed in the field of environmentally friendly urban renovation. The Heinrich Böll Foundation has conducted a study on how suitable start-up financing can mobilize large-scale private investments. The most promising option seems to be a system that rewards ambitious investment in energy savings. Using a similar model to the Renewable Energy Act, financing could come from a surcharge on the price of fossil fuels (heating oil, natural gas).[17]

Technology and financing are two crucial factors in the move toward a CO_2-neutral city, but ultimately the development of an environmentally friendly construction culture depends on the various players whose interaction shapes urban development: investors, architects, construction companies, citizens' action groups, urban planners and big politics, which provides the framework for local stakeholders. For a long time energy efficiency and sustainability barely played any role in construction. That has changed. Nowadays those in the industry are expected to know about energy balance sheets and environmentally friendly building materials. In 2009 the Association of German Architects presented the Federal Minister for the Environment, Nature Conservation, Building and Nuclear Safety with a manifesto signed by numerous architects, engineers and landscape architects entitled "Reason for the World." In it they commit to sustainable planning and construction, not only with regard to the ecological optimization of individual buildings, but also changes to urban landscapes and infrastructure reform.[18] Forward-thinking policy, economic incentives, legal standards and clear priorities for urban development must be established if they are to succeed.

A City for All

Modern metropolises—particularly the megacities in Asia, Latin America and Africa—are too complex for centralized, top-to-bottom management. Of course there is a need for integrated planning that takes into account construction, transportation, energy and water supplies, schools and social services, but such planning will be impossible to implement without the early involvement of citizens in decision-making processes. Stuttgart 21, a controversial railway and urban development project in Germany, was a particularly potent wake-up call in this respect. City dwellers are becoming more self-reliant; in many cases citizens' action groups have as much (or even more) expertise than the authorities. Thanks to the Internet traditional forms of assembly democracy are being supplemented with new media for the presentation of information and discussion of public affairs. Details of construction plans, transportation projects and budgetary decisions can be put online and discussed ahead of time. In setting central targets and drawing up frameworks some room must be left for self-government, proactivity and competition over the best solutions.

A city's greatest potential lies in a lively civil society: citizens' action groups, foundations, neighborhood projects, self-managed social and cultural institutions, clubs, self-help groups and cooperative projects make up the social and cultural capital that is no less important to flourishing cities than investments in real capital. Businesses must become good corporate citizens who get involved in public affairs: as sponsors, but also as partners for schools, universities, theaters, cultural centers, social projects and sports clubs.

Urban ecological modernization is unlikely to succeed unless we act to overcome the ever-widening social divide. When cities break down into islands of prosperity and zones of impoverishment the effects reach all the way to their transport structures: When social contrasts become more pronounced and uncertainty increases, the affluent withdraw into their sedans. Political backing for public transport funding disappears and the quality of service drops, driving away even more passengers. Landlords in socially precarious areas of cities are less likely to invest in their buildings. A downward spiral sets in. Public space becomes desolate. It takes a concerted effort from both citizens and public authorities to reverse the trend. Improvements to buildings, neighborhood initiatives, residents' gardens, sports clubs, cultural projects, the establishment of small businesses and consistent action against violence and vandalism can help to stabilize communities. The key, however, lies in education and vocational training—the only things that help people escape poverty and a lack of prospects once and for all. Sustainable urban modernization is labor intensive. It provides numerous jobs for people with a whole range of skills, including builders, plumbers, energy and buildings engineers, horticulturists etc. Though the protagonists of the green city are generally middle class, it is not a project carried out by the haves at the expense of the have-nots. Low earners in particular cannot afford to live in badly insulated buildings with high heating costs. Prioritizing public property, from municipal kindergartens to affordable and well-developed public transport, is in the interests of the less fortunate.

Chapter 9

Ecocapitalism

Capitalism—or, more specifically, antipathy to capitalism—is all the rage at the moment. At conferences and in theaters the whole system is being called into question, and no wonder: with the financial markets in chaos, the centers of capitalism are in crisis. Occupy Wall Street! The protests are targeted at the heart of the beast. Admittedly revolution has been postponed for now, not least for the lack of a revolutionary subject and a halfway convincing alternative. But what remains is an enduring crisis of legitimation for market economics. There is a deeply rooted impression that unscrupulous gamblers have brought whole economies to the edge of the abyss. When the financial bubble burst, states had to jump in. The costs of the bailout were socialized—the usual story. The crisis thus further intensified the social inequality that had already been corroding Western society since globalization began to gather pace in the 1990s. Those were the best of times for capital and the worst of times for those with little more than the shirts on their back to bring to market. Highly skilled workers were in demand, while unskilled labor became dirt cheap. The economy grew, but the profits were concentrated at the top of the income pyramid. In the United States today 20 percent of households account for

60 percent of income (before government benefits); the top percent earns (if you can call it that) much more than the bottom 40 percent. The imbalance in the distribution of wealth is even more extreme. More than a third of the country's total wealth is in the hands of 2 percent of the population. In Germany too, income inequality has grown significantly since the 1990s. In 2011 the top 10 percent of earners in Germany made approximately eight times as much as the bottom 10 percent. In the 1990s the ratio was only six to one. The current average in the industrial nations is nine to one.[1]

Extremely unequal distribution of income intensifies inequality of opportunity, abrogating one of the main promises of capitalism: that everyone makes his or her own luck. The idea of working your way up is both the core of the American dream and a powerful impulse for a dynamic economy. If this principle ceases to apply, if capitalism cannot guarantee equal opportunity, it loses the main justification for its existence. If that happens there will be no use in evoking the past triumphs of an economic system that has catapulted prosperity to previously unknown heights—particularly when suspicion is rife that this progress is destroying its natural foundations. A socioeconomic system is not judged on its past successes but on its prospects for the future. And for more and more people those seem bleak: the expectation that the future will be better than the past is giving way to increasing worry about what is going to happen to us and our children, at least in old Europe. In the young societies of the south, which have only just entered the global capitalist economy, optimism still prevails.

The deformities of financial capitalism are not only economic in nature. A section of the capitalist elite has freed itself from all ties: from ties to a concrete community (a city or country) as well as ties to the honor code of respectable businesspeople. The true function of entrepreneurs lies in value creation: they make profit by bringing to market products and services that have added value for society. The exchange value of a product can only be realized if it has a use value. In order to succeed in the long run, companies must be both innovative and respectable. That is the only way to keep hold of old clients while also attracting new ones. Though this sounds like a fairy tale from times past, in essence it still applies. It is the reality of millions of small and large businesses that are working to better themselves every day. They must define the face of capitalism once more.

The separation of profit from value creation that has taken place in the financial industry corresponds to a separation of profit from accountability. This double isolation lies at the very heart of the financial crisis that has been breaking in wave after wave since the American real estate bubble burst. When losses are no longer borne by companies but instead picked up by public authorities, a casino mentality spreads. Reputable businesspeople aim to balance risks and opportunities. There is no trace of that prudence in the modern alchemy labs of investment banking. The prospect of absurd bonus payments combined with the knowledge that in case of doubt the state would jump in led to the abandonment of all safeguards in the run up to the crisis. Any lasting reform of the financial sector must thus restore the liability of banks and hedge funds, right up to the personal accountability of the management. It corrupts any corporate culture when managers responsible for losses caused by speculation are bid farewell with a golden handshake.

In spite of all the criticism, it is too early to sound the death knell of capitalism. To do so would indicate a failure to recognize the enormous transformative capacity of its mode of production. The combination of capitalism and democracy is an adaptive system. Marx thought that capitalist relations of production would quickly become too restrictive for the further development of its productive forces, ushering in revolution as the midwife of a new, socialist society. In fact capitalism has shed its skin and emerged rejuvenated after every crisis it has faced. In this regard critiques of capitalism have helped make it successful, whereas real socialism has disappeared—it lacked both the dynamism of market economics and the corrective power of democracy.

Capitalism as an Adaptive System

We do environmentalism no favors when we use it as a Trojan horse to subvert capitalism. By becoming entrenched in our old attitudes we waste opportunities to form alliances with corporations. The economy is not monolithic. Some businesspeople gain from environmental transformation while others lose out, some are potential allies and others stubbornly defend outdated business models. In between there is a whole host of companies who are fighting stricter environmental regulation with one hand and yet already working on green innovation with the other. It would be naive to expect enthusiasm for the green revolution from the coal industry, multinational oil firms or the old electricity monopolists. They are afraid that their capital will depreciate and they will lose their markets. Unless they reinvent themselves they will gradually disappear. The same process has been repeated at every new stage of the Industrial Revolution. Many companies, however, are undergoing technological and cultural change. They are preparing for a future with radically reduced CO_2 emissions. We need to let go of old grudges and support this transformation process. The left has traditionally embraced the state. To the extent that political action is needed to steer the economy in a sustainable direction it is right to do so. But it is a mistake to treat all corporations as opponents with whom we must take as hard a line as possible. Instead we should see them as a productive force. Innovative products and technologies do not come from government.

The founding fathers of socialism fundamentally underestimated the mutability of capitalism, which is characterized above all by its capacity to transform any opposition into innovation.

- The labor movement led to the welfare state and social market economics; the resulting increase in mass purchasing power did much to rejuvenate capitalism. As hard fought as the concessions obtained from corporations were, the capitalist economy profited from the rising education standards, improved heath and growing income of the labor force.
- The antiauthoritarian rebellion of 1968 galvanized individualization and creativity. From an economic perspective it advanced the expansion of the service sector and the culture industry. It paved the way for a new corporate culture more suited to a modern, knowledge-based economy than the old hierarchical order: patriarchal leadership was replaced by participatory models, decentralization and a transition to team-oriented work structures.
- The change in traditional gender roles and the push for equal opportunities for women in the workplace are increasing the talent reserves of companies. A work–life balance, variable working hours for parents and

help with childcare have become standard features of modern human resources policy.

- The consumer protection movement is helping to improve the quality of groceries, equipment and consumer goods of all kinds. Hard regulatory policy (safety and hygiene regulations), expanded liability law and a wide range of consumer information are all playing a part. Although price competition is still a factor, companies in the middle and upper segments of the market are generally competing to provide better quality products rather than cheaper ones.
- Environmental and human rights groups are increasingly putting multinational concerns under pressure to take more responsibility for the social and ecological footprints of their products. In today's market companies like Adidas, Nestlé and Apple can no longer afford to ignore outrageous conditions among their suppliers. Child labor, the exploitation of convicts and inhumane working conditions never remain hidden for long, and when exposed they cause scandals that damage companies' reputations and endanger their revenue. The same goes for practices that are damaging to the environment and human health, such as the unscrupulous implementation of pesticides or dangerous chemicals.

This increasingly moralistic tendency of markets is having a greater impact on companies at the end of the value chain than on the basic materials industry. Until now it has primarily been a phenomenon of the Western world, where companies have to compete in a democratic environment complete with free media and critical NGOs. All of which brings us to the significance of the political superstructure for the concrete nature of the capitalist mode of production: social and environmental progress result from the combination of market economics and democracy. Even before the establishment of general, free and fair elections, Germans had unions and socialist parties, a halfway pluralistic press, freedom of assembly (up to a point) and enforceable civil liberties. It was against this background that the struggle for the eight-hour day, for social security and political freedom unfolded, and these things are just as important today. Anyone outraged by the ruthless exploitation of humans and nature in the raw materials mines of Africa, by inhumane working conditions in the sweatshops of Asia or by the disdain for the land rights of indigenous people prevalent in South America must campaign for human rights, the freedom to unionize, an independent justice system and a free press. These are the most effective barriers to exploitation and plunder.

The Soviet brand of real socialism failed for reasons other than just the inefficiency of its bureaucratic planned economy. It also failed because it lacked the critical and corrective mechanisms of democracy. There is an inherent link between political and economic freedom. A functioning market economy requires due process, a critical public, equal opportunities for businesses and a functional separation of the economy from the state. Monopolies and cartels; nepotism; corruption; despotism from the police, the justice system and the tax authorities as well as favoritism toward particular economic groups at the cost of others override the regulatory mechanisms of markets. As the example of China shows, when an economy is playing catch-up this kind of model can even produce high growth rates for a certain period of time, as long as it does not choke economic proactivity and guarantees a high investment ratio. But in the long term it leads to large amounts of social resources being wasted. Authoritarian regimes become dysfunctional as soon as economic development reaches the point where creativity and innovation are required above all else. There is plenty of evidence that a modern knowledge economy not only requires a high degree of legal certainty but cannot flourish in the long run without a critical public, freedom of opinion and political pluralism.

A Mixed Economy

What do we actually mean by the term capitalism? The capitalist mode of production—i.e. the combination of private property, markets as a coordinating force and competition as a process of optimization—varies greatly depending on the geographic, political and cultural context. It has generated a wide range of different systems: from the neoliberal Anglo-Saxon model to the Western European social market economy, the mixture of freestyle capitalism and state control in China and Russia's crony capitalism, which divides up its profits between private oligarchs and the ruling elite. They differ with respect to social justice, the role of the state, the relationship between private and community property, the degree to which they use taxes to redistribute wealth and the significance they place on public goods.[2]

No country has a purely capitalist, market driven system. Mixed economies, in which private enterprise coexists with state and charitable sectors, are found everywhere. In Europe many vital services are organized by the state rather than private companies. The education system, public safety and infrastructure are financed via taxes and deductions. The use of these goods is not regulated by the market; they are available to all citizens. Health care is also a civil right; the health system does include some private providers, but their prices are negotiated collectively and payments are means tested. The old-age pensions of a majority of the population are paid for by taxes or social charges. To a significant degree energy prices are administrative prices; the structure of the energy system is largely determined by state decisions—see the energy reform currently taking place in Germany, for example. The private sector is subject to many legal regulations and political stipulations: employment law, protection against unfair dismissal, environmental protection regulations, liability law and all kinds of other rules limit the authority of business owners.

In fact, in nearly all highly developed industrial nations politics is the ultimate authority—which is not to say that politicians can intervene in the economy at will and override the momentum of the markets. A system in which politicians had such absolute power would produce a state economy with comprehensive control over businesses and the aim of overriding the regulatory mechanisms of the market. Foreign trade would also have to be tightly controlled in order to prevent capital outflow. It would be a surefire path to self-isolation and impoverishment. But even though politics has to accommodate the internal logic of the markets, it is far from being at their mercy. The public expenditure quota of a country is a good way of measuring the influence of its government on economic activity. It reveals how much of a country's gross domestic product is consumed by the state and the social security system. In Western Europe it hovers at around 50 percent of GDP. In the Scandinavian countries it is higher and in Germany a little lower, at around 47 percent. Switzerland is unusual, with a public expenditure quota of just under 35 percent.

Contrary to common belief, at around 43 percent, the public spending of the US, the birthplace of individualism and free enterprise, is of almost European proportions.[3]

The New Face of Capitalism

Given the variety of forms capitalism takes in practice, its transformative capacity and its malleability, the old leftist distinction between system-immanent and system-transcending reforms is evidently misleading. The variant currently on the agenda is the *ecological transformation of capitalism*—or what the Greens have less dramatically called an ecological and social market economy. This transformation is already underway. Just as the labor movement of the nineteenth and twentieth centuries fought for social limitations on capitalism, the environmental movement is fighting for environmental boundaries. It is sharpening consumer consciousness, altering the consumption habits of millions upon millions of people and giving rise to new institutions: international treaties and conventions, environmental authorities, a dense web of laws and decrees, taxes and deductions related to environmental issues and a whole armada of environmental associations—not least new political organizations like the Green Party, whose name encapsulates the defining project of our age. An environmental transformation is likewise taking place in science; in addition to the expansion of the environmental sciences in the narrow sense of the term, environmental problems are being examined in traditional disciplines such as engineering and the natural sciences, economics and political science. Environmental issues are regularly covered in the media and countless educational institutions are working to better inform the public.

These changes in the cultural and political spheres are also having an impact on the economy. New markets are developing: for renewable energy sources, electric cars, organic food, energy-efficient appliances and environmentally friendly building renovation. The rise of renewable energy has already fundamentally altered the German energy market. The oligopoly of the electricity companies has been demolished. More than 50 percent of facilities for the production of green energy are owned by private individuals and farmers; in 2010 the share owned by the big four energy suppliers amounted to just 6.5 percent. New business models are emerging: fair trade, ecosupermarkets, citizens' power plants, car sharing, swap sites, free software, microloans and energy contracting.[4] The charitable sector is growing; collectives and cooperatives are experiencing a revival. In fact, according the German Ministry for the Environment the number of energy collectives doubled in 2011 and has multiplied tenfold in the last decade. With regard to the financial sector, in Germany alone there are 1,121 cooperative banks with total assets of €730 billion and a surplus of three billion euros. Cooperatives generally have a solid financial basis and are not dependent on bank loans. Culturally and economically they are geared more toward sustainable growth than profit maximization. The insolvency rate of cooperative businesses is just 0.1 percent. Almost a billion people worldwide—in Germany one in four—are members of cooperatives, which are most prominent in the construction, financial, agricultural and food industries. Around four hundred and forty thousand people work in this sector.[5]

Owing to growing environmental risks, expanding markets for green technologies and products, an environmentally conscious public and growing investor awareness when it comes to the CO_2 intensity of businesses, companies are increasingly investing in energy efficiency, waste reduction and emission control in order to reduce their environmental impact. Management systems like environmental balance sheets, mass throughput analyses and ecoaudits are part of this trend. Green cultural change is also having an effect on the economy, as evidenced by the numerous environmentally oriented associations and initiatives being set up and awards being given for environmentally friendly corporate management and green innovation. The German Association of Environmental Management, which was founded back in 1984, has 550 member companies. The foundation 2° is an initiative made up of CEOs, executives and family businesses who believe it's their responsibility to combat climate change.

The fact that businesses are cooperating with environmental and human rights organizations—for instance in developing common standards for environmentally and socially sustainable products—is a further reflection of the new corporate culture. One of the best-known examples of this is the Forest Stewardship Council (FSC), the first worldwide body for the certification of sustainable forestry and the products obtained from it (wood for construction, furniture, paper etc.). The impetus for this initiative came from human rights and environmental organizations, merchants and industrial businesses in California at the beginning of the 1990s. Since then representatives of indigenous peoples have also become involved. Today the organization has over five hundred members worldwide; in 2010 more than one hundred and twenty million hectares of forest were cultivated in accordance with FSC criteria.[6] Another such project is the Extractive Industries Transparency Initiative, which brings leading oil and gas concerns together with governments, civil organizations, investors and development banks to make the cash flows from oil and gas projects in resource-rich countries more transparent. The Ethical Trading Initiative and the Fair Labor Association work to ensure compliance with the core employment standards established by the International Labour Organization. In the diamond industry the Kimberley Process introduced a certification system for raw diamonds that is designed to combat the distribution of blood diamonds.

In many cases these initiatives have been criticized for not setting sufficiently strict criteria and handing out their certificates too easily. Collaboration between profit-oriented companies and environmental associations is always something of a tightrope walk. But unless we are content merely to pontificate about the sins of others we have to take a chance on cooperation with business. In the process we will discover that companies are not one-dimensional profit machines but complex entities that employ many people who are concerned about tomorrow's world. Collaboration between consumer associations, environmental initiatives, human rights organizations, unions and corporations is giving rise to a new form of *cooperative market regulation* in areas where there is not (yet) sufficient consensus to establish binding supranational regulations. As imperfect as it may be, it is doing a lot to ensure that ethical questions are taken into consideration in economic decision-making processes.

One of the most interesting developments is taking place on the *financial markets*. Stock markets, rating agencies, insurance companies and investment funds are seismographs for future developments and trends. A number of big reinsurance companies, for example, grew wise to climate change years ago. They are funding research into climate change, educating the public and getting involved in sustainable investment schemes. Multinational companies like Munich Re and Swiss Re cannot afford to dismiss the greenhouse effect as irrelevant: they face horrendous compensation claims in the event of hurricanes or tidal waves. The ratings of institutional investors are of crucial importance to every internationally active company, and since the turn of the century sustainability indicators have taken on growing weight in such ratings. Pension funds refer to their "fiduciary duty" to reduce investor risk. The CO_2 balance of a company plays a central role in determining its future prospects. The higher the carbon dioxide emissions of its production processes and the carbon content of its products, the more vulnerable it is to political regulation and public campaigns. The coal industry, for example, could be left economically devastated by CO_2 taxes or a massive reduction in emissions allowances. Car companies with no energy-efficient models in the pipeline risk their access to the Chinese and the Californian markets.

Up to now the most successful association of institutional investors has been the Carbon Disclosure Project (CDP), a nonprofit organization founded in 2000 with the goal of making companies' greenhouse gas emissions more transparent. The project is founded on the conviction that reducing carbon emissions increases companies' long-term earning power. Once a year the CDP surveys the five hundred largest publicly traded companies about their CO_2 emissions, climate risks and reduction goals. Nowadays it also includes cities in its investigations.[7] The information it gathers has been used to produce the largest database of its kind in the world. The projects is supported by more than six hundred and fifty-five institutional signatory investors. Altogether these investors manage wealth amounting to more than seventy-eight trillion dollars and represent a majority of the highest-earning listed companies in the world.[8] The CDP is independent. Its financing comes from a broad range of sponsors as well as from membership fees and various projects. The yearly reports are published on the Internet, while members of the organization also receive access to information that is not made public. The reports influence company ratings and the choices of investors. The CDP has increased the pressure on corporate executives and accountants to develop transparent standards for reporting on climate risks.

We could dismiss these initiatives and projects as Potemkin villages constructed to conceal the same old grubby capitalism as ever. This is certainly a popular view in Germany, with its deep-rooted anticapitalist tradition on both the left and the right. Often enough there is some truth to accusations of greenwashing. Nevertheless, the allegation that environmentalism is nothing but a marketing trick for most companies betrays ignorance. It demonstrates a lack of awareness of how open to social questions many companies have become nowadays and how important a role environmental issues play in their corporate structures. Environmentally ignorant companies risk both losing moral capital and missing out on the markets of tomorrow.

The Economics of Sharing

You want to spend your holiday in a foreign city but don't want to pay for a hotel room? No problem: look for someone to swap your apartment with! Collaborative consumption is a new trend that is growing in popularity around the world.[9]

We have the Internet to thank for this development: swap sites make it quick and easy to find people who have things you need. The spread of digital models for borrowing, renting and exchanging is giving rise to new business models founded on trust: trust between swappers that each will treat the belongings of the other with respect, despite the fact that they have never laid eyes on one another. More and more new Internet companies and charitable initiatives are springing up with the aim of bringing together people with things to exchange, share or give away. *Time* has even identified this new type of consumption as one of the ten big ideas that will change the world.

Cooperative forms of use are not new: apartment sharing, libraries, laundromats, carpooling, returnable packaging systems and agricultural machinery syndicates are all based on the concept of communal use. Second-hand shops are also a way of sharing and exchanging things. At a given level of private consumption sharing reduces waste of scarce resources. Take the example of a privately owned drill: on average drills are used for 45 hours over the course of their lives. But they *can* be used for over three hundred hours. One machine circulated between different users can replace five to six further devices, saving money, raw materials and energy. The only overheads involved are those required to get the device from the person who had it last. As more users take part and more devices become available, the chance of getting one exactly when you need it improves. Machinery rental is a commercial variant of this model. Until now this kind of consumption has had a rather niche existence. The inconvenience of lending and exchanging as well as the high availability of cheap products have stood in its way. The idea of cooperative use really began to gather momentum with the advent of online swap sites. In 2009 in Germany, three students founded a clothes exchange site called Kleiderkreisel. Three years later the site had 380,000 (mostly young and female) members wanting to sell, exchange or even give away old clothes. The project has an anticonsumerist streak (the website declares the aim of fighting waste in style) and caters to a desire for distinctive fashion and individual style: instead of buying clothes off the rack, women put together outfits from the comprehensive selection on offer.[10] As well as providing a forum for the exchange of goods, Kleiderkreisel serves as a social network where tips can be exchanged and various topics discussed.

One of the first people to identify this new culture of sharing was Rachel Botsman, the Harvard graduate and author of the book *What's Mine is Yours*. Today auction sites like e-bay are being joined by portals whose focus is on sharing and reuse rather than ownership. A culture of sharing allows for consumption with a good conscience: someone else gets the things I no longer want or need. The Internet is playing a central role in its growing popularity. The web is built on the principle of sharing information, texts and music, whether in a commercial capacity or not. New information and communications technologies have significantly reduced transaction costs and caused supply to snowball. According to the online platform mesh-it, 7,377 companies in 136 countries have now committed to cooperative consumption.[11]

Having come from small beginnings, car sharing—i.e. making use of a shared fleet of vehicles when the need arises—has developed into a booming business in which even Deutsche Bahn and major car companies are now involved. The newest trend is called car2go: when you need to drive somewhere you use a smartphone to locate an available rental car, open the car using an electronic seal, enter your personal PIN number and then off you go. You simply leave the car at your destination: use instead of ownership. Payment, which is calculated by the minute, is made by direct debit. The same principle can be applied to electric bikes or scooters. Half a year after the Daimler subsidiary car2go opened for business in Berlin around twenty-five thousand customers had registered. They have 1,200 city cars at their disposal. With other car companies offering similar services, automobile manufacturers are transforming from vehicle sellers into providers of mobility services. That might sound futuristic, but it corresponds to a real growing trend among young city dwellers. The car is no longer a status symbol that people simply have to own. It is there to be used when needed; otherwise there are bikes and the subway.

The concept of using rather than owning can also be applied to the relationships between companies and customers. Leasing is already a common practice: in exchange for a fee lessees are given access to office buildings, cars, machinery, telephone systems, computers or medical technology for a certain period of time. During this time they are responsible for maintenance and repairs. Afterwards the leased objects are returned to the manufacturer (or the rental company). One advantage of the take-back obligation is that manufacturers and merchants retain responsibility for the entire life cycles of products. It is thus in their interests to make their products as durable, low-maintenance and recyclable as possible. This helps to counteract our cheap, throwaway culture and leads to more efficient use of resources. Recently even chemical leasing—not the leasing of chemicals, but of chemical services such as car-body painting or cleaning/waterproofing services for materials—has become a possibility. Once the lease period is up the substances used are taken back and recycled.

The interest of the provider thus shifts from maximizing the amount of chemicals sold to ensuring that they are handled as efficiently as possible. A study conducted by the Institute for Prospective Technological Studies calculated the revenue potential for chemical leasing in the EU to be €77 billion. That corresponds to approximately 14 percent of the revenue of the European chemical industry.[12]

Chapter 10

The Politics of Environmental Transformation

A good economic order is strengthened by the "imperative of responsibility."[1] This is true at every level of the system, from the countless everyday decisions of consumers to the investment decisions of large companies. One of the reasons decentralized market economies are superior to planned economic systems is that they hold consumers and corporations responsible for their actions. Where this principle is suspended—as in broad segments of the financial sector—market failure is inevitable. Anyone who is in favor of self-organizing systems should also be able to get on board with the idea of the market as a decentralized system of control predicated on the interaction of numerous producers and consumers whose talents, capabilities, preferences and value judgments are reflected in supply and demand. Pricing reduces a range of data and qualities to quantitative values, thus allowing them to be compared. No planned economy can match the complexity and elegance of markets. However, even markets require certain things that they cannot provide for themselves.

These include the ecological building blocks of all economic activity (soil, air, water and a climate favorable to human life), but also a whole series of social conditions: legal certainty, nonviolence, a well-trained labor force, modern infrastructure, a stable financial system, market transparency, the free flow of information and equality of competition. To this extent, functioning *markets* always require a functioning *state*. Hardly any companies pay their taxes willingly, but they are all dependent on efficient government. The Scandinavian model shows that a high public expenditure quota can even benefit private enterprise when tax revenue is invested in well-developed public services rather than wasted.

Environmental crises such as climate change build up over decades. Most companies are not even operational for that long. Their horizons are determined by the time they have to generate a return on their investments. If that time is cut short under the pressure of the financial markets, the scope for entrepreneurial action is also reduced: short-term returns trump long-term thinking. The risk that climate change may spiral out of control is thoroughly pertinent information for many companies. They are beginning to examine the risks involved for them and are looking for alternative business models, but ultimately it is the political framework that will determine how quickly the switch to climate-friendly operations and technologies takes place. If process and product innovations do not become profitable (or take a very long time to do so) companies have limited room for maneuver. The task of environmental regulatory policy is to strike an optimal balance between micro- and macroeconomic good.

The political scientist Claus Leggewie makes a subtle distinction between limits *to* growth and limits *for* growth.[2] The difference is bigger than it at first seems.

Which do we have to restrict: economic growth per se or the consumption of natural resources? Here the concept of environmental guardrails—indicators for sustainable growth deduced from the limits of the biosphere—comes into play. The guardrails include upper limits for greenhouse gas emissions as well as targets for reducing land use, increasing energy efficiency and recycling raw materials. It must be left to competition to determine how these goals can best be reached. In ordoliberal terms this approach can be described as a regulatory framework for an environmentally friendly market economy.[3] It aims to steer economic growth in a sustainable direction while actually accelerating it: the transition to a carbon-neutral mode of production requires an increase in innovation and entrepreneurial spirit in the best sense of the word.

The task of the state is not to slow the change taking place in the structure of the environment due to the activities of established sectors and providers, but to moderate it so that it can proceed in a social acceptable way. Subventions for old industries are counterproductive when they result in the preservation of uncompetitive technologies and products instead of facilitating their transformation. In promoting a thriving economy, governments should above all be aiming to promote innovation. In the short term greater tax relief for research and development spending reduces tax revenue, but it pays off in the long term. The more investors and companies believe that the future of the economy lies in sustainable products, technologies and services, the more money they will invest in this area. Politics must consequently send clear signals to the markets that only environmentally friendly solutions will succeed in the long run. It must create reliable conditions for long-term investment profitability. Investment security has up to now been the big advantage of the German

Renewable Energy Act over the kind of short-term government support renewable energy receives in the US, where Congress must reapprove the extension of tax credits for wind and solar installations each year. We must not squander this advantage.

Instead of coming up with more and more tricks to restrict, regulate and control enterprises and consumers our goal should be to make allies of them, and even pioneers of solutions to the environmental questions at hand.[4] That of course means treating them as potential contributors to environmental change rather than our principal opponents. Corporations bring together a wealth of skills and innovation power. In order for them to make sustainable use of these capacities, markets must be modeled in such a way as to make ecointelligent investments cost-effective. There is a whole range of methods that can be combined to achieve this: resource taxes; levies on emissions; more costly CO_2 allowances; higher efficiency standards for vehicles, buildings and devices; sustainable research and infrastructure policy; financial support for pilot projects and demonstration facilities; expanded corporate liability and environmentally friendly public procurement policy.

High environmental standards initially involve additional costs. As a result they do not usually meet with enthusiasm among trade associations. Energy and resource-intensive companies are usually the ones to raise alarm and warn about serious competitive disadvantages. Yet the German case shows that ambitious standards improve the competitiveness of industry in the long run: they advance process and product innovations, increase resource efficiency, lower the costs of waste disposal and generate pioneer profits on the global market. Environmental innovation pays off on a macroeconomic level too. Better air quality reduces the need for health care spending, while a growing renewable energy quota lowers the import bill for oil, gas and coal and boosts domestic value creation. The British economist Nicholas Stern has shown that preventative action against climate change pays off: the longer we wait to reduce greenhouse gas emissions, the greater the resulting growth and prosperity losses for the global economy are. Taking no action is the most expensive option. Investments in alternative energy, resource efficiency and environmentally friendly technologies secure the basis for long-term growth.[5]

Environmental regulatory policy requires a legal framework that guarantees long-term commitment to sustainability, independent of administration changes. The balanced-budget rule recently introduced into the German constitution—which obligates the federal government as well as the 17 states to close the gap between regular revenue and expenditure—provides this kind of security in matters of fiscal policy. A comparable commitment to environmental goals has not yet been established. The Stability and Growth Act of 1967, which is still in force today, describes four desirable policy outcomes: economic growth, a high employment rate, low inflation and a balance between exports and imports. There is nothing wrong with these goals in themselves, but they miss out something crucial: they completely ignore environmental considerations and likewise engender no obligations with respect to social participation and the (in)equality debate. A reform of the law to bring it up to date is overdue. It must be centered around the three pillars of sustainable development: economic, social and environmental sustainability.[6]

Prices Must Tell the Environmental Truth

In order for markets to function effectively, the state—in its capacity as "the ideal personification of the total national capital" (Engels)—must guarantee certain conditions, including the availability of transparent product information and undistorted prices that reflect the real cost of goods and services. Currently it is not doing a very good job of meeting either condition. The amount of information manufacturers are required to provide must be increased in order to give consumers more freedom of choice. For instance, it should be made obligatory for all electric goods to be labeled with details of their energy efficiency, as is already common with household appliances. The climatic and social balance of consumer goods must likewise be made as transparent as possible. That can best be achieved by way of certificates providing information about environmental quality and social criteria—including fair working conditions as defined by the ILO. You can't tell by looking at a football whether or not it was manufactured in a Chinese penal camp. If importers are forced to reveal the origin of their products many consumers will listen to their consciences rather than simply opting for the cheapest price. To be on the safe side they should choose products labeled as fair trade, organic, recyclable etc.

Even more important than product-specific information, however, are the prices themselves. In order for market prices to act as a regulatory mechanism they must represent the costs of products as completely as possible. Allowing companies to use the atmosphere as a free dumping ground for their CO_2 emissions leads to fossil fuels being overused. If the cost of long-distance transportation only reflects a fraction of the resulting environmental damage the structure of the economy becomes extremely transport intensive. This is why from early on the green movement has called for prices that tell the environmental truth. Politicians should not set prices, but they can send price signals—for example by imposing taxes and levies designed to make environmental consumption more expensive. Since the primary aim here is to minimize environmental consumption rather than to create additional income for the public purse, income taxes or social security contributions can be lowered in return. This is the basic idea behind environmental tax reform—providing economic incentives to use resources more efficiently and thus steering innovation in a sustainable direction.[7]

Owing to the price relationship between labor and natural resources, in recent decades average labor productivity has risen much faster than productivity in the use of raw materials. Nature does not send invoices or make labor agreements, which tends to mean that producers pay less for natural resources (soil, water, forests, fish etc.) than they are worth: they pay for making resources economically usable but not for their regeneration. The taxation system further intensifies the disparity in price between resources and labor. In Germany more than 60 percent of public-sector financing comes from taxes and deductions on earned income, which drives up wage costs. This kind of system is economically irrational. It raises the entry threshold to the job market, particularly for less-qualified workers, and increases the incidence of irregular working conditions. In contrast, taxes on environmental pollution or the consumption of resources contribute just over 5 percent to the national income. This disparity is further intensified by numerous environmentally counterproductive tax credits and subsidies, including subsidies for coal mining, commuter tax credits, a tax exemption for aviation fuel and tax breaks for high-powered company cars. We should at least begin to dismantle these benefits. Half of the resulting additional income could go to paying off debts, with the other half being used to boost green innovation.

Protecting the Global Commons

By agreeing to fiscal discipline, the Eurozone countries have voluntarily shackled themselves in order to limit the temptation of debt. The same kind of obligation should apply to environmental sustainability. What might a balanced-environmental-budget provision look like? There is certainly no general formula for the sustainable use of natural capital. But it is entirely possible to set quantitative limits to deal with certain environmental problems—particularly climate change. Given the correlation between global warming and the enrichment of greenhouse gases in the atmosphere, it is possible to deduce upper limits that future emissions must not exceed if we are to preserve our livelihood. The big difficulty lies in reaching a global consensus as to what this maximum should be and how it should be divided between almost two hundred countries. Up to now diplomacy has failed to cope with the challenge of climate change. The United Nations Climate Change Conference scheduled to take place in Paris in December 2015 might be the last chance to reach a binding agreement—and not a moment too soon. Yet, central players in the global economy still perceive a binding convention—one that would stipulate drastic reduction obligations for the OECD countries as well as a cap on emissions for the developing countries—as a threat to their growth prospects. In this regard they are unfortunately of one mind with critics of growth who argue that a shrinking economy is the only way out of the global environmental crisis. It is thus all the more important that economic growth be separated from CO_2 emissions on a broad scale—that will help smooth the way to a global climate treaty.

It is possible to take the analogy with financial policy even further: do we need new, independent authorities to guarantee environmental stability just as the central banks preserve financial stability? Central banks are (at least ideally) beyond the direct reach of parliaments and governments. Their governing bodies are appointed rather than elected. They stand outside representative democracy. This flaw is accepted in order to provide a corrective to the profligate tendencies of political systems. The independence of central banks is intended to prevent governments from simply printing money to finance their spending. Applying this notion to the problem of climate stability, the question arises: what institutional provisions are necessary to prevent an inflationary increase in CO_2 emissions? Might the answer lie in an international climate bank charged with guarding climatic stability? Like a central bank it would have the sole right to grant CO_2 allowances and reduce them where necessary to avoid overheating the earth. This kind of climate bank (or climate agency) could act as the custodian of a global climate treaty. In order for it to do so the nations of the world would have to come to an agreement over its mandate and mode of operation. It would be naive to think that it could be entirely independent: it is hard to imagine states agreeing to transfer so much of their sovereignty to an authority over which they have no influence. Nongovernmental organizations, scientists and other civil institutions could be involved in an advisory function, as is the case with UN institutions.

Another idea in the same vein would be to establish an international ocean authority to grant fishing rights, regulate the exploitation of maritime raw materials and thus preventing overuse of the seas. It could be set up on the basis of the United Nations Convention on the Law of the Sea, which already builds on the idea of a common human heritage. This notion underlies the three international institutions that were set up to enforce the convention and handle disputes: the International Tribunal for the Law of the Sea, the International Seabed Authority and the Commission on the Limits of the Continental Shelf.

The Arctic will be the next flash point in the conflict between climate protection and raw materials production. According to the estimates of the United States Geological Survey, up to 30 percent of the world's natural gas reserves and approximately 13 percent of its as yet untapped oil reserves lie in the northern polar region. Around 80 percent of these resources are believed to be in the natural mineral deposits of the Arctic Sea.[8] Competition over the the Arctic's resources has already begun, helped by the rising temperatures that are causing the ice on the edges of the Arctic Ocean to melt, at least in summer, and opening the sea route between northern Europe, the northeast coast of America and Asia. The time for a general protection convention analogous to the Antarctic Treaty has probably already passed. In that treaty, which was signed back in 1959, the neighboring countries agreed to suspend their territorial claims to the Antarctic, preserving the uninhabited territory between 60 and 90 degrees south latitude for international research and keeping it free of military activity. The Protocol on Environmental Protection to the Antarctic Treaty, which came into effect in 1991, reinforces the area's character as a nature reserve and forbids the extraction of raw materials.[9] Now that the neighboring countries—Russia, the US, Canada, the Scandinavian countries and Iceland—have already tasted blood, it may no longer be possible to establish a similarly far-reaching agreement for the northern polar region. The minimum goal must be an international framework convention limiting the exploitation of raw materials, establishing binding safety standards, laying down rules for sustainable use and guaranteeing international monitoring—rules and standards that could also check the looming militarization of the Arctic. We are already seeing the first signs of a potential armament led by Russia. Currently there is only the Arctic Council, a loose forum for coordination between the riparian states. That is not enough to guarantee the protection of sensitive Arctic ecosystems, particularly given the attractive raw material deposits and potential for profits it holds. Developing a common Arctic policy for the European Union, Norway and Iceland could be the first step to international regulation.[10]

Regardless of what form they ultimately take, the challenges of the twenty-first century require a new level of *global cooperation* and *transnational institutions* to protect the global commons on which human civilization depends: the sea, which helps to regulate the global climate and is a valuable source of protein; old-growth forests, which are the green lungs of the earth and a treasure chamber of evolution; and the atmosphere, which provides a protective medium between us and space. Because they do not belong to anyone they have been badly treated up to now. They have served as a source of raw materials and a dump for pollutants. The future stability of the ecosphere depends on whether or not a resilient authority can be established in the coming years to protect global public property from overuse and ensure its sustainable reproduction. Such a regime will require the prioritization of international cooperation over national selfishness, legally binding conventions and the capacity to enforce them.

The Green New Deal

In order for industrial society to make the transition to a sustainable economic system there must be an *increase in the pace of innovation and in investment*, in both the private and public sectors. Ecological transformation means far-reaching reorganization of the industrial apparatus and of public infrastructure, similar to what took place during the rapid phases of modernization at the end of the nineteenth century and after the Second World War. It is worth reviewing some of the necessary changes in order to illustrate the extent of the challenge we face: The capacity of rail networks must be doubled (at least) to facilitate an appreciable shift away from automobile transport. In addition there must be investment in regional public transport in order to relieve cities of car traffic. The rate at which old buildings are modernized must rise to 2 percent per year in order to make building stock as energy efficient as possible by the middle of the century. Ongoing energy reform calls for enormous investment in the further expansion of renewable energy sources, highly efficient gas power plants and the expansion of electricity storage facilities. Regional and supraregional electricity networks must be expanded. A zero-waste economy needs a comprehensive system of reuse and recycling. The development of second-generation biofuels must be advanced. The transition to electromobility requires highly efficient battery technology and a far-reaching reorganization of the car industry. In order to increase energy efficiency there must be continuous investment in buildings and industrial processes. The chemical industry must replace oil with organic raw materials. Biotechnological processes will revolutionize industrial process engineering. In the agricultural sector organic cultivation methods must be substituted for chemical fertilizers and pesticides. Agriculture and industry will be linked in synergetic cycles. High-tech city farms will supply fresh vegetables and fruit to surrounding areas. And the physical world will be interconnected by a worldwide information and communications network.

This all requires massive investment in research and development as well as in the modernization of real capital. In order to achieve an 85 percent reduction in CO_2 emissions by 2050, it is estimated that the German energy sector alone requires investment of five hundred billion euros. The lion's share (three hundred million euros) is needed to improve the energy efficiency of buildings. Other areas where large investments are required include railway infrastructure and electromobility. It should be noted that these figures refer only to the additional expenditure needed over and above a less ambitious scenario with a reduction in CO_2 emissions of 62 percent.[11] Improved energy efficiency and the expansion of renewable energy are connected with high initial investments that pay for themselves over time thanks to reduced energy imports and lower operating costs. According to various studies, energy savings will surpass additional investments from the mid-2030s onwards. In 2011 the cost of OECD oil imports alone came to the unbelievable sum of a trillion dollars. Add gas and coal imports and you have enormous potential savings that could be converted into domestic investment and jobs. Thanks to the expansion of renewable energy sources and increased energy efficiency Germany avoided imports valued at €7.4 billion in 2010.[12]

In a growing economy higher investments can be financed from current revenue. In contrast, in stagnant or shrinking economies private and public spending must be drastically reduced to finance rising investment. In aging societies, where pressure on state benefits is high, this is an almost impossible political goal. Conversely, rising investment leads to higher employment, rising demand and increased revenue. It drives economic growth, as evidenced by the strong correlation between investment ratios and growth rates. Green growth is essentially the product of higher (and, compared to current levels, rising) investment and a higher pace of innovation. "Green growth means altering the course of economic growth so that the investments it requires accelerate growth and create new jobs."[13] The environmental economist Carlo Jaeger calculates that net investment must be raised from the current level of 5 percent to around 8 percent of the national income over the coming decades if the ecological transformation is to be successful. Even in rich countries like the US, Germany or Japan an increase in net investment ratio of just over 50 percent would significantly increase economic growth.

How should and can these additional investments be financed? A least for the public sector, going further into debt is not an option. The mutually agreed balanced-budget rule will drastically limit the German government's room for maneuver in this respect. By 2020 the federal states will be obliged to balance their budgets. There is no way around the fact that a higher share of national income must be productively invested: "Since net investments are mostly financed by investment income, the amount of investment income that must be productively invested also has to rise."[14] Interest, dividends and other investment income makes up 30 percent of the national income. Only a sixth of this is reinvested. The Renewable Energy

Act, which has made millions of citizens coowners of the means of energy production, is an example of the successful mobilization of private investments. Better tax relief options for investments in research and development could lead to similar success. The other option is to increase taxes for the rich in order to finance investment in education, science and environmental innovation. Asking more from those who are better off is not merely a question of distributive justice; as long as the additional income is invested productively it increases the potential for innovation and growth.

Contrary to past practice, governments must set clear priorities for investments in future prosperity. Education, research and the modernization of public infrastructure must take priority over transfer payments. That might sound heartless to some people, but given the demographic change taking place in Europe it is the only way to ensure the continued existence of the welfare state.

European countries will only escape the debt trap with a combination of fiscal discipline and sustainable economic growth. Consolidation and investment are two sides of the same coin. Our continent still has what it takes to keep up with global innovation competition: industrial competence, highly innovative companies, a dense network of universities and research institutions and a skilled workforce. What it lacks are ambitious European projects capable of catalyzing the green industrial revolution, e.g.:

- the expansion of the transnational electricity grid as the nervous system for a network of renewable energy sources stretching from Scandinavia to North Africa,
- the modernization of European rail transport,
- a collective European initiative to promote electromobility and

- the expansion of European research programs on key environmental technologies.

Germany can play a pioneering role in all this. The decision to phase out nuclear power was critical: it has accelerated the move toward a resource-efficient solar-powered society. Other industrial nations are watching very closely to see how we fare. We do not have to return to a way of life shaped by self-denial, prohibition and bitter distribution conflicts. It is possible to create a world in which nine billion people lead contented, self-determined lives. If in future Europe wants to be more than just a large open-air museum, it must lead the way toward ecological modernity.

Notes

Introduction The Decline of Modernity or the Beginning of a New Chapter?

1 See Werner Plumpe, "Konjunkturen der Kapitalismuskritik (Cycles in the Critique of Capitalism)," *Merkur: Deutsche Zeitschrift für europäisches Denken* 757 (2012): 523–30.
2 It is not the "clash of civilizations" identified by Samuel Huntington as the new axis of conflict in world politics that is shaping the global situation, but the conflict between modernity and restoration taking place within individual societies. Its battlegrounds are the relationship between church and state, the struggle for gender equality and clashes between pluralism and homogenization, liberal democracy and authoritarian rule.
3 Paul J. Crutzen, "Geology of Mankind," *Nature* 415 (2002): 23.
4 Christian Schwägerl, *The Anthropocene: The Human Era and How It Shapes Our Planet* (Santa Fe: Synergetic Press, 2014). Schwägerl quotes from Erle Ellis and Navin Ramankutty, "Anthropogenic Biomes," The Encyclopedia of Earth, accessed November 15, 2014, http://www.eoearth.org/view/article/150128/.
5 Johann Wolfgang von Goethe, *Faust I & II*, trans. Stuart Atkins (Cambridge, MA: Suhrkamp/Insel, 1984), 291.
6 *Frankenstein* appeared in 1818, while *Faust II* was published in 1832, a few months after Goethe's death. He had completed the first part in 1805, only resuming work on the material 20 years later.

7 See the critical discussion of the concept of the green economy in Barbara Unmüßig et al., *Critique of the Green Economy: Toward Social and Environmental Equity* (Berlin: Heinrich Böll Foundation, 2012). As much as we require a more rigorous concept of green economics, it would be wrong to abandon the idea altogether.

8 See Tim Jackson (professor of sustainable development at the University of Surrey, UK), *Prosperity without Growth: Economics for a Finite Planet* (London and New York: Earthscan, 2009).

9 Wolf Biermann is a German singer and poet who became famous for his opposition to the government of the former East Germany.

10 Meinhard Miegel in an interview with the *Frankfurter Allgemeine Zeitung* newspaper, August 11, 2012, 33.

11 Martin Jänicke, "Radikal schrumpfen, radikal wachsen (Radical Shrinkage, Radical Growth)," *Böll.Thema,* May 2011, 30–31. Jänicke has been involved in environmental innovation policy for decades. See his book *Megatrend Umweltinnovation: Zur ökologischen Modernisierung von Wirtschaft und Staat* (The Megatrend of Environmental Innovation: On the Ecological Modernization of Economies and States) (Munich: Oekom, 2008).

12 2010 weekly report no. 24, German Institute for Economic Research, accessed November 15, 2014, http://www.diw.de/documents/publikationen/73/diw_01.c.357505.de/10-24-1.pdf.

13 The United Nations Environment Programme (UNEP) defines a green economy as an economic system that contributes to greater human well-being and social equality, reduces environmental risk and works to avoid shortages of natural resources.

14 Cf. Ottmar Edenhofer and Michael Jacob, "Die Illusion grünen Wachstums (The Illusion of Green Growth)," *Frankfurter Allgemeine Zeitung,* March 2, 2012. The authors argue that a move toward resource efficiency and renewable energy sources is not enough to stop climate change on its own: given that the supply of fossil fuels is so huge, there is urgent need for a global climate convention limiting access to it. "Green growth cannot replace this kind of regulatory framework. It can, however, help to bring it about."

15 See the study *International Resource Politics: New Challenges Demanding New Governance Approaches for a Green Economy* (Berlin: Heinrich Böll Foundation and Wuppertal Institute for Climate, Environment and Energy, 2012).
16 A wealth of concrete examples of how efficiency is being revolutionized in the twenty-first century is provided in Ernst Ulrich von Weizsäcker et al., *Factor Five: Transforming the Global Economy through 80 % Resource Productivity* (London and Sterling, VA: Earthscan, 2009).
17 German CO_2 emissions rose slightly in 2013–14, primarily because around half of the country's nuclear power plants have been shut down in recent years and partially replaced with electricity from coal-fired plants. They will fall again as renewable energy sources increasingly replace coal-fired electricity and the energy efficiency of the construction and transportation sectors improves—the goal is a 40 percent reduction by 2020.
18 See Paul Hawken et al. in the classic text *Natural Capitalism: Creating the Next Industrial Revolution*, rev. ed. (London and Washington, DC: Earthscan, 2010), 2.
19 See Ernst Ulrich von Weizsäcker, *Earth Politics* (London: Zed Books, 1994).
20 "Noosphere"—derived from the Greek for "mind"—is a concept that was first used by the Russian geochemist Vladimir Ivanovich Vernadsky back in the 1920s. In the 1970s the media theorist Marshall McLuhan used it to refer to the global network of electronic information systems that form the world's technological brain.
21 See Hans-Josef Fell, *Global Cooling: Strategies for Climate Protection* (Leiden and New York: CRC Press, 2012).

Chapter 1 A Changing World

1 Interview printed in the *Frankfurter Allgemeine Zeitung*, October 20, 2012, accessed November 16, 2014, http://www.faz.net/aktuell/wirtschaft/recht-steuern/gespraech-mit-patentamt-chef-battistelli-wir-patentieren-niemals-nur-die-gene-allein-11931412.html.

2 Robert W. Fogal, "Capitalism and Democracy in 2040: Forecasts and Speculations" (working paper, National Bureau of Economic Research, Cambridge, 2007).

3 Helmut Wiesenthal, "(Irr-)Wege in die inklusive Arbeitsgesellschaft (How (Not) to Build an Inclusive Labor Society)," paper presented on May 15, 2012, accessed November 16, 2014, https://www.boell.de/sites/default/files/assets/boell.de/images/download_de/wirtschaftsoziales/Wiesenthal_Irrwege_Juni_2012.pdf.

4 Carlo Jaeger, *Wachstum—wohin?* (Growth—Where Now?) (Munich: Oekom, 2011), 18.

5 Ramesh Ponnuru, "China's Population Crash Could Upend US Policy," Bloomberg, April 30, 2012, accessed November 16, 2014, http://www.bloomberg.com/news/2012-04-30/china-s-population-crash-could-upend-u-s-policy.html.

6 See Jonathan Watts, "China's Big Spend on Green Power," Chinadialogue, May 2, 2012, accessed November 16, 2014, https://www.chinadialogue.net/article/show/single/en/4903-China-s-big-spend-on-green-power.

7 Ibid.

8 "China will die Umwelt schützen (China Wants to Protect the Environment)," *Die Welt,* November 15, 2012, accessed November 16, 2014, http://www.welt.de/print/die_welt/politik/article110844414/China-will-die-Umwelt-schuetzen.html.

9 So writes Matthias Braun, an executive with the pharmaceutical group Sanofi-Aventis, in an essay for the anthology *Die Modernität der Industrie* (The Modernity of Industry), ed. Birger P. Priddat and Klaus-W. West (Marburg: Metropolis, 2012), 295.

10 Jaeger, *Wachstum—wohin?*, 15.

11 Ibid., 20.

12 See http://www.footprintnetwork.org/en/index.php/GFN/page/footprint_basics_overview/, accessed November 17, 2014.

13 Carlo Jaeger, an economist at the Potsdam Institute for Climate Impact Research, expects nominal GWP to increase sixfold by the middle of the century, from around sixty-five billion dollars today to just under four hundred billion.

14 Rudolf Bahro, *Elemente einer neuen Politik: Zum Verhältnis von Ökologie und Sozialismus* (Elements of a New Politics: On the Relationship between Environmentalism and Socialism) (Berlin: Olle und Wolter, 1980), 194.
15 See the warning from Frank Drieschner, an editor at the German newspaper *Die Zeit*, in the October 11, 2012 edition of the paper: "Der große Selbstbetrug," accessed November 19, 2014, http://www.zeit.de/2012/41/Vier-Grad-Klimapolitik-Klimawandel.
16 Graphic illustrating global population development, accessed November 19, 2014, http://www.faw-neu-ulm.de/sites/default/files/Weltbev%C3%B6lkerung.pdf.
17 See the study on China's population development conducted by the Berlin Institute for Population and Development, accessed November 19, 2014, http://www.berlin-institut.org/fileadmin/user_upload/handbuch_texte/pdf_Taubmann_Bevoelkerungsentwicklung_China.pdf.
18 *Bevölkerung Deutschlands bis 2050* (Population Development in Germany to 2050) (Wiesbaden: Statistisches Bundesamt, 2006), 5.
19 "Demografischer Wandel in Deutschland (Demographic Change in Germany)," German Federal Agency for Civic Education, accessed November 19, 2014, http://www.bpb.de/politik/innenpolitik/demografischer-wandel/75997/sozialeauswirkungen.

Chapter 2 The Limits to Growth – The Growth of Limits

1 Donella H. Meadows et al., *The Limits to Growth: A Report for the Club of Rome's Project on the Predicament of Mankind* (New York: Universe, 1972).
2 Ibid., 127–28.
3 See Barbara Paul and Marcel Wagner, "Der kranke Wald: ein Mythos von gestern? (The Ailing Forest: Yesterday's Myth?)", accessed November 19, 2014, http://www.swr.de/unser-wald/oekosystem/waldsterben-debatte/-/id=3927758/nid=3927758/did=3873062/4di2nb/index.html.

4 See http://de.wikipedia.org/wiki/Waldsterben, accessed November 19, 2014.
5 See "Uno Bericht: Europas Wälder wachsen (UN Report: Europe's Forests are Growing)," *Der Spiegel*, June 15, 2011, accessed November 19, 2014, http://www.spiegel.de/wissenschaft/natur/uno-bericht-europas-waelder-wachsen-a-768498.html.
6 Meadows et al., *The Limits to Growth*, 154.
7 Ibid., 169.
8 Ibid., 158 ff.
9 Dennis Meadows in an interview with the magazine of the Smithsonian Museum, published March 16, 2012, accessed November 19, 2014, http://www.smithsonianmag.com/science-nature/Is-it-Too-Late-for-Sustainable-Development.html?c=y&page=1.
10 Interview to mark the 40th anniversary of *The Limits to Growth*, *Frankfurter Allgemeine Sonntagszeitung*, March 4, 2012, 43.
11 Günter Anders, *Die Antiquiertheit des Menschen: Über die Seele im Zeitalter der zweiten industriellen Revolution* (The Obsolescence of Mankind: Reflections on the Soul in the Age of the Second Industrial Revolution) (Munich: Beck, 1956).
12 Jørgen Randers, "Ein guter Diktator: Das ist der Gipfel (A Benevolent Dictator: That is the Ideal)," *Tagesspiegel*, June 17, 2012, accessed November 19, 2014, http://www.tagesspiegel.de/politik/rio-20-ein-guter-diktator-das-ist-der-gipfel/6760528.html. Randers was chosen to write the follow-up report for the 40th anniversary of *The Limits to Growth*, which is entitled *2052: A Global Forecast for the Next Forty Years* (White River Junction, VT: Chelsea Green, 2012).
13 Details taken from the German Wikipedia entry for the Three Gorges Dam, accessed November 25, 2014, http://de.wikipedia.org/wiki/Drei-Schluchten-Talsperre.
14 Reported by *Spiegel* Online, June 11, 2012, accessed November 19, 2014, http://www.spiegel.de/wissenschaft/

natur/forscher-entdecken-riesige-luecke-in-chinas-co2-bilanz-a-838183.html.

15 Meadows et al., *The Limits to Growth*, 54 ff.

16 Bjørn Lomborg, "Environmental Alarmism, Then and Now," *Foreign Affairs*, July/August 2012, 24 ff. Lomborg downplays the dramatic extent of climate change as well as the degradation of agricultural land and the looming water crises facing populous regions. The real environmental problem, he argues, is air pollution, for which we are paying a high price in sickness and death around the world.

17 See *International Resource Politics: New Challenges Demanding New Governance Approaches for a Green Economy* (Berlin: Heinrich Böll Foundation and Wuppertal Institute for Climate, Environment and Energy, 2012), 22.

18 See Heidi Feldt, *The German Raw Material Strategy: Taking Stock* (Berlin: Heinrich Böll Foundation, 2012), accessed November 19, 2014, http://www.boell.de/sites/default/files/txt_120822_the_german_raw_materials_strategy_taking_stock_hf_v100.pdf. The author criticizes inconsistency between development and raw materials policies.

19 *International Resource Politics*, 51–52.

20 See Steve Kretzmann, "Oil's New Supply Boom Is a Bust for the Climate," Oil Change International, accessed November 19, 2014, http://priceofoil.org/2012/10/25/oils-new-supply-boom-is-a-bust-for-the-climate/.

21 Oil report published by Erste Group Research, March 5, 2012, http://www.erstebank.hr/hr/Downloads/ bdfcaf10-2da3-467c-a446-be8e0eeba40d/2012_03_05_EN_Report_Oil_2012.pdf.

22 See James Burgess, "Saudi Arabia Could Become a Net Oil Importer by 2030," September 5, 2012, accessed November 19, 2014, http://oilprice.com/Latest-Energy-

News/World-News/Saudi-Arabia-Could-Become-a-Net-Oil-Importer-by-2030.html.

23 *Frankfurter Allgemeine Sonntagszeitung*, March 4, 2012, 45.

24 See http://theenergycollective.com/josephromm/2146821/methane-leaks-wipe-out-any-climate-benefit-fracking-satellite-observations-confir?ref=popular_posts, accessed November 19, 2014.

25 "'Fracking' nur unter strengen Auflagen (Fracking Only under Strict Conditions)," Deutsche Presse-Agentur, September 6, 2012, accessed November 19, 2014, http://www.faz.net/aktuell/politik/inland/gasfoerderung-fracking-nur-unter-strengen-auflagen-11881112.html.

26 "ExxonMobil Departure Unsettles Outlook for Shale Gas Exploration," *Financial Times*, October 31, 2012, 3.

27 *Handelsblatt*, October 8, 2012, 1.

28 According to Steve Levine in an article for America's leading foreign affairs magazine *Foreign Policy*. "The Era of Oil Abundance," July 17, 2012, accessed November 19, 2014, http://www.foreignpolicy.com/articles/2012/07/17/the_era_of_oil_abundance.

29 A 2008 Republican campaign slogan.

30 See http://de.wikipedia.org/wiki/Kohleverfl%C3%BCssigung, accessed November 19, 2014.

31 *Weser-Kurier*, April 3, 2012, 22.

32 Julian L. Simon, *The Ultimate Resource* (Princeton: Princeton University Press, 1981). Even the first sentence of the introduction is typical of Simon's laconic style: "Is there a natural-resource problem now? Certainly—just as always."

33 See http://en.wikipedia.org/wiki/Julian_Simon, accessed November 19, 2014.

34 A similar summary can be found on page 33 of the Lomborg article quoted above. The figures are based on the raw materials price index of the *The Economist* and the International Monetary Fund.

35 "Was die Nahrungspreise treibt (What Drives Food Prices)," *Frankfurter Allgemeine Zeitung*, August 14, 2012, 11.
36 "Minenwerte unter Druck (Mining Stocks under Pressure)," *Frankfurter Allgemeine Zeitung*, August 11, 2012, 22.
37 Quoted in John J. Lalor, ed., *Cyclopædia of Political Science, Political Economy and the Political History of the United States by the Best American and European Writers* (New York: Maynard, Merrill & Co., 1899), 3: 297.
38 See the statistics collected by the German Federal Employment Agency, accessed November 19, 2014, http://statistik.arbeitsagentur.de/Navigation/Statistik/Statistik-nach-Themen/Beschaeftigung/Beschaeftigung-Nav.html.
39 LOHAS: Lifestyle of Health and Sustainability—the lifestyle of environmentally enlightened urban professionals. Like almost all current cultural trends, it originated in America.

Chapter 3 The Malaise of Modernity

1 See Charles Taylor, *The Malaise of Modernity* (Concord, Ont.: Anansi, 1991). Taylor criticizes what he sees as Western civilization's cult of self-fulfillment.
2 English translation by George C. Schoolfield taken from Ingrid Walsøe-Engel, ed., *German Poetry: From the Beginnings to 1750* (New York: Continuum, 1992), 229.
3 The American economist David S. Landes entitled his monumental history of the scientific and industrial revolution *The Unbound Prometheus* (Cambridge: Cambridge University Press, 1969).
4 Paul M. Schafer, ed., *The First Writings of Karl Marx* (Brooklyn, NY: lg Publishing, 2006), 90.
5 Johann Wolfgang von Goethe, *Faust I & II*, trans. Stuart Atkins (Cambridge, MA: Suhrkamp/Insel, 1984), 42.

6 Benjamin von Blomberg, a dramaturge at the Thalia Theater in Hamburg who staged a *Faust* marathon under the direction of Nicolas Stemann.
7 Goethe, *Faust I & II*, 257.
8 Ibid., 290.
9 Joseph Schumpeter, *The Theory of Economic Development: An Inquiry into Profits, Capital, Credit, Interest, and the Business Cycle* (Cambridge, MA: Harvard University Press, 1934), 93.
10 Ibid., 258.
11 Ibid., 292.
12 Ibid.
13 Ibid., 290.
14 Hans Christoph Binswanger, "Geld und Magie (Money and Magic)" (essay for the *Faust* marathon program, Hamburg, 2011). Binswanger goes into more detail in *Money and Magic: A Critique of the Modern Economy in Light of Goethe's Faust*, trans. J. E. Harrison (Chicago: University of Chicago Press, 1994).
15 Binswanger, *Money and Magic*, 60.
16 Landes, *The Unbound Prometheus*, 555.
17 Wikipedia defines this break as a "transition between forced adaption to the environment and a dynamic process of rapidly rising productivity driven by momentous ingenuity." Accessed November 19, 2014, http://de.wikipedia.org/wiki/Neolithische_Revolution.
18 Binswanger, *Money and Magic*, 40.
19 Ibid, 42.
20 Goethe, *Faust I & II*, 291.
21 Binswanger *Money and Magic*, 43.
22 Ibid., 44.
23 "Danke, wir verzichten," *Frankfurter Allgemeine Zeitung*, December 27, 2009. The editors of the *FAZ*'s feature

section promote the idea of postgrowth society, while its economic editors oppose it. The dispute between apologists for growth and those turning their back on it will remain pointless until the *quality* of growth is discussed.

24 Printed in the newspaper *Die Welt*, December 17, 2009, accessed November 19, 2014, www.welt.de/die-welt/debatte/article5556427/Wie-gross-ist-gross.html.

25 Historically, however, Calvinism did not insist on detached inwardness. In fact it had a pronounced entrepreneurial streak, deeming acquisitiveness pleasing to God and teaching that anyone successful in this world could also expect to be one of the chosen ones in the afterlife.

26 Peter Sloterdijk, *You Must Change Your Life* (Cambridge, UK and Malden, MA: Polity, 2013), 347.

27 Interview with *Evonik Magazine*, 2/2012, 27.

28 Trotsky in a speech to representatives of a Danish student organization in November 1932, quoted in Sloterdijk, *You Must Change Your Life*, 316.

29 Bahro, *Elemente einer neuen Politik: Zum Verhältnis von Ökologie und Sozialismus* (Berlin: Olle und Wolter, 1980), 125.

30 Ibid., 113.

31 Ibid., 114.

32 Rudolf Bahro, *Logik der Rettung: Ein Versuch über die Grundlagen ökologischer Politik* (Stuttgart: Weitbrecht, 1987).

33 Jan Robert Bloch and Willfried Maier, eds., *Wachstum der Grenzen: Selbstorganisation in der Natur und die Zukunft der Gesellschaft* (Frankfurt am Main: Sendler, 1984).

34 From Sloterdijk's Copenhagen speech.

Chapter 4 The Green Industrial Revolution

1 Ernst Ulrich von Weizsäcker et al., *Factor Five: Transforming the Global Economy through 80% Improvements in Resource Productivity* (London and Sterling, VA: Earthscan, 2009), 1–3.
2 Michael Braungart, "Ein Rohstoff ist ein Rohstoff ist ein Rohstoff (A Raw Material is a Raw Material is a Raw Material)," *Earnest & Algernon: Dream & Reality*, 3/2012, 28 ff.
3 Martin Jänicke, *Megatrend Umweltinnovation: Zur ökologischen Modernisierung von Wirtschaft und Staat* (Munich: Oekom, 2008), 16.
4 See "Philips: Absatz von grünen Produkten erreicht Rekordniveau (Philips: Sales of Green Products Reach Record Levels)," Nordic Market, February 29, 2012, accessed November 19, 2014, http://www.nordic-market.de/news/2707/philips_absatz_von_gruenen_produkten_erreicht_rekordniveau.htm.
5 Interview with the radio station Deutschlandfunk on June 17, 2012.
6 See www.blueeconomy.eu, accessed November 19, 2014.
7 The expression "green revolution" was first used to describe the efforts of the World Bank and other international agencies to improve the food situation in developing countries by introducing industrial agricultural technologies. That revolution began around 1960.
8 Gunter Pauli, *Neues Wachstum: Wenn grüne Ideen nachhaltig "blau" werden* (New Growth: When Green Ideas Go "Blue") (Berlin: Konvergenta, 2010), 19.
9 Joseph A. Schumpeter, *Capitalism, Socialism and Democracy* (New York and London: Harper, 1942).
10 Landes, *The Unbound Prometheus*, 5.
11 Weizsäcker et al., *Factor Five*, 10–11.

12 Harald Welzer, *Climate Wars: What People Will Be Killed for in the 21st Century* (Cambridge, UK and Malden, MA: Polity, 2012), 171.
13 See Michael Jacobs, "Green Growth: Economic Theory and Political Discourse" (working paper no. 108, Centre for Climate Change Economics and Policy, October 2012).
14 See Weizsäcker et al., *Factor Five*, 15 ff.
15 Quotation taken from http://en.wikipedia.org/wiki/The_Coal_Question, accessed November 19, 2014.
16 An overview of the various forms the rebound effect can take is found in Tilman Santarius, *Der Rebound-Effekt: Über die unerwünschten Folgen der erwünschten Energieeffizienz* (The Rebound Effect: On the Undesired Consequences of Energy Efficiency) (Wuppertal: Wuppertal Institut für Umwelt, Klima, Energie, 2012).
17 See "Ein Lob auf die deutsche Industrie (Praise for German Industry)," *Frankfurter Allgemeine Sonntagszeitung*, October 21, 2012, 33.
18 "Der geplatzte Traum vom Energiesparen (The Shattered Dream of Energy Savings)," *Die Welt*, August 25, 2012. See the graphic at http://www.welt.de/wirtschaft/energie/article108796448/Der-geplatzte-Traumvom-Energiesparen.html?wtmc=nl.wdwbaufmacher, accessed November 19, 2014. The title of the article does not give an accurate idea of its content.
19 Verband der Automobilindustrie, *Jahresbericht 2012* (2012 Annual Report of the German Automotive Industry Association), 114.
20 See the German Chemical Industry Association's 2011 profile of the country's chemical and pharmaceutical sectors, accessed November 19, 2014, https://www.vci.de/downloads/BP2011.pdf.
21 See http://www.nachhaltigkeit2011.bayer.de/de/oekologie.aspx, accessed November 19, 2014.

22 Weizsäcker et al., *Factor Five*, 158 ff.
23 Gunter Pauli, *Neues Wachstum*, 65.
24 Jänicke, *Megatrend Umweltinnovation*, 18.

Chapter 5 Bioeconomics

1 Study commissioned by the German Federal Ministry of Food and Agriculture concluded in February 2012, accessed November 19, 2014, http://www.bmelv.de/SharedDocs/Downloads/Ernaehrung/WvL/Studie_Lebensmittelabfaelle_Kurzfassung.pdf?__blob=publicationFile.
2 Facts and Figures from the previously cited book *Neues Wachstum: Wenn grüne Ideen nachhaltig "blau" werden* (Berlin: Konvergenta, 2010) by Gunter Pauli, 61.
3 Jan Robert Bloch and Willfried Maier, eds., *Wachstum der Grenzen: Selbstorganisation in der Natur und die Zukunft der Gesellschaft* (Frankfurt am Main: Sendler, 1984), 21.
4 See Frederic Vester, *Neuland des Denkens: Vom technokratischen zum kybernetischen Zeitalter* (A New Way of Thinking: From the Technocratic to the Cybernetic Age) (Stuttgart: Deutsche Verlags-Anstalt, 1980).
5 The Bioeconomy Council was set up in 2009 as an initiative of the German government under the control of the National Academy of Science and Engineering. Since then it has published a series of recommendations.
6 See "Statusbericht Bioraffinerie (Biorefinery Status Report)," Process, March 22, 2010, accessed November 19, 2014, http://www.process.vogel.de/anlagen_apparatebau/engineering_dienstleistung/bioanlagen/articles/ 256058/.
7 See the report *Weiße Biotechnologie: Chancen für eine biobasierte Wirtschaft* (White Biotechnology: Prospects for a Biobased Economy) published by the German Federal Ministry of Education and Research in 2012, 33.

8 The website of the Swiss development aid coalition Alliance Sud provides an introduction to the subject with numerous references and links. Accessed November 19, 2014, http://www.alliancesud.ch/de/dokumentation/e-dossiers/land-grabbing.

9 Interview with Eduardo Rojas-Briales, acting general secretary of the FAO and head of the Global Forest Partnership, accessed November 19, 2014, http://www.spiegel.de/wissenschaft/natur/welt-waldbericht-unser-sorgenkind-ist-lateinamerika-a-743093.html.

10 See http://www.rspo.org/, accessed November 19, 2014.

11 "Gift für Brasiliens Regenwald (Poison for Brazil's Rain Forest)," *Zeit* Online, February 8, 2010, accessed November 19, 2014, http://www.zeit.de/wissen/umwelt/2010-02/studie-biosprit-urwald/komplettansicht.

12 See the study conducted by the German National Academy of Sciences on the prospects for and limits of bioeconomics, *Bioenergie: Möglichkeiten und Grenzen (2012/2013)*, http://www.leopoldina.org/uploads/tx_leopublication/2013_06_Stellungnahme_Bioenergie_DE.pdf.

13 See http://www.biotechnologie.de/BIO/Navigation/DE/root, did=153182.html, accessed November 19, 2014.

14 See http://www.focus.de/wissen/technik/erfindungen/tid-11316/neue-energie-hat-biosprit-eine-gute-klimabilanz_aid_321536.html, accessed November 19, 2014.

15 "Neue CO_2-Berechnung: Biosprit ist Gift für die Umwelt (New CO_2 Figures: Biofuel is Poison for the Environment)," *Financial Times Deutschland* Online, September 14, 2011.

16 See http://de.wikipedia.org/wiki/Richtlinie_2009/28/EG_%28Erneuerbare-Energien-Richtlinie%29, accessed November 19, 2014.

17 Winand von Petersdorff, "In die Biotonne (Into the Organic Waste)," *FAZ* Online, July 28, 2012, accessed

November 19, 2014, http://www.faz.net/aktuell/politik/inland/bioenergie-in-die-biotonne-11835386.html.

18 Seehttp://www.sueddeutsche.de/wirtschaft/nahrungsmittel-statt-biosprit-gefangenin-der-ethanol-falle-1.1438888-2, accessed November 19, 2014.

19 See http://www.leopoldina.org/uploads/tx_leopublication/201207_Stellungnahme_Bioenergie_kurz_de_en_final.pdf, accessed November 19, 2014.

20 Ottmar Edenhofer et al., eds., *Renewable Energy Sources and Climate Change Mitigation: Special Report of the Intergovernmental Panel on Climate Change* (Cambridge and New York: Cambridge University Press, 2012).

21 See http://de.wikipedia.org/wiki/Biokraftstoff, accessed November 19, 2014.

22 Susanne Kilimann, "Benzin aus der Biotonne (Gasoline from the Organic Waste)," *Die Zeit* Online, July 12, 2011, accessed November 26, 2014, http://www.zeit.de/auto/2011-07/pflanzenkraftstoff-biomasse.

23 Ernst Ulrich von Weizsäcker et al., *Factor Five: Transforming the Global Economy through 80% Improvements in Resource Productivity* (London and Sterling, VA: Earthscan, 2009), 178.

24 "Kraftwerk lässt Abgas durch Algen filtern (Power Station Uses Algae to Filter Exhaust Gas)," *Handelsblatt* Online, November 6, 2008, accessed November 19, 2014, http://www.handelsblatt.com/technologie/energie-umwelt/umwelt-news/co2-reduzierung-kraftwerk-laesst-abgas-durch-algen-filtern/3049646.html.

25 See www.biokon.net, accessed November 19, 2014—a rich and interesting source.

26 Kay Dohnke, "Abgeguckt," *mobil* (the Deutsche Bahn magazine), 1/2012. The following examples are taken from the same article.

27 See http://www.proplanta.de/Agrar-Nachrichten/Pflanze/25-Jahre-Verwirrungstechnik-in-der-Schweiz_article1313310484.html, accessed November 19, 2014.

28 "Termiten als Treibstoffproduzenten (Termites as a Source of Fuel)," note on the technology website Haute Innovation, accessed November 19, 2014, http://www.haute-innovation.com/de/magazin/energie/biowasserstoff.html.

29 See http://www.wissenschaft.de/wissenschaft/news/315648.html, accessed November 19, 2014.

30 "Die Natur als Vorbild (The Example of Nature)," *Forum: Das Wochenmagazin*, May 25, 2012, 84 ff.

31 See http://www.lanuv.nrw.de/veroeffentlichungen/malbo/malbo20/malbo20s611s634.pdf, accessed November 19, 2014.

32 See http://www.biospektrum.de/blatt/d_bs_pdf&_id=1008981, accessed November 19, 2014.

33 Dohnke, "Abgeguckt," 71.

34 See *Spiegel* Online, January 3, 2012, accessed November 19, 2014, http://www.spiegel.de/wissenschaft/natur/0,1518,806859,00.html.

35 See http://de.wikipedia.org/wiki/Synthetische_Biologie, accessed November 19, 2014.

36 See http://www.synbiosafe.eu/, accessed November 19, 2014.

37 See Raymond Fismer et al., "Die Thermodynamik und das Weltgesetz der Entropie (Thermodynamics and the Global Law of Entropy)," in Bloch and Maier, eds., *Wachstum der Grenzen*, 295 ff.

38 Hanno Charisius, "Das grüne Wunder," accessed November 19, 2014, http://www.spiegel.de/wissenschaft/natur/forscher-arbeiten-an-kuenstlicher-photosynthese-a-820372.html. The following examples are taken from this article.

39 Ibid.
40 *Süddeutsche Zeitung*, July 25, 2011, http://www.sueddeutsche.de/wissen/energiegewinnung-sprit-aus-licht-1.1124182.
41 See the company's website, http://www.sunfire.de, accessed November 19, 2014.
42 See Freeman J. Dyson, *The Sun, the Genome and the Internet: Tools of Scientific Revolutions* (Oxford and New York: Oxford University Press, 1999).
43 See the science section of the *Frankfurter Allgemeine Zeitung*, April 18, 2012.
44 Charisius, "Das grüne Wunder."
45 The International Rice Research Institute is a charitable organization that houses the world's largest rice bank, with over one hundred and ten thousand types from around the world. It provides seeds to researchers free of charge, subject to certain contractual conditions. See the information on the IRRI website, http://irri.org/, accessed November 26, 2014.
46 Weizsäcker et al., *Factor Five*, 175.
47 See the article on this subject in *Die Welt*, September 11, 2007, accessed November 19, 2014, http://www.welt.de/welt_print/article1174263/Wissenschaft-kompakt.html.
48 See the graphic on the tipping points of the global climate at *Spiegel* Online, accessed November 19, 2014, http://www.spiegel.de/flash/0,5532,17184,00.html.
49 See Sebastian Matthes and Susanne Donner, "Der Klimakiller als Rohstoff (The Climate Killer as a Raw Material)," *Wirtschaftswoche*, May 24, 2012, accessed November 19, 2014, http://www.wiwo.de/technologie/forschung/co2-recyclingder-klimakiller-als-rohstoff-seite-all/6642990-all.html.
50 Uta Bilow, "Vom Abgas zum wertvollen Rohstoff (From Exhaust Gas to a Valuable Raw Material)," *Frankfurter Allgemeine Zeitung*, October 31, 2012, N2.

51 See "Grünes Benzin aus Kohlenstoffdioxid (Green Gasoline from Carbon Dioxide)," accessed November 19, 2014, www.energie-und-technik.de/energiequellen/news/article/89167/0/Gruenes_Benzin_aus_Kohlenstoffdioxid/.

52 See http://www.process.vogel.de/anlagen_apparatebau/effizienzsteigerung/verfahrenseffizienz/articles/300140/, accessed November 19, 2014.

Chapter 6 The Future of Agriculture

1 Figures from the website www.green-economy.de, "Agrar- und Forstwissenschaften globale Situation."

2 "Wetten auf den Hunger," *Frankfurter Allgemeine Zeitung*, September 14, 2012, 23.

3 Information from the German Wikipedia article on organic farming, accessed November 22, 2014, http://de.wikipedia.org/wiki/%C3%96kologische_Landwirtschaft#cite_note-Goklany 2002-66.

4 Jan Grossarth, "Getreide für Brot, Tierfutter und Strom," *Frankfurter Allgemeine Zeitung*, September 14, 2012, 17.

5 Dietrich Schulz, "Die Rolle der Landwirtschaft beim Klimawandel," http://www.boelw.de/uploads/media/pdf/Veranstaltungen/Herbsttagung_2007/BOELW-Herbsttagung_07_Vortrag_Schulz.pdf.

6 See http://www.verbraucherfuersklima.de/cps/rde/xchg/projektklima/hs.xsl/die_lange_reise_bis_zum_kochtopf.htm, accessed November 23, 2014.

7 Jesko Hirschfeld et al., *The Impact of German Agriculture on the Climate: Main Results and Conclusions* (Berlin: Institut for Ecological Economy Research, 2008).

8 See http://de.wikipedia.org/wiki/%C3%96kologische_Landwirtschaft, accessed November 26, 2014.

9 See http://www.sciencedirect.com/science/article/pii/S03 08521X1100182X, accessed November 23, 2014.

10 Verena Seufert, Navin Ramankutty, Jonathan Foley, "Comparing the Yields of Organic and Conventional Agriculture," *Nature* 485 (2012): 229–32, cited in Andrew C. Revkin, "Study Points to Roles for Industry and Organics in Agriculture," accessed November 23, 2014, http://dotearth.blogs.nytimes.com/2012/04/25/study-points-to-roles-for-industry-and-organics-in-agriculture/.

11 Information taken from Peter Clausing, "Reale Alternativen (Real Alternatives)," accessed November 23, 2014, http://www.welt-ernaehrung.de/2009/11/18/reale-alternativen/.

12 One of many facts provided by Joachim Müller-Jung, the science editor of the *Frankfurter Allgemeine Zeitung* in "Kränkelnde Krume (Ailing Topsoil)," *Frankfurter Allgemeine Zeitung*, August 22, 2012, N1.

13 Bernhard Kegel, *Epigenetik: Wie Erfahrungen vererbt werden* (Cologne: DuMont, 2009), 292.

14 See Volker Stollorz, "Das Leben, einmal neu redigiert (Life, Reedited)," *Frankfurter Allgemeine Sonntagszeitung*, August 26, 2012, 53—an informative overview of new methods of genetic engineering.

15 Ibid.

16 See http://de.wikipedia.org/wiki/Gr%C3%BCne_Gentechnik, accessed November 23, 2014.

17 See the German Federal Agency for Nature Conservation's policy on global food provision, biodiversity and genetic engineering, accessed November 23, 2014, http://www.bfn.de/fileadmin/MDB/documents/themen/agrogentechnik/PositionspapierWelternaehrungGT.pdf.

18 See http://www.bdp-online.de/de/Pflanzenzuechtung/Methoden/Smart_Breeding/, accessed November 23, 2014.

19 Bertolt Brecht, *The Threepenny Opera*, trans. Ralph Manheim and John Willett (New York: Arcade, 1979), 55.

20 See http://www.brot-fuer-die-welt.de/fileadmin/mediapool/2_Downloads/NIFSA/NIFSA_Kampagnenblatt_Fleischkonsum.pdf.

21 A German public television documentary about Wiesenhof, Europe's largest poultry corporation, throws industrial animal breeding into sharp relief, http://mediathek.daserste.de/Reportage-Dokumentation/ARD-exclusiv-Das-System-Wiesenhof/Das-Erste/Video?documentId=8068044&topRessort=tv&bcastId=799280.

22 Seehttp://www.wiwo.de/unternehmen/muhammad-yunus-der-nimbus-des-nobelpreistraegers-verblasst-seite-2/5234936-2.html, accessed November 23, 2014.

23 Müller-Jung, "Kränkelnde Krume."

24 Ernst Ulrich von Weizsäcker et al., *Factor Five: Transforming the Global Economy through 80 % Resource Productivity* (London and Sterling, VA: Earthscan, 2009), 184 ff.

25 See http://www.umweltdialog.de/umweltdialog/branchen/2012-08-17_Intensive_Hochleistungs-Landwirtschaft_versagt_in_Trockenzeiten.php, accessed November 23, 2014.

26 See http://www.oeig.at/oecd-israelische-landwirte-verbrauchen-am-wenigsten-wasser/, accessed November 23, 2014.

27 *OECD Environmental Outlook to 2030* (Washington, DC: OECD Publishing, 2008), 306.

28 Freeman J. Dyson, *Heretical Thoughts about Science and Society* (Boston: Boston University, Frederick S. Pardee Center for the Study of the Longer-Range Future, 2006), cited in Carlo Jaeger, *Wachstum—wohin?* (Munich: Oekom, 2011), 59.

29 "Why trees matter," accessed November 23, 2014, http://www.nytimes.com/2012/04/12/opinion/why-

trees-matter.html?src=me&ref=general. One of Dyson's unconventional ideas is the suggestion that genetic engineering should be used to accelerate tree growth so that more CO_2 can be bound.

30 See http://www.foresteurope.org/state-europes-forests-2011-report.

31 In a report for the radio station Deutschlandfunk, Volkart Wildermuth describes a pilot project run by the Brandenburg agricultural cooperative Forst. The report can be found at www.dradio.de/dlf/sendungen/wib/1811734/drucken/, accessed November 23, 2014.

32 Cited in a Deutschlandfunk report on August 9, 2012: "Mit Pflanzen gegen Wüstenbildung (Using Plants to Fight Desertification)."

33 For more details see the Deutschlandfunk report "Schwarze Revolution (Black Revolution)," which was broadcast on May 13, 2012.

34 Ibid.

35 See the website of Wageningen University and Research Center, http://www.wageningenur.nl/nl/Expertises-Diens tverlening/Onderzoeksinstituten/Alterra.htm.

36 Presentation given by the Dutch agricultural expert Dr. Peter Smeets at an innovation convention organized by the Heinrich Böll Foundation that took place in Berlin on May 9, 2012.

37 See http://www.hydroponische-pflanzenzucht.de, accessed November 23, 2014.

38 "Vertical Farm in Abandoned Pork Plant Turns Waste into Food," *Japan Times*, July 8, 2012, 8.

39 A detailed video about the project can be found on the website of the Leibniz Institute of Freshwater Ecology and Inland Fisheries, accessed November 23, 2014, http://www.igb-berlin.de/astafpro.html.

40 See http://www.ecf-center.de/ecf-stadtfarm/, accessed November 23, 2014.
41 See http://www.fraunhofer.de/de/publikationen/fraunhofer-magazin/2012/weitervorn_2-2012_Inhalt/weiter-vorn_2-2012_16.html, accessed November 23, 2014.
42 Some of these designs can be viewed on YouTube, accessed November 23, 2014, http://www.youtube.com/watch?v=TBrgRsjR-JQ&feature=relmfu.
43 See http://www.uni-muenster.de/NiederlandeNet/nl-wissen/wirtschaft/vertiefung/landwirtschaft/schweine.html, accessed November 23, 2014.

Chapter 7 An Energy Revolution

1 See "Länder-Wettlauf um die EEG-Förderung (Interstate Competition for Energy Act Funding)," *Frankfurter Allgemeine Zeitung*, August 20, 2012, 11. The article analyzes how the distribution of costs associated with the Renewable Energy Act across all Germany's energy consumers benefits states with access to a high volume of wind and solar power. The act established a transfer system between the federal states. The financially weak states in the northeast of Germany were not the only ones to benefit from this—thanks to its high solar power density Bavaria also profited.
2 Federal Environment Agency press release of March 26, 2012.
3 Numbers are for 2011. See page 3 of the April 2012 report from the German Federal Ministry of Economic Affairs and Technology on the state of the German photovoltaic industry, accessed November 23, 2014, http://www.bmwi.de/BMWi/Redaktion/PDF/B/bericht-des-bmwi-

zur-lage-der-deutschen photovoltaikindustrie,property=pdf,bereich=bmwi2012,sprache=de,rwb=true.pdf.

4 See *FAZ* online, October 15, 2012, accessed November 23, 2014, http://www.faz.net/aktuell/wirtschaft/wirtschafts politik/energiepolitik/oekostrom-eeg-umlage-steigt-auf-5-3-cent-11926353.html.

5 The feed-in tariffs for rooftop photovoltaic installations with a capacity of over a megawatt fell from 54 cents per kilowatt-hour in 2004 to 12.85 cents in July 2012.

6 New additions include the poultry concern Wiesenhof, dairies and municipal public transport providers.

7 See *12 Thesen zur Energiewende: Ein Diskussionsbedarf zu den wichtigsten Herausforderungen im Strommarkt* (Berlin: Agora Energiewende, 2012).

8 The term "negawatt" was coined by the American physicist and environmental visionary Amory Lovins to refer to the enormous potential of energy-saving measures, which can generally be implemented more cheaply than new power plants can be built.

9 Cf. the ideas of Felix Matthes, an energy expert at the Institute for Applied Ecology, on reforming the Renewable Energy Act, accessed November 23, 2014, www.oeko.de/oekodoc/1545/2012-405-de.pdf.

10 Cf. Sascha Müller-Kraenner and Susanne Langsdorf, *A European Union for Renewable Energy: Policy Options for Better Grids and Support Schemes* (Brussels: Heinrich Böll Foundation, 2012). This publication summarizes the outcomes of a series of meetings between experts organized by the European office of the Heinrich Böll Foundation in Brussels.

11 See the website of the Desertec Foundation, accessed November 23, 2014, http://www.desertec.org/en/.

12 "Schwellenländer überholen Industriestaaten bei der Energiewende (Emerging Nations Overtake

Energy Reform of Industrial States)," accessed October 31, 2014, http://www.manager-magazin.de/unternehmen/energie/schwellenlaender-ueberholen-industriestaaten-bei-energiewende-a-999680.html.

13 See http://www.erene.org/, accessed November 23, 2014. The concept for a European community for renewable energy (ERENE) was developed by former EU commissioner Michaele Schreyer and the scientist Lutz Metz on behalf of the Heinrich Böll Foundation.

14 International Energy Agency, *World Energy Outlook 2012*, accessed November 23, 2014, http://www.iea.org/publications/freepublications/publication/English.pdf.

15 The numbers cited here are taken from the essay "Cleaning up Coal" by Richard Morse, which was published in the July/August 2012 issue of *Foreign Affairs*. Morse is director of research for the Program on Energy and Sustainable Development at Stanford University in California.

16 International Energy Agency, *World Energy Outlook 2012*.

Chapter 8 The Postfossil City

1 The proceedings of an international conference organized by the Heinrich Böll Foundation give an idea of the diverse ways in which cities around the world are developing and of the recurring issues in the debate on urban development: *Urban Futures 2050: Szenarien und Lösungen für das Jahrhundert der Städte* (Scenarios and Solutions for the Century of Cities) (Berlin: Heinrich Böll Foundation, 2011), accessed November 23, 2014, http://www.boell.de/publikationen/publikationen-11972.html.

2 See http://www.iclei.org/our-activities.html.

3 Herbert Girardet, one of the masterminds of sustainable urban development, has coined the phrase "from petropolis to ecopolis" to describe the impending structural change. See his article "Creating Regenerative Cities" in *Urban Futures 2050*, 22–26.

4 Today the German middle class is characterized by green values and an environmentally enlightened, cosmopolitan and tolerant lifestyle. This is the basis for the level of success being enjoyed by green candidates in mayoral elections—a level of success that at first glance seems astonishing. The fact that in the fall of 2012 both the head of the Baden-Württemberg state government and the mayor of Stuttgart were Greens is evidence of the party's potential—as long as the right people are involved.

5 Friedrich von Borries, "Zehn Thesen für die Stadt von morgen," in *Perspektiven einer nachhaltigen Entwicklung: Wie sieht die Welt von morgen aus?* (The Outlook for Sustainable Development: What Will Tomorrow's World Look Like?), ed. Harald Welzer and Klaus Wiegandt (Frankfurt am Main: Fischer, 2011), 40–63.

6 Ernst Ulrich von Weizsäcker et al., *Factor Five: Transforming the Global Economy through 80 % Resource Productivity* (London and Sterling, VA: Earthscan, 2009), 67.

7 See http://www.thehighline.org/about/park-information/, accessed November 23, 2014.

8 See Jeremiah Moss, "Disney World on the Hudson," op-ed in the *New York Times*, August 21, 2012, accessed November 23, 2014, http://vanishingnewyork.blogspot.de/2012/08/disney-world-on-hudson.html.

9 See Bright Farms press release of February 5, 2014, http://www.brightfarms.com/s/#!/news/d/579.

10 See http://berlin.nabu.de/themen/Artenschutz/countdown2010/#header, accessed November 23, 2014.

11 See Weizsäcker et al., *Factor Five*, 108.

12 See R. Frechette and R. Gilchrist, "Towards Zero Energy: A Case Study of the Pearl River Tower, Guangzhou, China," accessed November 23, 2014, http://ctbuh.org/LinkClick.aspx?fileticket=%2bpedN46s7Es%3d&tabid=486&language=en-US/.

13 See http://www.dezeen.com/2009/12/10/urban-forest-by-mad/, accessed November 23, 2014.

14 One of the many interesting facts found on Sonnenseite, the website of the journalist and solar technology pioneer Franz Alt. Accessed November 23, 2014, http://www.sonnenseite.com/Aktuelle+News,Hochhaus+in+solarer+Pracht,6,a22499.html.

15 See http://dabonline.de/2009/09/01/form-follows-energy/, accessed November 23, 2014.

16 There are around forty million apartments in Germany. Only two hundred thousand are currently under construction.

17 *Strategien zur Modernisierung I: Neue Finanzierungsmodelle für einen klimaneutralen Gebäudebestand* (Modernization Strategies I: New Funding Models for a Climate-Neutral Building Stock) (Berlin: Heinrich Böll Foundation, 2012), accessed November 26, 2014, http://www.boell.de/publikationen/publikationen-finanzierungsmodelle-klimaneutraler-gebaeudebestand-14802.html.

18 See http://www.klima-manifest.de/praeambel.html, accessed November 23, 2014.

Chapter 9 Ecocapitalism

1 See the statement "Divided We Stand: Why Inequality Keeps Rising" put out by the OECD on December 5, 2011.

2 See William J. Baumol et al., *Good Capitalism, Bad Capitalism: The Economics of Growth and Prosperity* (New Haven: Yale University Press, 2007). The authors distinguish between four models of capitalism: entrepreneurial, big-firm, state-guided and oligarchic varieties.

3 See http://de.wikipedia.org/wiki/Staatsquote, accessed July 30, 2014.

4 Energy contracting is the outsourcing of energy management to external service providers who take a cut of the energy costs saved.

5 See "Business Briefing Nachhaltige Investments (Sustainable Investments)," *Handelsblatt* November 9, 2012.

6 See the FSC's international website, accessed November 26, 2014, https://ic.fsc.org/.

7 See https://www.cdproject.net/en-US/Pages/HomePage.aspx, accessed November 24, 2014.

8 See http://de.wikipedia.org/wiki/Carbon_Disclosure_Project, accessed November 24, 2014.

9 See the study by Karolin Baedecker et al. *Nutzen statt Besitzen: Auf dem Weg zu einer ressourcenschonenden Konsumkultur* (Use, Don't Own: Toward a Resource-Efficient Consumer Culture) (Berlin: Heinrich Böll Foundation/Naturschutzbund Deutschland, 2012).

10 See www.kleiderkreisel.de.

11 Jutta Maier, "Second-Hand-Paradies Internet (Online Second-Hand Paradise)," *Frankfurter Rundschau* Online, October 7, 2012, accessed November 24, 2014, http://www.fr-online.de/wirtschaft/internet-plattform-kleiderkreisel-second-hand-paradies-internet,1472780,20290260.html.

12 See Baedecker et al., *Nutzen statt Besitzen*, 42.

Chapter 10 The Politics of Environmental Transformation

1 This is the title of a famous book by Hans Jonas that had a formative influence on the green movement: *The Imperative of Responsibility* (Chicago: University of Chicago Press, 1984). In an allusion to Kant, Jonas formulates a new "ecological imperative": "Act so that the effects of your action are compatible with the permanence of genuine human life" (11).

2 Claus Leggewie in the *Frankfurter Allgemeine Sonntagszeitung* on March 4, 2012.

3 The concept of ordoliberalism was developed by Walter Eucken and the Freiburg School. It provided the theoretical basis for Germany's postwar social market economy. The goal of ordoliberalism is an economic order in which state regulatory policy guarantees the conditions for economic competition and citizens' economic freedom.

4 As argued by the American ecovisionaries Paul Hawken, Amory Lovins and Hunter Lovins in their seminal text *Natural Capitalism: Creating the Next Industrial Revolution*, rev. ed. (London and Washington, DC: Earthscan, 2010).

5 Nicholas Stern, *The Economics of Climate Change: The Stern Review* (Cambridge and New York: Cambridge University Press, 2007).

6 Sebastian Dullien and Till van Treeck, "Ein neues 'magisches Viereck': Ziele einer nachhaltigen Wirtschaftspolitik und Überlegungen für ein neues 'Stabilitäts- und Wohlstandsgesetz'" (A New "Magic Square": Goals for a Sustainable Economic Policy and Thoughts on a New "Stability and Prosperity Law") (working paper 2, Denkwerk Demokratie, October 2012).

7 Cf. Damian Ludewig et al., *Nachhaltig aus der Krise: Ökologische Finanzreform als Beitrag zur Gegenfinanzierung des Krisendefizits* (Sustainable Recovery: Ecological Financial Reform as a Means of Funding the Deficit) (Berlin: Heinrich Böll Foundation, 2010), accessed November 24, 2014, http://www.boell.de/oekologie/marktwirtschaft/oekologische-marktwirtschaft-oekologische-steuerreform-8742.html.

8 See Shell, *Sustainability Report 2011*, http://reports.shell.com/sustainability-report/2011/servicepages/welcome.html.

9 See the relevant information on the protection of the Antarctic at http://www.umweltbundesamt.de/antarktis/index.htm, accessed November 24, 2014.

10 See Roderick Kefferpütz and Danila Bochkarev, *Wettlauf um die Arktis: Empfehlungen an die EU* (Race for the Arctic: Recommendations to the EU) (Brussels: Heinrich Böll Foundation, 2009), http://ru.boell.org/sites/default/files/wettlauf_um_die_arktis2009.pdf.

11 Results of a study conducted by Prognos, EWI and GWS on behalf of the German government, cited in Jürgen Blazejczak and Dietmar Edler, *Strukturwandel und Klimaschutz: Wie Klimapolitik Wirtschaft und Arbeitswelt verändert* (Structural Change and Climate Protection: How Climate Policy is Changing the Economy and the Workplace) (Berlin: Heinrich Böll Foundation, 2011).

12 Press release from the German Renewable Energy Federation, accessed November 26, 2014, http://www.bee-ev.de/3:662/Meldungen/2011/Erneuerbare-Energien-2011-Energieimporte-in-Hoehe-von-7.4-Mrd-Euro-vermieden.html.

13 Carlo Jaeger, *Wachstum—wohin?* (Munich: Oekom, 2011), 36.

14 Ibid., 37.

Bibliography

Agora Energiewende. *12 Thesen zur Energiewende: Ein Diskussionsbedarf zu den wichtigsten Herausforderungen im Strommarkt*. Berlin: Agora Energiewende, 2012.

Anders, Günter. *Die Antiquiertheit des Menschen: Über die Seele im Zeitalter der zweiten industriellen Revolution*. Munich: Beck, 1956.

Baedecker, Karolin, Kristin Leismann, Holger Rohn and Martina Schmitt. *Nutzen statt Besitzen: Auf dem Weg zu einer ressourcenschonenden Konsumkultur*. Berlin: Heinrich Böll Foundation/Naturschutzbund Deutschland, 2012.

Bahro, Rudolf. *Elemente einer neuen Politik: Zum Verhältnis von Ökologie und Sozialismus*. Berlin: Olle und Wolter, 1980.

———. *Logik der Rettung: Ein Versuch über die Grundlagen ökologischer Politik*. Stuttgart: Weitbrecht, 1987.

Baumol, William J., Robert E. Litan and Carl J. Schramm. *Good Capitalism, Bad Capitalism: The Economics of Growth and Prosperity*. New Haven: Yale University Press, 2007.

Binswanger, Hans Christoph. *Money and Magic: A Critique of the Modern Economy in Light of Goethe's Faust*. Chicago: University of Chicago Press, 1994.

Blazejczak, Jürgen and Dietmar Edler. *Strukturwandel und Klimaschutz: Wie Klimapolitik Wirtschaft und Arbeitswelt verändert*. Berlin: Heinrich Böll Foundation, 2011.

Bloch, Jan Robert and Willfried Maier, eds. *Wachstum der Grenzen: Selbstorganisation in der Natur und die Zukunft der Gesellschaft*. Frankfurt am Main: Sendler, 1984.

Borries, Friedrich von. “Zehn Thesen für die Stadt von morgen.” In *Perspektiven einer nachhaltigen Entwicklung: Wie sieht die Welt von morgen aus?*, edited by Harald Welzer and Klaus Wiegandt, 40–63. Frankfurt am Main: Fischer, 2011.

Braun, Matthias. “Die Industrie als intelligenter ökologischer Problemlöser.” In *Die Modernität der Industrie*, edited by Birger P. Priddat and Klaus-W. West. Marburg: Metropolis, 2012.

Braungart, Michael. “Ein Rohstoff ist ein Rohstoff ist ein Rohstoff.” *Earnest & Algernon: Dream & Reality*, 3/2012.

Brecht, Bertolt. *The Threepenny Opera*. Translated by Ralph Manheim and John Willett. New York: Arcade, 1979.

Brown, Lester R. *Eco-Economy: Building an Economy for the Earth*. New York: Norton, 2001.

Bundesministerium für Bildung und Forschung. *Weiße Biotechnologie. Chancen für eine biobasierte Wirtschaft*. Berlin: Bundesministerium für Bildung und Forschung, 2012.

Bundesministerium für Wirtschaft und Technologie. *Bericht zur Lage der deutschen Fotovoltaikindustrie*. April 2012.

Dohnke, Kay. “Abgeguckt.” *mobil* (Deutsche Bahn Magazine), 1/2012.

Dullien, Sebastian and Till van Treeck. “Ein neues ‘magisches Viereck’: Ziele einer nachhaltigen Wirtschaftspolitik und Überlegungen für ein neues ‘Stabilitäts- und Wohlstandsgesetz.’” Working Paper 2, Denkwerk Demokratie, October 2012.

Dyson, Freeman J. *The Sun, the Genome and the Internet: Tools of Scientific Revolutions*. Oxford and New York: Oxford University Press, 1999.

———. *Heretical Thoughts about Science and Society*. Boston: Boston University, Frederick S. Pardee Center for the Study of the Longer-Range Future, 2006. Cited in Carlo Jaeger: *Wachstum—wohin?*

Edenhofer, Ottmar, R. Pichs-Madruga, Y. Sokona, K. Seyboth, P. Matschoss, S. Kadner, T. Zwickel, P. Eickemeier, G. Hansen, S. Schlömer and C. von Stechow, eds. *Renewable Energy Sources and Climate Change Mitigation: Special Report of the Intergovernmental Panel on Climate Change*. Cambridge and New York: Cambridge University Press, 2012.

Feldt, Heidi. *The German Raw Material Strategy: Taking Stock.* Berlin: Heinrich Böll Foundation, 2012.

Fell, Hans-Josef. *Global Cooling: Strategies for Climate Protection.* Leiden and New York: CRC Press, 2012.

Fismer, Raymond et al. "Die Thermodynamik und das Weltgesetz der Entropie." In *Wachstum der Grenzen,* edited by Jan Robert Bloch and Willfried Maier, 295 ff. Frankfurt am Main: Sendler, 1984.

Fogal, Robert W. "Capitalism and Democracy in 2040: Forecasts and Speculations." Working Paper 13184, National Bureau of Economic Research, Cambridge, June 2007.

Girardet, Herbert. "Creating Regenerative Cities." In *Urban Futures 2050: Szenarien und Lösungen für das Jahrhundert der Städte,* 22 ff. Berlin: Heinrich Böll Foundation, 2011.

Goethe, Johann Wolfgang von. *Faust I & II.* Translated by Stuart Atkins. Cambridge, MA: Suhrkamp/Insel, 1984.

Hass, Hans H. "Joseph A. Schumpeter: Innovation und schöpferische Zerstörung: Der Unternehmer als Motor der Entwicklung." *E + Z – Entwicklung und Zusammenarbeit* 7/8 (1999): 215–18.

Hawken, Paul, Amory Lovins and Hunter Lovins. *Natural Capitalism: Creating the Next Industrial Revolution.* rev. ed. London and Washington, DC: Earthscan, 2010.

Heinrich Böll Foundation. *Strategien zur Modernisierung I: Neue Finanzierungsmodelle für einen klimaneutralen Gebäudebestand.* Berlin: Heinrich Böll Foundation, 2012.

———. *Urban Futures 2050: Szenarien und Lösungen für das Jahrhundert der Städte.* Berlin: Heinrich Böll Foundation, 2011.

Heinrich Böll Foundation and Wuppertal Institute for Climate, Environment and Energy. *International Resource Politics: New Challenges Demanding New Governance Approaches for a Green Economy.* Berlin: Heinrich Böll Foundation and Wuppertal Institute for Climate, Environment and Energy, 2012.

Hirschfeld, Jesko et al. *Klimawirkungen der Landwirtschaft in Deutschland.* Berlin: Institut für ökologische Wirtschaftsforschung, 2008.

Institut der deutschen Wirtschaft Köln. *Wirtschaftswachstum? Warum wir wachsen sollten und warum wir wachsen können.* Cologne: Institut der deutschen Wirtschaft, 2012.

Jackson, Tim. *Prosperity without Growth: Economics for a Finite Planet*. London and New York: Earthscan, 2009.

Jacobs, Michael. "Green Growth: Economic Theory and Political Discourse." Working Paper no. 108, Centre for Climate Change Economics and Policy, October 2012.

Jaeger, Carlo. *Wachstum—wohin?* Munich: Oekom, 2011.

Jänicke, Martin. *Megatrend Umweltinnovation: Zur ökologischen Modernisierung von Wirtschaft und Staat*. Munich: Oekom, 2008.

———. "Radikal schrumpfen, radikal wachsen." *Böll.Thema* (Magazine of the Heinrich Böll Foundation), 2/2011, 30.

Jonas, Hans. *The Imperative of Responsibility*. Chicago: University of Chicago Press, 1984.

Kefferpütz, Roderick and Danila Bochkarev. *Wettlauf um die Arktis: Empfehlungen an die EU*. Brussels: Heinrich Böll Foundation, 2009.

Kegel, Bernhard. *Epigenetik: Wie Erfahrungen vererbt werden*. Cologne: DuMont, 2009.

Lalor, John J., ed. *Cyclopædia of Political Science, Political Economy and the Political History of the United States by the Best American and European Writers*. New York: Maynard, Merrill & Co., 1899.

Landes, David S. *The Unbound Prometheus*. Cambridge: Cambridge University Press, 1969.

Lomborg, Bjørn. "Environmental Alarmism, Then and Now." *Foreign Affairs*, July/ August 2012.

Ludewig, Damian, Bettina Meyer and Kai Schlegelmilch. *Nachhaltig aus der Krise: Ökologische Finanzreform als Beitrag zur Gegenfinanzierung des Krisendefizits*. Berlin: Heinrich Böll Foundation, 2010.

Malthus, Thomas. *Essay on the Principle of Population*. London, 1798.

Matthes, Felix Christian. "Einordnung der aktuellen Debatte um den Flankierungsrahmen für die Stromerzeugung aus erneuerbaren Energien." Working Paper, Institute for Applied Ecology, Berlin, 2012.

Meadows, Dennis L. "Wir sollten uns nicht um den Planeten sorgen, sondern um die Spezies Mensch" (Interview). *Evonik Magazine*, 2/2012, 26-27.

Meadows, Dennis, Donella Meadows and Jørgen Randers. *Beyond the Limits: Confronting Global Collapse, Envisioning a Sustainable Future*. Post Mills, VT: Chelsea Green, 1992.

Meadows, Donella H., Dennis L. Meadows, Jørgen Randers and William W. Behrens III. *The Limits to Growth: A Report for the Club of Rome's Project on the Predicament of Mankind*. New York: Universe, 1972.

Morse, Richard. "Cleaning Up Coal." *Foreign Affairs*, July/August 2012.

Müller-Kraenner, Sascha and Susanne Langsdorf. *Eine Europäische Union für erneuerbare Energien: Politische Weichenstellungen für bessere Stromnetze und Fördersysteme*. Brussels: Heinrich Böll Foundation, 2012.

Nietzsche, Friedrich. *Thus Spoke Zarathustra*. Translated by Walter Kaufmann. New York: Modern Library, 1995.

Nordhaus, Ted and Michael Shellenberger. *Break Through: Why We Can't Leave Saving the Planet to Environmentalists*. Boston: Mariner Books, 2009.

OECD Publishing. *OECD Environmental Outlook to 2030*. 2008.

Pauli, Gunter. *Neues Wachstum: Wenn grüne Ideen nachhaltig "blau" werden*. Berlin: Konvergenta, 2010.

Pfaller, Robert. *Wofür es sich zu leben lohnt: Elemente materialistischer Philosophie*. Frankfurt am Main: Fischer, 2011.

Plumpe, Werner. "Konjunkturen der Kapitalismuskritik." *Merkur: Deutsche Zeitschrift für europäisches Denken* 757 (2012): 523–30.

Randers, Jørgen. *2052: A Global Forecast for the Next Forty Years*. White River Junction, VT: Chelsea Green, 2012.

Rifkin, Jeremy: *The Third Industrial Revolution: How Lateral Power is Transforming Energy, the Economy and the World*. New York: Palgrave Macmillan, 2011.

Santarius, Tilman. *Der Rebound-Effekt: Über die unerwünschten Folgen der erwünschten Energieeffizienz*. Wuppertal: Wuppertal Institut für Umwelt, Klima, Energie, 2012.

Schafer, Paul M., ed. *The First Writings of Karl Marx*. Brooklyn, NY: Ig Publishing, 2006.

Schumpeter, Joseph A. *Capitalism, Socialism and Democracy*. New York and London: Harper, 1942.

———. *The Theory of Economic Development: An Inquiry into Profits, Capital, Credit, Interest, and the Business Cycle.* Cambridge, MA: Harvard University Press, 1934.

Schwägerl, Christian. *The Anthropocene: The Human Era and How It Shapes Our Planet.* Santa Fe: Synergetic Press, 2014.

Simon, Julian. *The Ultimate Resource.* Princeton: Princeton University Press, 1981.

Sloterdijk, Peter. "Wie groß ist 'groß'?" *Die Welt,* December 17, 2009.

———. *You Must Change Your Life.* Cambridge, UK and Malden, MA: Polity, 2013.

Statistisches Bundesamt. *Bevölkerung Deutschlands bis 2050.* Wiesbaden: Statistisches Bundesamt, 2006.

Stern, Nicholas. *The Economics of Climate Change: The Stern Review.* Cambridge and New York: Cambridge University Press, 2007.

———. *The Global Deal: Climate Change and the Creation of a New Era of Progress and Prosperity.* New York: Public Affairs, 2009.

Taylor, Charles. *The Malaise of Modernity.* Concord, Ont.: Anansi, 1991.

United Nations Environment Programme. *Towards a Green Economy: Pathways to Sustainable Development and Poverty Eradication.* Nairobi: UNEP, 2011.

Unmüßig, Barbara, Wolfgang Sachs and Thomas Fatheuer. *Critique of the Green Economy: Toward Social and Environmental Equity.* Berlin: Heinrich Böll Foundation, 2012.

Verband der Automobilindustrie. *Jahresbericht 2012.*

Verband der chemischen Industrie. *Chemie-Industrie: Branchenporträt der deutschen chemisch-pharmazeutischen Industrie.* 2011.

Vester, Frederic. *Neuland des Denkens: Vom technokratischen zum kybernetischen Zeitalter.* Stuttgart: Deutsche Verlags-Anstalt, 1980.

Watts, Jonathan: "China's big spend on green power." Chinadialogue, May 2, 2012.

Weizsäcker, Ernst Ulrich von. *Earth Politics.* London: Zed Books, 1994.

Weizsäcker, Ernst Ulrich von, Karlson Hargroves and Michael Smith. *Factor Five: Transforming the Global Economy through 80% Improvements in Resource Productivity*. London and Sterling, VA: Earthscan, 2009.

Welzer, Harald. *Climate Wars: What People Will Be Killed for in the 21st Century*. Cambridge, UK and Malden, MA: Polity, 2012.

———. "Futur Zwei: Die Wiedergewinnung der Zukunft." In *Der Futurzwei Zukunftsalmanach 2013: Geschichten vom guten Umgang mit der Welt*, edited by Harald Welzer and Stephan Rammler. Bonn: Bundeszentrale für politische Bildung, 2013.

About the Author

Ralf Fücks is the president of the Heinrich Böll Foundation and has been a member of the German Green Party since 1982. He has served as leader of the national Green Party in Germany and as senator for the environment and urban development in the state of Bremen. He writes widely on matters of the environment and public policy, and also edited the book *Sind die Grünen noch zu retten?* (Does the Green Party Have a Future?).

Anthony Giddens is the former director of the London School of Economics and Political Science. He has written over thirty books, including seminal works on modernity, globalization and political thought; his *The Politics of Climate Change* offers models for a new kind of politics to confront this global threat.

Index